Blood Feud: Mary Queen of Scots and the Earl of Moray

Steven Veerapen

Table of Contents

Prologue

On a cold January day in 1570, a shot rang through the chilly air of Linlithgow. The townspeople rushed towards the sound, eager to find its source. To their shock, the victim was James Stewart, the earl of Moray, regent of Scotland and half-brother to their quondam queen, Mary. When he died that night, he became the first recorded victim of assassination by gunfire. By the end of the month, the news had reached the captive queen, who was reported to have felt 'sorrow for his sudden and timely cutting off, wishing rather that he might have been spared for repentance and acknowledgement of his faults'. [1] Mary was quick to write a letter to her brother's widow, in which she expressed sympathy mingled with a posthumous rebuke for Moray's ingratitude and unnatural offences. In short order, the veneer of sisterly sorrow had all but vanished and the queen of Scots organised a pension for the assassin.

What brought about this strange reaction in a woman noted for her compassion? The answer lies in the tumultuous relationship between Mary and her illegitimate brother, which moved from affection to mutual dependence to outright antipathy.

The relationship between Mary Queen of Scots and her half-brother has not been ignored by historians. However, it has been either simplified or recounted under the weight of prejudice. To those who condemn Mary as either a Catholic temptress or a scatter-brained fool, Moray offers a cool, Protestant hero. To those who view her as a tragic heroine, he provides a Machiavellian schemer, ceaselessly plotting at her downfall. Even in more modern, less partisan accounts of Mary's life, Moray is almost without exception depicted as ambitious and calculating (which, it must be stressed, were no bad things in sixteenth-century politics). Thus, to Allan Massie, Moray 'may have had an affection for Mary, but, resenting his own illegitimacy, he could not but think that he would have made a better king than she a queen'.[2] To Robert Stedall, he is calculating and cynical.[3] In his exemplary history of Mary, John Guy asserts Moray's dour Protestantism and accuses him of plotting his sister's downfall. In older sources the criticism is more pronounced still. Agnes Strickland, that arduous recorder of the lives of queens, cites an unnamed contemporary source who denounced him as 'her perfidious brother' (a description which she found so apt she used it herself repeatedly). Such descriptions stand in contradistinction to those of Mary: according to Guy, she was 'shrewd and charismatic'. [4] To Strickland, she was 'the beautiful and unfortunate mother of our royal line'.[5]

If Mary has her supporters and Moray his detractors, the attitudes of each might easily be flipped. Thus, Andrew Lang, in his deep studies of Mary's life and reign, documents unattractive behaviours of Moray with the addendum, 'such worldliness is to be regretted in so good a man'. 'His ambition,' states Lang, 'was probably more limited than his covetousness, and the suspicion that he aimed at being king, though natural, was baseless'. Of Mary, Lang is less sanguine, noting that while she was 'sensitive, proud, tameless, fierce, and kind', her 'woman's weapon … was deceit'. This certainly is a good deal more balanced than Marjorie Bowen, who provides the following withering condemnations:

Like many another reckless and artful woman, Mary's ready wit in a crisis was as notable as was her folly in bringing a crisis about. Her cleverness was very superficial and only exercised in emergencies, or she would have seen long before Rizzio was murdered that she was playing an impossible game between favourite, husband, and the Lords who were aided by such a man as Moray.[6]

To this, Bowen adds that Mary 'showed those extremes of conduct that are acknowledged to be feminine characteristics; a foolish, wilful drifting to disaster, a bold ability, a fertile resource when disaster arrived'. In the sexist language of another age, both Lang and Bowen are largely in agreement. Lang perhaps sums up the attitude that dominated secular critical attitudes until Antonia Fraser's magisterial biography: 'one thing this woman wanted,' he writes, '[was] a master'.[7] Nor are modern historians who criticise Mary kinder. To Jenny Wormald, Scotland's most famous daughter was 'profoundly irresponsible', 'dismal', and 'unfit to rule'.

As will become apparent, a master is exactly what Mary Stewart did not want. That her brother tried, and ultimately failed, to master her (only to be succeeded by Darnley, in an even less effectual way and for an even shorter period) is part of what contributed to her downfall. Whilst her contemporary, Elizabeth I, found means of making many Englishmen fall into grinning servility under a staunch schoolmistress, Mary was to find her Scottish subjects less willing to conform. She did, however, attempt an ever more ground-breaking method of providing for her country's succession without sacrificing power than ever Elizabeth did.

Criticism of James Stewart has not, as we will see, been confined to historians. His contemporaries, saddled with their own agendas, can be found to have laid bare their own opinions on his ambitions. To loyal Marian Lord Herries, he was therefore 'ambitious of a croune, nothing can satiffie but a croune! Many,' Herries went on, warming to his theme, 'supposed it was the croune that Lord James aimed at from the beginning, as was observed by the course of all his actions'.[8] On numerous occasions during his lifetime, various politicians were to make similar claims. Yet these can be deconstructed. Herries, writing years after the death of Moray, was an outspoken critic. Those who sounded out the possibility of his desire for crown when he was alive were often outside the Scottish political sphere (amongst them the constable of France, and England's secretary, William Cecil). Interestingly, Cecil was to remark in 1560 that James himself was 'a man not unlyke ether in person or qualitees to be a Kyng soone'.[9] Although he would undoubtedly have liked nothing better than to see a pro-English Protestant puppet on the throne, the secretary did not take into consideration the attitudes of the political community of Scotland. As a result, he displayed an almost Henrician ignorance of Scottish sovereignty, perhaps born of his working under a queen who had herself been legally bastardised.

The tendency to portray Mary and her brother's relationship in black-and-white has not been limited to historians but generations of filmmakers, novelists, and playwrights. Whether it was the gruff turn by Patrick McGoohan in *Mary, Queen of Scots* (1971) or Ian Keith menacing a plucky Katharine Hepburn in *Mary of Scotland* (1936), screen portrayals of Moray have tended to promulgate the stereotype of the Shakespearean Edmund, haunted by his illegitimacy and eager to take the throne for himself. But to what extent is this true? To what extent was James Stewart an ambitious climber, obsessed with securing the power that he felt was only denied him by his parentage? And what role did his relationship with his half-sister have in the tragedy of Mary Queen of Scots?

The study of brothers and sisters in the early modern world has been limited. Certainly, the pages of history are littered with stories of brothers who feuded (consider, for example, Edward IV and the duke of Clarence, or the Seymour brothers, Thomas and Edward). Sisters, too, have been the subject of scholarly attention, notably Mary Tudor and her sister Elizabeth. The ideal relationship between brother and sister, however, is more obscure, and that between half-brother and half-sister more puzzling still. In conventional terms, in the absence of a father it was the duty of a brother to see that his sister married well and in a way that might bring prestige, wealth, or advancement to the family. When the sister was a queen and the brother a bastard, the conventional power dynamic was somewhat destabilised. So it was in the case of Queen Mary, younger than James Stewart, but outranking him by virtue of her legitimacy and crown. It was in large part their inability to negotiate an acceptable rebalancing of the brother-sister relationship in light of their positions which ultimately led to the downfalls of both. Thus, as we will see, Mary's attempt to marry without her brother's permission and approval led to war, and her decision to follow a policy independent of his guidance marked a turning point in her personal reign.

One of the joys of writing this book has been the research involved. For source material, both primary and secondary on Mary, there is a wealth. A number of accounts of events (of varying reliability) were produced during her lifetime, and an extraordinary number of her letters survive. Of her modern biographers, Lady Antonia Fraser, Alison Weir, and John Guy provide the most engaging books. In terms of her detractors, Jenny Wormald's provocative study continues to inspire debate, and it remains wonderfully readable. There are dozens if not hundreds more.

If books on Mary are too many, books on her brother are too few. His only biographer, Maurice Lee, provides the most thorough account of his life (albeit the primary purpose of his text is to situate James within the wider Scottish reformation). This made it an invaluable tool both in tracing the chronology and in sourcing primary material (Lee was meticulous in providing references). However, throughout, I strongly frequently with his arguments, and have indicated where and why I find his interpretations unconvincing. Ultimately, his central thesis is that Moray was the most important figure in the reformation: a man who provided stable governance in spite of his murderous sister. Combatting the semi-hagiographical treatment afford by Lee is Claire Webb's excellent PhD thesis, 'The 'gude regent?': a diplomatic perspective upon the Earl of Moray, Mary, Queen of Scots and the Scottish Regency, 1567-1570'. Webb's pendulum swings the other way, and although her focus is on Moray's regency rather than his wider life, her argument is primarily that the queen's brother was hungry for power and that, once he gained it, he did everything in his power to hold on to it. This is true. However, her contention that he was never reluctant is problematic, the reasons for which can only be understood by study of his cautious character and his concomitant desire to rule without ultimate responsibility.

In tracing the intertwined narratives of Mary and James, I found that their similarities and differences made them each deeply fallible, and yet each deserving of credit. Taken together, their stories parallel one another's, with tragedy stemming from the fact that although their formative experiences were similar, they were pulled in different religious directions.

It will be the purpose of this study to strip away the layers of stereotype and chart the real relationship between royal sister and base-born brother. In doing so, what will emerge is a thoroughly sixteenth-century story: one of thrones, double-dealing, plots, and murder.

This is the story of a brother and sister, united in blood but divided by religion, suspicion, and politics.

A Bastard Born

The winter of 1542 was unusually fierce, even for Scotland. The water in the great fountain at Falkland palace had frozen, and a biting wind whistled through the tennis court. The builder of these innovations, thirty-year-old King James V, was lying in his bedchamber, broken in spirit and breaking in body. His councillors crowded him, trying to elicit some sense out of their king, but it was obvious to all that he was past the help of physicians. As dangerous as the physical illness that was ravaging Mary and James Stewart's royal father was the simple fact that he had lost the will to fight it. As tradition has it, he turned his face to the wall and died. So began his daughter's reign, and the relationship with her base-born brother that was to play such a key and, ultimately, tragic role in it.

Any study of the relationship between Mary Queen of Scots and her notorious half-brother must begin with consideration of their enigmatic father's life and mysterious death. Born of the famous marriage between the thistle and the rose - the match between James IV and Margaret Tudor - King James V was a puzzling personality. As was common with Scottish monarchs, his upbringing was not an easy one. His father was drawn into the early military endeavours of Henry VIII. When England's boisterous young king invaded France, James IV was compelled to invade England in support of her ancient ally. This resulted in his death at Flodden in 1513, along with the loss of the flower of Scotland's nobility. The shadow of Flodden Field was to cast a long shadow over sixteenth-century Scotland, and it should not later surprise us to find an unwillingness on the part of Scots to engage in further military campaigns against England in France's interest.

The death of James IV left his son, the one-year-old James V, king of Scots. Naturally, toddlers have a disinclination to govern, and so his mother Margaret assumed the reins as 'tutrix' or regent, ruling on his behalf. This she was singularly unable to do, for a variety of reasons. Her rapid remarriage to Archibald Douglas, the handsome young earl of Angus, provided an excuse to oust her (her regency being predicated on her remaining a widow). In desperate need of a man to rule, the Scottish political community sent a request to France, where the duke of Albany lived. Albany was a charming Frenchman, and the son of James III's exiled brother. With the French king's permission, he departed for Scotland, and thereafter the country was governed on-and-off by him. Albany's rule was relatively stable, and to his credit he made genuine efforts to understand his ancestral kingdom. He was, however, opposed in his political manoeuvrings by Angus, and in his military ambitions by the Scots themselves. When Queen Margaret (whose romantic life gave her brother, Henry VIII, a run for his money) fell out with Angus, she fell in with Albany. Together the pair were able to accuse Angus of high treason, forcibly exiling him to France. Albany's own rule only came to an end when the ambitious Margaret and her supporters then turned on and got rid of him too, sending him back to France himself and declaring the twelve-year-old James V a competent adult ruler. One can only imagine that Albany, who was famed for throwing his hat in the fire when annoyed, might have thrown it in the air in joy at the prospect of leaving the turbulent politics of Scotland behind.

In the same year Albany was overthrown, 1524, Angus returned to Scotland via London. During his time in England's capital, he had won the support of Henry VIII, with the two men agreeing to engineer the overthrow of the woman who was wife to one and sister to the other. Capturing Edinburgh, Angus outflanked Margaret and assumed power. He built this up until in 1526 he was able to gain the guardianship of the fourteen-year-old King James V. The young king was not, however, a lover of captivity. Indeed, the effect on his psychology of Angus' guardianship – though it does not seem to have been in any way cruel or physically traumatising – was to leave James V with a long-lasting and deadly hatred of the whole Douglas clan.

James V's captivity lasted until 1528, when he was able to effect an escape, taking refuge with his mother in the fastness of Stirling castle. Immediately he outlawed and proscribed his stepfather, forbidding all Douglases to come near his presence. Angus fled back to England, where he sheltered under the increasingly-capacious wing of Henry VIII until 1543. With him went his daughter by Margaret Tudor, Margaret Douglas, who was to have an interesting career of her own (of which more must be said later).

Thus James V was able to assume the power he had nominally been granted by his mother in 1524, when she had banished Albany. The stage was set for the young king to flourish. He had a great deal to live up to; his father, after all, had been arguably Scotland's best-loved Stewart king. The country waited with bated breath to see if its ruler, freed from the iron grip of regents and guardians, would be another renaissance prince, or a distrusted James III. It would not be long before key aspects of his personality would become apparent. From his father he seems to have inherited political acumen and a passion for architecture; from his mother he inherited a flair for the dramatic and a streak of viciousness. How these traits were to be manifested in Mary Queen of Scots and James Stewart will later become apparent.

James V's reign was to witness a continuation of building work, with the famous Stirling heads and the beautiful palace buildings at the same castle completed. So too was the hunting lodge of Falkland transformed into a fairy-tale palace, and the palace of Linlithgow beautified. Alongside such princely pursuits, however, the king was to be found milking money from the church, supporting heresy trials, and executing foes and former friends on trumped up charges. In one particularly unpleasant episode, he had Janet, Lady Glamis, burned on the esplanade of Edinburgh Castle on a charge of witchcraft, with her son forced to watch. His friend and Master of Building Works, Sir James Hamilton of Finnart, was likewise executed, albeit by the axe, after having gained too much power and wealth. James V was throughout susceptible to flattery and the influence of strong personalities, whether it be his chief cleric, David Beaton, or his untrustworthy favourite, Oliver Sinclair. This susceptibility was to be inherited by his son and daughter.

In all, Mary and James Stewart's father was a man of extremes. His surviving portraits glare out suspiciously from deep-set, weary eyes, but so too is there strength of character in the firm set of his lips. His reputation amongst his people remained high, however. It was said that he walked amongst ordinary Scots in disguise, frequently pretending to be the 'gudeman o' Ballengiech'. This love of guising and, with it, mingling amongst commoners was something later taken to by his successor, Mary. Whilst in disguise, it was the prerogative of the king to seek out and remedy injustices. Indeed, Leslie states that 'he was a manteiner of justice, an executor of the lawis, a defender of the innocent and pure. Quhairthrough he was namet commounlie be [by] his special nobilitie the pure [poor] manis king'.[10] Yet his desire to see justice done in the shires led also to extremes in behaviour: Buchanan attests that he was 'eager and over violent' in his pursuit of order.[11] This trait was to rise in James Stewart during his period as regent of Scotland.

By all accounts handsome and charming, James V was also prone to depression, bloodthirst, and, it must be said, he was no slave to chastity.

During a flyting (something of an early modern poetry slam session with witty insults exchanged) with his friend Sir David Lindsay of the Mount, the latter somewhat startlingly accused the king of raping a serving woman, condemning the incident as denigrating the king (rather than the poor woman). Although the specific incident is likely an exaggeration given James' tastes in women, the warnings issued by Lindsay ring true: King James was frequently to be found with a woman, the pair 'swettering like twa swine'.[12]

Scotland's Stewart (later altered to the more Francophone Stuart) kings were never, of course, noted for their marital fidelity. King James V was no exception, with Elizabeth Schaw, Elizabeth Carmichael, Elizabeth Bethune (or Beaton), Euphemia Elphinstone, and Margaret Erskine counted amongst his known lovers. Given that these women were of noble or gentle blood, it might be fairly said that the king had high tastes. He was, however, exceptional in appearing to have had no official mistresses during his marriages to Madeleine of Valois or Mary of Guise.[13] Instead, the sexual awakening encouraged in the king during his captivity brought about a brood of illegitimate children before his royal marriages took place. Indeed, by the time King James married, a veritable brace of bastard offspring had been produced. Playing with wooden swords and being clothed at the king's expense were Adam; James (not, oddly, the subject of this study, but a half-brother with the same name); Jean; another James (again, not our man; giving children the same name was not uncommon in the period); Robert; John; another Robert; and our James, later earl of Moray. Notably, each of these children was given the Stewart surname; unlike in England, where the name Fitzroy designated a base-born royal child, illegitimate offspring were not so-marked north of the border.

It was with the reputedly beautiful daughter of Lord Erskine, Margaret, who was already married to Sir Robert Douglas, that the king sired little James Stewart in 1531.[14] Margaret is known to history as King James' favourite mistress, and rumours have flown down the centuries that the king intended to end her marriage to Douglas so that he might take her as his bride. However, the likelihood of this being true is slim. Sixteenth-century monarchs married less for love than for the glory of foreign alliances, and James was outspoken in his desire to make a grand match with a European superpower. As R. H. Mahon puts it, 'royal alliances were first and last matters of political negotiation and national advantage' and there was little national advantage in marrying a divorced native Scotswoman whose son with the king was beyond question illegitimate.[15] Though Andrew Lang records that James broke off his French negotiations in 1536 in order to consult the pope about the possibility of granting Margaret a divorce, and whatever he might have felt for her, it is unlikely that his intention was ever to marry his son's mother.[16] Far more likely is that he briefly entertained the possibility as a last resort, or even that he intended for whispers of his potential marriage to Margaret Erskine to step up negotiations with a more serious candidate. Although the king's biographer, Caroline Bingham, mounts a spirited defence of the Margaret Erskine marriage, pointing out that earlier Stewart kings had married native noblewomen, and that Henry VIII chose the native-born Anne Boleyn, Jane Seymour, Katherine Howard, and Katherine Parr as wives, the suggestion remains problematic.[17] Certainly Henry's repudiation of a European wife in favour of an Englishwoman can hardly have provided an encouraging lesson in 1536 (the year of the supposed eagerness to wed Margaret Erskine). More critically, in the early modern period Scottish kings were engaged in a process of strengthening the prestige of the crown in order to try (with limited success) to shake off the medieval foundations of the *primus inter pares* (or first amongst equals) Scottish system. To marry a noblewoman, whilst it may not have constituted a *mésalliance*, would have been to undo James' policy of using his marriage to make clear that Scotland's kings were equal to those on the continent.[18]

Equally unlikely is the supposition of Maurice Lee that such a marriage would have led to little James Stewart becoming king.[19] Although the birthdates of the illegitimate brood cannot be known for certain, we can be sure that our James Stewart was not, as is sometimes claimed, the king's eldest son.[20] Even were King James V to have married Margaret Erskine, the throne would have passed to any issue following that marriage, with the king disinclined to revive the murky hereditary and legitimacy confusion which followed Robert II's marital adventures. In short, James V's marriage to Margaret Erskine was never a likely prospect; and even if it had happened, it would not have put the crown within touching distance of James Stewart.

At any rate, James V was to make his grand French alliance when he wed King Francis I's favourite daughter, the fragile beauty Madeleine, who was to die of tuberculosis only weeks after her arrival in Scotland in 1537. During her brief period in the palace of Holyroodhouse, it is unlikely that she got to know, or even met, any of her husband's illegitimate children, and their thoughts on their glamorous but sickly stepmother are not recorded. In the subsequent search for a replacement, James does not appear to have looked backwards, but instead kept his eyes firmly on France, securing the widowed Duchess of Longueville, Mary of Guise, who reluctantly left her own infant son to become his queen in 1538.

An attractive, willowy brunette, Mary of Guise was to be a more direct, external influence on the lives of her daughter and stepson. Of the up-and-coming Guise family (which was to play a major role in French, English, and Scottish politics in the coming decades), the charming and elegant Mary has won near-universal praise from historians, including those hostile to her daughter. In this remarkable woman was to be found a canny politician, albeit one who sought to bring Scotland into what she thought was a positive French sphere of influence, and an able leader. She was, in time, to become an icon to her daughter and, despite their ultimate estrangement, a figure of admiration and respect to James Stewart. At the outset of her marriage, however, her political abilities were nascent; she appears to have been content to fulfil the obligations of any sixteenth-century queen consort: to provide heirs and to enable an artistic and cultural side to her husband's court. The former she did with admiral rapidity, giving birth to Prince James in 1540 and Prince Robert in 1541.

Whilst King James sought a foreign bride, increased taxation on the church, and began a campaign of Renaissance palace-building, his illegitimate children were raised in honourable estate. Although it is tempting to imagine that the taint of bastardy might have been something shameful, to be a royal bastard was on the contrary something of a boon. It is from a later period (and another country) that we find attitudes such as that of Louis XIV: 'no issue', said Louis of his illegitimate children, 'should come of such species'.[21] In sixteenth-century Scotland, a quiver of bastards proved that the king was fertile. Further, it provided him with a solid stock of loyal adherents who might be – and were – provided with clerical appointments. No fewer than five of King James' illegitimate sons were preferred to priories, including our James, whom the king successfully made prior of St Andrews when he was seven. The benefit of advancing young children to high clerical positions was obvious. Throughout his adult reign, King James followed a policy of allowing bishops, abbots and priors to feu-farm ecclesiastical land. This was a type of tenure by which the landowner might lease land in perpetuity to tenants (and at ever-inflating rental costs). By ensuring that the landowning ecclesiastics were his own children, the king could be assured that they controlled and raised money which would find its way into his own treasury via taxation. It was a neat trick, if highly unpopular. It was partly thanks to such corrupt practices, however, that the whole edifice of the Catholic Church in Scotland came to be in a parlous state by the time of the reformation.

We can confidently say that the young Prior James was well cared for by his father, who, according to the Treasurer's Accounts, provided clothing suitable for a noble child. Like most royal children, legitimate or otherwise, his contact with his father would have been severely limited, and thus it is doubtful that the king imprinted on his son any great mark of personality. This he was to have in common with Mary Queen of Scots, who never knew James V. Very likely the first decade of James' life was split between his mother's domicile on her island castle of Lochleven (which was to play a major role in Queen Mary's story, as the site of one of the ugliest scenes ever played out between brother and sister) and St Andrews, his ecclesiastical seat, which lay about thirty miles distant. In the earliest years of his life, it is likely that James inhabited an exclusively female world, ruled over by his mother and a number of her female attendants, who would have served him as wet nurses and governesses. Such was the life of any boy born into the aristocracy of early modern Europe. The break with the world of the feminine came only with the 'breeching', when the child was taken out of childish skirts and put into breeches. Probably this occurred for James at or shortly before he was promoted to the priory of St Andrews. Following his move into the masculine sphere, it is likely that he was introduced to his future home: the St Andrews grammar school attached to his benefice.

St Andrews in the sixteenth century was a small, grey town composed of three main streets: Market Street, South Street, and North Street. It was dominated entirely by its coastal university, its forbidding clifftop castle, and the magnificent Romanesque cathedral which was to be James' ecclesiastical seat.[22] When visiting and studying in the grammar school there, James – like any child – is likely to have been impressed by the scale of the buildings and the sense of grandness they inspire (even in their modern, ruinous state). However, he seems to have been singularly unaffected by the religious life of the monastics over whom he was apparently destined to rule.

When living at or subsequently visiting Lochleven, James would have been confronted with a vibrant and sociable woman. His mother had, after all, been a king's lover, and was reputed to have been a potential queen (however unlikely). There is a tradition that Margaret brooded resentfully over her son's illegitimacy, retaining an especial dislike for Mary as her son's rival, which communicated itself to James, firing his ambitions. There is no contemporary evidence that this is the case. Instead, it seems probable that James had a positive relationship with his mother – it was certainly one that was only to end with his death. We can thus dispense with the idea that a domineering mother fostered her son's ambition.

If at any point in James' life there was a possibility of his somehow becoming king (without resorting to deposition or murder), it would have been in brief the period between April 1541 and December 1542. For, in 1541, King James V lost both his legitimate sons by Mary of Guise. The new-born duke of Albany and the infant duke of Ross were both found dead within hours of one another. The effect of the loss of both children on their parents cannot be overestimated in this or any period. King James V seems to have taken the news particularly badly, whilst Mary of Guise sought solace in her faith. As Margaret Tudor, nearing the end of her own life and by then a grumbling, ill-tempered, rather pitiable woman, was to write, 'the queen is very sickly and full of heaviness'. She could not resist including the usual salacious gossip that the princes' deaths were due to poison. In terms of the country's future, however, the still-young king and queen were back to where they had been at the outset of their marriage: heirless.

It is tempting here to imagine that the loss of the two legitimate princes heralded an ambition for the crown amongst the illegitimate brood. However, this must be avoided. In England, of course, Henry VIII had, near contemporaneously, considered the legal means by which he might legitimise his bastard son, Henry Fitzroy, in order to provide for the succession prior to the birth of Prince Edward. But Scotland was not England. In the northern kingdom, there existed two clearly-delineated alternatives to the direct Stewart line: the Hamilton family (whose head, the earl of Arran, was a grandson of Princess Mary, sister to James III) and the Lennox Stewarts (whose head, the earl of Lennox, was similarly descended, albeit through the female line). There was therefore never any need or inclination to legitimise bastards; the Stewart kings, certainly, did not show Henry VIII's propensity for exterminating rival claimants (the Stewarts' place on Scotland's throne being far more secure than the Tudors' place on that of England). Furthermore, there existed in Scotland a peculiar attachment to the legitimate line of sovereigns, with the monarchs personifying the country's independence. One need only turn to the plethora of books and treatises which blossomed in the sixteenth century and before, each proudly – and often falsely – lauding the unbroken line of descent from the mythical King Fergus down to James V, for evidence that the Scots of the period were not likely to substitute a bastard child for a legitimate claimant.[23] Though it is easy to scoff at pseudohistorical claims that the Scots were descended from Scota, an Egyptian princess, to do so is to underestimate the power of national and dynastic myth-making in the early modern period. Yet texts such as Andrew of Wyntoun's *Orygynale Cronykil of Scotland*, Fordun's *Chronica Gentis Scotorum*, and Boece's

Historia Gentis Scotorum were part of the national fabric, as were the English beliefs promulgated vigorously by the Tudors that their dynasty formed a legitimate line from Cadwallader and King Arthur. The fact that James V instituted two royal commissions to translate Boece's work from Latin to Scots, and that he carried one of these into France to give as a gift to Francis I, suggests strongly that the Scottish monarchy was closely concerned with protecting the honour and reputation of its place in the country's history.[24]

Once again, the idea that James Stewart coveted the Scottish throne must be recognised for what it is: a false premise, at least at this stage. Even when it was theoretically possible that a bastard (and there existed elder male bastards) might inherit in light of the sudden loss of the two legitimate heirs, there is no reason to believe that the vocal Hamilton and Lennox Stewart claimants would have sat idly by whilst the throne fell to an illegitimate child. If, in later life, James was ever to seek the throne, it would require the discrediting if not the utter ruination of these two noble houses.

In addition to being ravaged by the loss of its princes, the Scotland in which James Stewart spent the first decade of his life was an outward-looking European nation, albeit on the fringes. It was thus touched by the winds of religious reform which had been blowing across the continent from the bellows of Martin Luther's Ninety-five Theses. The country was bisected by a jagged west-to-northeast line, above which were the semi-autonomous Highlands and below which were the Lowlands and Borders. The spirit of reform entered through the Lowland ports, but received only scattered, rudderless support throughout the country, likely due to its associations with the 'auld enemy', England. Throughout his life King James V remained a staunch Catholic, as did the majority of his nobility in this decade. With the zealous support of Cardinal David Beaton, the political community thus resisted reform, which was even then sweeping England under Henry VIII. It would not be until the 1550s that James became not simply an opponent of the Catholic Church, but a leading proponent of Protestantism.

Though the Catholic Church itself had been inadvertently weakened by James V and his covetous dealings with successive popes, it remained standing and largely unopposed whilst the king lived and his little son grew up under royal protection and in the embraces of a loving mother. But his place in the world, and that world itself were about to change drastically.

After King James refused (probably wisely) to meet with his Uncle Henry at York, relations between reformist England and Catholic Scotland soured. Despite Henry's entreaties, James V steadfastly refused to countenance religious reform – likely due to a combination of sincere religious belief, which he was to pass on to Mary and James Stewart in very different ways, and a disinclination to jeopardise the lucrative position he had achieved within the Catholic system of worship and governance. The two countries entered a state of cold war, livened by intermittent raids. After an early victory at Haddon Rig, Cardinal Beaton urged the king to take the war to England, and King James obliged. With something of the complexion of a Holy War, the Scottish cohort marched south, eager to mount a raid on their southern neighbour. Whilst James V remained at nearby Lochmaben, his forces were routed in the unfamiliar, marshy bog-land by Lord Wharton's Englishmen. Though casualties were few, the defeat was an exercise in humiliation, and the English were able to take a significant number of Scottish notables hostage, shuttling them south to be bribed by King Henry to press England's interests on Scotland's king. No fewer than twenty-three high-ranking Scots were taken first into custody in the Tower of London, and then on a tour of Henry's palaces over the festive period. With characteristic unpredictability, Henry thus turned prisoners into honoured guests. As he filled their bellies and their pockets, the English king's goal was to convert them to his newfound cause: convincing their Scottish peers to accept a marriage between Mary Stewart and Edward Tudor. By doing so he could work towards a long-held dream of assuming direct power over Scotland. However, his houseguests were no strangers to unpredictability themselves. They took Henry's money, assured him of their determination to help him achieve his dynastic goal, and were freed to Scotland the following year, there to pay lip service to the tyrannical English king. Travelling north with them would be the Douglas brothers, who were only able to return to Scotland when the disaster of Solway Moss claimed the life of the country's king.

James V was understandably crushed by the latest humiliation, and he seems to have sunk into a deep depression, which cannot have been helped by a bout of dysentery or the severe winter conditions crowding in during December 1542. The news that Mary of Guise, pregnant again, had delivered a healthy baby did little to rouse him: the child was a daughter. In failing spirits, King James returned north, eventually taking to his bed at Falkland Palace. There, it is said (probably apocryphally) that his dynasty 'cam' wi' a lass and will gang wi' a lass'. If he did speak these words, first recorded by John Knox, he was possessed of remarkable foresight. The Stewart line, begun with the marriage of Marjory Bruce, did indeed end with a lass, but it was not his daughter; the unfortunate Queen Anne (d. 1715) was to be the last of the direct Stewart line of anointed monarchs.

In the wake of the king's sudden death, the chess board of politics was wiped clean, and required reassembly. To little James Stewart, then only ten or eleven, his father's death can have meant little. He was, after all, living in comparative luxury and comfort, and had ahead of him a glittering career in holy orders. For certain, there is no reason to believe that he was nurtured in resentment at his station. The birth of his first legitimate sister, who was almost immediately made his sovereign lady, was to have far greater and longer lasting an effect on them both.

Hail Mary!

As Marcus Merriman colourfully puts it, the only job of the new-born Mary Queen of Scots was to eat, sleep, and survive. During her infancy, her elder brother was embarking on his university education at St Andrews. Around both, however, the country was undergoing some of the most convoluted political shenanigans in an already-tortuous history.

Following the king's death, his chief advisor, Cardinal Beaton, forged or embroidered a will, purporting to be the late monarch's final wishes for the country's governance during Mary's minority. The will unceremoniously cut out the earl of Arran, who was widely recognised as the heir presumptive should anything untoward happen to the baby queen; instead it suggested a council of regency. Naturally, Arran was nonplussed, and by the end of January, he and the cardinal, who was a cousin to him, were at loggerheads. The impasse culminated in Arran's victory; he managed to have Beaton arrested for his forgery during a council meeting and seized power himself.

James Hamilton, earl of Arran, was condemned in his time as a vacillating young man; even his ally, Sir George Douglas (brother to Archibald, earl of Angus) was to state that he was 'the most wavering and unstable person in the world, and the soonest would be altered and changed with every man's flattery or fair speech'.[25] Yet he was undoubted heir presumptive, the whisper of illegitimacy owing to his parents' dubious marital history being the only blot on his position (further evidence, if it were needed, of the need for legitimacy in the

Scottish succession). This whisper Arran was keen to dampen, and he did so via a parliament called for March 1543. This parliament recognised him formally as governor and second person of the realm, passing legislation also that allowed the Bible to be translated into Scots and English. As wavering in religion as he was in allegiance, this short period was to become known as the governor's 'godly fit'; later, he was to renounce reform and embrace Catholicism once again.

Whilst Beaton languished in increasingly loose confinement at the Douglas castle of Dalkeith, followed by the state prison at Blackness, Mary of Guise and her baby daughter were either chased or fled to the dowager's palace at Linlithgow, leaving Governor Arran to parade in princely splendour in the great Stewart palace of Holyroodhouse. The queen dowager maintained contact with Beaton, and together the pair formed an uneasy alliance aimed at thwarting Arran's pro-English and pro-Protestant policies. This involved their getting the king of France's approval to recall Matthew Stewart, the earl of Lennox, as a counterweight to Arran. Battle-lines were thus drawn. With the queen of Scots an infant, Henry VIII had decided to court Arran, hoping to win Scotland for his son by marriage between Edward and young Mary. It was certainly a far more pleasant plan than his previous attempts at conquest. However, the means by which he had his unreliable Solway Moss captives – accompanied by the Douglas brothers – return north to argue in favour of another thistle and rose marriage betray his utter incompetence. As part of the marriage negotiations, he demanded that certain strategic Scottish fortresses be given into English hands and forbade the Scots from making any foreign policy without his approval. The frontal attack on Scottish independence was a foolish and iron-fisted move, but hardly a surprising one. Henry VIII's policy towards Scotland had ever been misguidedly proprietorial. At the time of Solway Moss he had told James V's herald that 'I am the very owner of

Scotland, and he holdeth it of me by homage'.[26] Henry might well have been fooled by the perfidy of his long-time guest, Angus, who had promised to 'make unto us the oath of allegiance, and recognise us as supreme Lord of Scotland, and as his prince and sovereign'.[27]

Mary of Guise and the Scottish parliament were sagacious enough to play along with Henry VIII's demands. In March 1543, Sir Ralph Sadler, a doyenne of Scottish affairs, was to give Mary Queen of Scots her first audience. In the nursery at Linlithgow, the child was divested of her swaddling garments and, according to Sadler, appeared to be 'as goodly a child as I have seen of her age, and as like to live, with the grace of God'.[28]

A marriage between Mary Queen of Scots and Prince Edward, however, was unlikely to receive genuine support from anyone other than the English king and those he paid. As Henry VII had foreseen, union between the kingdoms would undoubtedly result in the smaller kingdom being swallowed up by the larger. As even Sadler, tasked with winning agreement to the marriage, was to record, the Scottish lawyer Adam Otterburn pointed out:

Our people do not like of it. And though the Governor and some of the nobility have consented to it, yet I know that few or none of them do like of it; and our common people do utterly mislike of it. I pray you give me leave to ask you a question: if your lad was a lass, and our lass were a lad, would you then be so earnest in this matter? And lykewise I assure you that our nation will never agree to have an Englishman king of Scotland. And though the whole nobility of the realm would consent, yet our common people, and the stones in the street would rise and rebel against it.[29]

With marriage to Edward, Mary would become the subordinate partner, and given Henry's already-bellicose attitude towards his northern neighbour, the realm's hard-fought independence would be lost. Thus, although the Treaty of Greenwich, which assured the marriage, was drawn up and approved by the Scottish parliament and ratified in August 1543, by late December of the same year it was a dead letter. Against this backdrop, the baby queen was crowned with great festivity at Stirling, but without the presence of Governor Arran, who was nominally in favour of the English match and thus eager that the child should be sent south. Not one to give up, Henry VIII reached for the sword where his ham-fisted diplomacy and bribery had failed, and so began a period of Anglo-Scottish war which was to become known as the 'rough wooing' of Mary Queen of Scots.[30]

Whilst his new sister warbled in her cradle at Linlithgow and then Stirling (where she and her mother fled in July 1543), James Stewart was looking forward to enrolment at the University of St Andrews.[31] Comprised of two colleges, St Leonard's and St Salvator's, the university was the oldest and arguably the most prestigious in Scotland. In the period, boys embarked on their university education far younger than students today; typically they matriculated in their early or mid teens, following the conclusion of their grammar school education. It was necessary that the lessons of the grammar school were well learned, for at the university all conversation within the college precincts were to take place in Latin.[32]

Whilst at university, James would have imbibed all of the ideas which typically motivate students: radical thinking and a disapproval of authority. St Andrews had in its recent history attracted scholars on international repute – men such as the Provost of St Salvator's College, John Mair, who displayed an early commitment to the idea of union between Scotland and England. At St Leonard's College, reformist ideas were certainly in circulation, though officially disapproved of; so it was that those who expressed reformist sympathies in mid-sixteenth-century Scotland were popularly said to have 'drunk of the well of St Leonard's'.[33]

University life in the 1540s, though, was difficult. Roderick Graham usefully compares it to monasticism, citing the spartan conditions and long hours. As a son of the late king and a grandson of the Lord Erskine – not to mention being himself the prior of St Andrews – James would have been placed far above the ranks of the humble bursar or fee-paying student. Nevertheless, he would have undergone a Catholic humanist education, which brought a knowledge of theology and classical literature, at St Leonard's, the newer, stricter college. The *Acta Facultatis Artium Universitatis S. Andre* tells us that 'things were done to improve discipline [at St Leonard's] under Alexander Mylne, Abbot of Cambuskenneth, who in 1539 was appointed Administrator for the King's son, James Stewart, the child Commendator, afterwards earl of Moray'.[34] It is not difficult to imagine the young James, fresh from the schoolroom, sent across to the college, there to be inculcated in the merits of self-discipline, and in the fact of his administrator being a disciplinarian we can glimpse an early indication of his mind being moulded along the serious lines which were to become such an integral part of his character. To what extent, if any, doubts about the Catholic faith were sown in the youthful prior's mind during his education at St Andrews we cannot know. However, it is tempting to imagine that the university which had produced John Knox might have had some effect on his spiritual life. It is more likely that during this period James was to be strongly imbued with the sense of entitlement to power common to all aristocrats in the period. Whether he was a natural scholar or not is unknown, and hardly matters. In this he underwent an education similar to his sister; the children of James V were provided with the means of thorough instruction in all the areas considered necessary in the period, but were required to display no exceptional academic aptitude, their futures being already assured. What did matter was the boy's lineage, and as son of a king and prior of St Andrews, it was necessary only that he be seen to be educated. His later career suggests, however, that he had a talent for languages and diplomacy, and that he followed his father in developing an interest in the law. This should not surprise us. Clerics in the sixteenth century were part of a domineering institution which reached into the lives of citizens of all levels, through a system of ecclesiastical law courts which held jurisdiction over such diverse areas as property law, slander, and moral conduct. As Keith Brown has noted, 'a nobleman's education placed great emphasis on service and public duty to the king and commonweal, which was reinforced by the self-interest of individual nobles, their kinsmen and their clients who saw benefits in exercising government at the highest levels'.[35] The service and public duty expected of a queen regnant's brother and prior of a nation's main ecclesiastical seat would have been of great importance: James was to serve both the Stewart dynasty and the country by means of exercising government. To do so was both the purpose of his education and his right.

The ongoing war with England certainly made its mark on the university town, for it was an odd kind of war, fought with both pen and sword. The most brutal act was to take place in 1544, with the burning of Edinburgh by Henry VIII's sea-borne forces. The English king's infamous instructions to his lieutenant, the earl of Hertford, echo down the centuries as evidence of his chilling despotism:

Put all to fire and sword, burn Edinburgh, so razed and defaced when you have sacked and gotten what ye can of it, as there may remain forever a perpetual memory of the vengeance of God lightened upon (them) for their falsehood and disloyalty... the castle, sack Holyrood House and sack Leith and burn and subvert it and all ... as the upper stone may be the nether, and not one stick stand by another.[36]

The attack on Edinburgh was to leave an indelible stain (indeed, archaeological work on the palace of Holyroodhouse has uncovered scorching). As the citizens of the town gathered their belongings and fled as refugees into the countryside, the English troops arrived at Leith and put their torches to thatched roofs and timber frames. Not yet content, they moved onto the palace and adjacent abbey, smashing the recent tomb of James V. As far as sacking the cardinal's town went, Henry's orders were to remain unfulfilled. Nevertheless, it is clear that the town in which James was lodged was a target. Hertford neglected to follow up the burning of Edinburgh with further action; the time of year, the need to attend to Henry's campaigns in France, and a lack of resources forced him to withdraw his troops after they had wreaked havoc on the capital and surrounding hamlets. Whilst Mary Queen of Scots lay in safety behind the high walls of Stirling's great castle, James was to be protected by Henry VIII's financial woes and continental aspirations.

Touching St Andrews – and therefore James – more closely was the extraordinary murder of Cardinal Beaton in 1546. The most vocal opponent of the English match, the cardinal had amassed great wealth and with it a clutch of local enemies. A number of these, mainly lairds and other disgruntled gentry, entered his castle in the guise of builders and surprised the old man, who had only just seen his mistress out. Stabbing him to death and barricading themselves in with Governor Arran's son as a hostage, the assassins, who were to become known as the Castilians, displayed the ravaged corpse of Beaton from the battlements. A Protestant preacher in his early thirties called John Knox soon joined them, and Mary Queen of Scots and her mother were left without a pro-French, anti-English adherent. Nevertheless, the loss of the cardinal had no great effect on the immediate course of the war. Greater was Arran's gradual attenuation, which started when Mary of Guise began her political ascent, gaining access to the Lords of the Privy Council and cementing her place as the coming woman in Scottish politics. The Castilians were simply an inconvenience, and Arran made no serious attempt to dislodge them from the castle or the town. It was not to be until August of 1547 that the castle was taken by French forces led by Leone Strozzi, with Knox and his fellows forced into slavery in the French galleys.

Though Cardinal Beaton had been an enemy of Henry VIII, the old English warhorse can have taken little joy at his death, for he was not far from his own grave. For years the king of England had been morbidly obese, and in almost constant pain from a sore on his leg that refused to heal. By January 1547 he had begun to deflate, and he died on the 28th of the month. The suitor for Mary's hand was no longer Prince Edward but King Edward VI, who was to be raised a zealous Protestant by his uncle, the earl of Hertford who was in charge of the Scottish campaigns. Hertford lost no time in assuming the Protectorate of England, and still less in raising himself to the dukedom of Somerset. Under his direction, the old king's idiosyncratic form of religion was replaced by hard-line Protestantism, which was much to the taste of the boy king. Further, Henry VIII's death was to matter little in the grand scheme of bringing Scotland to heel. Somerset was to achieve his greatest victory over the Scots at the battle of Pinkie Cleugh on 10th September 1547. This rout was one of the bloodiest in Scotland's history, with the eyewitness William Patten recording:

Soon after this notable strewing of their footmen's weapons, began a pitiful sight of the dead corpses lying dispersed abroad, some their legs off, some but houghed, and left lying half-dead, some thrust quite through the body, others the arms cut off, diverse their necks half asunder, many their heads cloven, of sundry the brains pasht out, some others again their heads quite off, with other many kinds of killing. After that and further in chase, all for the most part killed either in the head or in the neck, for our horsemen could not well reach the lower with their swords. And thus with blood and slaughter of the enemy, this chase was continued five miles in length westward from the place of their standing ... In all which space, the dead bodies lay as thick as a man may note cattle grazing in a full replenished pasture.[37]

Though the retreating Arran was blamed for the defeat – losing credit as a result – of more immediate concern to the queen dowager was the safety of her daughter. Whilst Mary of Guise thus mourned the loss of security, James' mother, Margaret Erskine, was to mourn the loss of a husband. Amongst the slain at Pinkie was Lord Erskine, James' stepfather.

The war had directly touched both siblings. For the elder, it was to lead to his active involvement; for the younger, it was to lead to her passive removal from the country. Understandably terrified, the queen dowager stepped up negotiations to have Mary Queen of Scots, then five, sent to France. Growing up, the young Queen of Scots was remarkably lucky in having such a prolonged period of personal involvement with her mother (in addition to her personal nurse, Janet Sinclair). With the English threat underscored by the catastrophe of Pinkie, that period, which she was to look on with great affection, was about to come to an end. Although Somerset failed again to follow up victory, instead keeping to his plan of occupying strategic Scottish sites, the plan to evacuate Mary Queen of Scots went forward apace.

In the absence of the sword, the pen was employed by those in favour of the English match. During the later 1540s, the idea of union between the kingdoms was revived, with a series of tracts published exhorting the benefits of marriage between Mary Queen of Scots and Prince Edward. The remarkably titled *An Exhortacion to the Scottes to conforme themselfes to the honourable, Expedient, & Godly Union betweene the two realmes of Englande & Scotland* was to achieve little. It is interesting, however, in its framing of union as a religious act. During the war, those in favour of the match were predominantly Protestant. The author, James Henrisoun, was somewhat undermined by a renewed military attack masterminded by Somerset. *A similarly meretricious Epistle or exhortaction, to unite & peace, sent from the Lorde Protector, & others the kynges most honourable counsaill of England: To the Nobilities, Gentlemen, and Commons, and all others the inhabitauntes of the realme of Scotland* was a querulous and sanctimonious plea for the Scots to collaborate with the invaders (which a significant number did, becoming 'assured Scots'). Yet although England seemed to have the advantage, with Somerset organising an ingenious series of manned fortifications around the lowlands (to which sympathetic Scots were invited for their own protection from both armies), the mooted union was not to be. Perhaps more interesting is the emphasis in these tracts on the prospect of social as well as spiritual reformation in Protestant union. Though it was to be a desire rather than an actuality, even following the union of the crowns, we can trace in these tracts some of the seeds which were to flourish in James' mind and in those of his fellows in the next decade: in particular the idea that unity between Scotland and England, and the peace that should be attendant on it, would bring improvement to the lives of ordinary Scots.

In 1548 James was to make his first mark militarily, and brother and sister were to come together, possibly for the first time. The young prior of St Andrews joined Scottish forces in resisting English attacks in Fife at the beginning of the year and in St Monans in June. Whatever the complexion of the seventeen or eighteen-year-old's religious beliefs, at this stage his patriotic tendencies appear to have been at the fore. The fight, too, was inescapably personal: it was not just his sovereign but his sister whom the English sought by destruction, violence, and bribery. Though he can have had no close relationship with her, family ties in sixteenth-century Scotland mattered.

His studies at St Andrews now complete and with an early understanding of political resistance seeded, James was set to follow the traditional route of Scottish noblemen and continue his studies abroad (the universities in Scotland being deficient in broad legal training, and the Catholic church possessed of its own courts and legal system). Moreover, it was common for graduates of the period to embark on a cosmopolitan course of further study abroad, with many dispersing throughout the Netherlands, France, Italy and even Poland.[38] Thus, he was bound for Paris at the same time as his sister, negotiations with the new French king, Henry II, concluding in July with the Treaty of Haddington. Although the Anglo-Scottish war was to rumble on for a year and a half, it was to be without the presence in the country of the little queen.

Mary Queen of Scots set sail from Dumbarton on the 7th of August 1548, bidding a tearful farewell to her mother, who had herself just narrowly escaped death when an English cannonball landed near her as she climbed a tower in Haddington. In the queen's train was Lord James, and it is likely that this is the first time brother and sister spent any time together. It is interesting to speculate what the vivacious five-year-old and the scholarly teenager made of one another. For his part,

Mary was his undoubted sovereign, and the key to his future. As her half-brother, he could expect a significant say in the government of Scotland whilst she lived in France. For her part, he was likely introduced as a high-ranking cleric, to be of future use as she governed Scotland from afar. As her brother, she owed him affection, support, and advancement. In turn he owed her loyalty, love, and good counsel. Each was to give what they owed just as long as it suited them to do so.

The next decade was to shape the personalities and futures of both James and Mary. However, like their father given to listening to forceful personalities, brother and sister were to fall under the spells of very different men with competing religious, political, and ideological beliefs.

Broadening Horizons

Mary Queen of Scots was a good sailor. During the passage to France, it was reported that she alone amongst her train failed to succumb to seasickness. We can suppose that her brother shared in the general malaise, although it is to be hoped that his symptoms lessened with time; he was to cross between France and Scotland several times during the course of an education designed to outfit him for a career in the church. At any rate, our first glimpse of the young Mary's burgeoning personality comes from this episode. She is said to have good-naturedly taunted her shipmates for their weak stomachs.

Brother and sister stepped ashore at St Pol-de-Leon after a stormy, eighteen-day voyage. Each looking forward to very different futures, their reactions must have been mixed. For Mary, the daunting prospect of beginning a new life with new people lay ahead; her beloved mother lay behind. For James, far more mature, the trip represented only a further step up the career ladder; he might, and would be, returning home comparatively quickly.

Travelling with the siblings was a wider retinue comprising those chosen to be Mary's friends, keepers, and confidantes. These included her famous four Marys (Beaton, Seton, Fleming, and Livingston), and her governess, the attractive Lady Fleming (later a lover of the French king). Giving a masculine air to proceeding were not only James, but his grandfather, the elderly Lord Erskine. To greet the new arrivals were the queen's maternal grandparents, old Duke Claude and Antoinette de Bourbon; the latter, with characteristic hauteur, was to write of her pleasure in her granddaughter's appearance, but her distaste with the cleanliness of the party. Given that the Scottish contingent had just spent over two weeks at sea before arriving in a foreign country, one wonder what she was expecting.

Mary's retinue was bound for Paris. She herself was to join the French royal household at the splendid palace of St Germain-en-Laye. Overlooking the Seine, this magnificent chateau had been remodelled extensively by both Henry II and his father, Francis I. The sight of it must have drawn the collective breaths of the little queen's retinue; even Mary of Guise's Linlithgow could have fit fairly comfortably into its courtyard. Awe must have been mingled with sorrow, however. On the journey to St Germain-en-Laye, the brother of Mary Seton succumbed to illness and died.

Mary joined her new royal nursery-mates at Carrieres, outside of St Germain-en-Laye, before travelling on to the palace. Henry II was delighted with what he saw and insisted that the Scottish queen take precedence at court even over his own daughters, deferring only to himself and her future husband, the dauphin. The king said of the five-year-old, already showing signs of attaining the height of her mother, 'she is the most perfect child I have ever seen'. Remarkably, given her close relationship with her mother, Mary apparently arrived in her new home speaking little or no French. This naturally had to be remedied, and the queen was separated quickly from her Marys, her former playmates being sent to a convent to be educated. Leaving her too was her brother. Although he had been shown signal honour by being invited to accompany the royal train, and would undoubtedly have been treated with respect, his ostensible purpose in travelling was educational, and he was afforded no place in Henry II's court. Mary, however, was placed in the French king's royal household, where she became a surrogate sister to his children, Francis (her future husband), Elizabeth (rapidly her best friend), and Claude. Henry's queen,

43

Catherine de Medici, was at this stage in the political shadows: the Madame le Serpent of the popular imagination was, during Mary's time in France, eclipsed by her husband's beautiful, mature mistress, Diane de Poitiers. Further, as James departed, Mary was to meet another half-brother, this time from her mother's previous marriage: the young duke of Longueville, whom Mary of Guise had been forced to leave behind on her arranged marriage to James V. It might thus be fairly said that at her arrival in France, Mary Queen of Scots was not only given a royal welcome but provided with a new family. Thereafter, her relationship with the brother whom she had only recently got to know would be different. It would be less familial and more like the conventional relationship between a mistress and a servant. She had always been set apart from him by her sovereignty, but now she was to join a household filled with those of similar rank. A fondness for the smiling but solemn teenage boy she knew as a brother she might have felt; respect for him as an equal or peer she never could.

It was in an atmosphere of conviviality and glamour that Mary made her entry into France, and this was to set the tone for her life in what became her favourite country. Here she learned the graceful dances for which the French court was renowned (and which were later to be so roundly condemned by Scottish Calvinists). In the first few years of her time abroad, she was to become rapidly acclimatised to French culture, French tastes, and the French language. In this she was encouraged by Henry II, who clearly saw the need to turn the girl who was earmarked as his son and heir's bride to develop and maintain all the attributes of a French renaissance queen. His task was made easier by the girl's natural grace, eagerness to please, and willingness to learn. All three qualities were to recur throughout her life, not least when her time in France came to an end and she had to consider a return to Scotland.

Yet Henry II's process of systematic cultural stripping and refashioning was to have limited success. Mary never forgot her Scots and was to retain a careful interest in the activities of her Scottish friends and enemies. In all, the French king's manipulation of the royal household so that it incorporated the future dauphiness was, in the end, successful enough only to make her charmingly different to her Scottish and English friends, and conveniently alien to her enemies.

Equally impressed by the bright-eyed Scottish queen were her maternal uncles, the notorious Guise brothers. These included Charles, the cardinal of Lorraine, a voluptuary clad in scarlet; the battle-scarred Francis, who would become duke of Guise in 1550; and Claude, duke of Aumale. These men were to train their niece in the arts of statecraft, their goal being to ensure Guise power extended not only directly into the French monarchy, but throughout Europe. With the ability to make a mark directly on the queen of Scots' young mind, they were not slow to impress upon her the importance of family, loyalty to the Church of Rome, and that invaluable tool of sixteenth-century politics: dissimulation.

The world into which the little queen had stepped could scarcely have been more different from that she had known in Scotland. Despite James V and Mary of Guise's best efforts, the renaissance palaces they had constructed were small-scale in comparison to the chateaux of the Loire and the sprawling palace of the Louvre; that first glimpse of St Germain-en-Laye was to have set a precedent. Where once she had kept to the well-appointed chambers of Stirling, she was now free to walk the galleries and orchards of Chenonceaux and Chambord. Where once she had for scenery tight knot gardens and the forbidding sight of the Trossachs, now she had the wide Seine and the rolling plains of the Loire valley. Her cultural tastes were thus to be shaped by her time in France; although she was wisely to maintain a careful, pro-Protestant

45

policy when she assumed her personal reign in Scotland, her household was to glitter with continental aesthetes. In her most recent full-scale biographer's memorable phrasing, Mary's identity was to be 'altered if not entirely transformed' by her French education.

What lessons did she learn in this gilded schoolroom, and from whom? With her Guise relatives near at hand, it appears that Mary was given a crash course in the art of obeying wise heads. In the schoolroom itself, she embarked on a course of French lessons, soon becoming proficient, in addition to Latin, poetics, and a smattering of Greek. Often criticised as the intellectual inferior to her rival, that insatiable student Elizabeth I, it should here be noted that Mary was never earmarked to be a great scholar: she was in training to be a queen consort of France. Academia, however, was hardly neglected. Though she was never a particularly accomplished poet, she was certainly a patroness, helping Ronsard's work to publication. As tutors she was assigned Claude Millot and Antoine Fouquelin, and when the basics were exhausted she was allowed to study under the dauphin's tutor, Jacques Amyot. If, as Guy attests, her schoolroom efforts were largely banal and by-rote, we should not be too harsh. Mary's education tells us more about her willingness to learn – and to listen to others – than her natural abilities.

In addition to high-minded pursuits, Mary was also to enjoy embroidery – for which she displayed a singular talent – and the enjoyable pastime of baking. If this seems twee, that is because it was. For centuries French noblewomen and royalty were to be found playing at humble housewives, with specially constructed kitchens designed for them (not unlike the toy kitchens provided for children today). Remarkably, this little leisure pastime was to be of more use in a crisis than either her poetry (which was used against her) or Latin. After the murder of Riccio and wild flight to Dunbar in 1566, the queen was reported to have insisted on cooking eggs for her adherents.

Throughout her hours of study and leisure, it is notable that Mary became a firm friend to her future husband, the weak and stammering Dauphin Francis. Contemporaries remarked with fond smiles on the burgeoning relationship between the pair, which was more like brother and sister than lovers (and, indeed, more like siblings than the queen's relationship with her own half-brothers and -sisters). In short, Mary was a remarkable addition to the French royal house from moment of her entry.

Whilst Mary was thus becoming accustomed to her new life as a French dauphiness-to-be, her half-brother would have been looking forward to attendance at the prestigious Sorbonne. Here he was to develop his interest in law, and within the first couple of years of his studies we can find reference to the fruits of his labours. In 1550, the nineteen-year-old James was to make his first serious attempts to enter the marriage market. The object of his desires – it cannot be said affections – was one Christian Stewart, a daughter of the master of Buchan who had fallen at the battle of Pinkie. The girl stood as the sole heir to the vast estates and, under sixteenth-century Scots law, they would fall to her husband on her marriage. James seems to have made serious inroads in courting her, and on the successful contract of marriage, she was sent to live with his mother at Lochleven. Although the marriage was not to come to pass, James pursued every legal avenue available in subsequent years in ensuring that the right of redemption of the mortgaged lands became his. These lands he was to covet until his sister was in a position to grant the whole estates of the earldom to him over a decade later.

The fact that James was pursuing marriage at this stage is doubly interesting not only for the light it sheds on his desire for land and revenue, but because it illustrates that his interests were secular rather than strictly religious. His position as a cleric was, even at this early stage, secondary to his acquisitive nature, and he was thus in the ranks of the commendators – those secular holders of benefices who controlled the revenue of abbeys and priories without being ordained priests. His studies at the Sorbonne coincided with a growth in religious reform across France and Scotland, and his mind seems to have been ripe for inculcation in the Protestant faith, which positively encouraged clerical marriage. Further, he studied, however briefly, at the prestigious Collège de Presles under the noted humanist Petrus Ramus.[39] The great scholar was no stranger to controversy. He had been accused of undermining religion and barred from lecturing in 1544, only being received back into the French academic world after the death of Francis I. Like his student, Ramus was ultimately to be won away from Catholicism. Praying in his lodgings during the St Bartholomew's Day Massacre of Huguenots in 1572, he was stabbed to death by rampaging Catholics. The effect of another worldly figure on James Stewart – and one who courted controversy – can only be guessed at.

The purpose of a continental education was not, of course, strictly academic (and it certainly was not in James' case). The prior of St Andrews had swapped the wind-whipped grey buildings of his ecclesiastical town for another world, much as his sister had. Here he would have found even greater boundaries of thought; here he would have witnessed not simply a small number of faculty and students drinking bad beer, but a powerhouse of intellectuals debating amidst an entire quarter dedicated to students, bookshops, and stationery.[40] The horizons of brother and sister had been irrevocably altered by their travels, and this widening of worlds was to have significant repercussions for both. For Mary, her time as an honorary and then an actual princess of France was to shape her attitude to her own station in life; for James, his time in one of Europe's premier university town was, as Andrew Lang puts it, to contribute to his own sense of superiority and 'worldliness'. Ever afterwards, he was to be at home in Scotland, France, and England, and to be as willing to turn his mind to state affairs as he was organising regional and local disputes.

Yet it would be a mistake to assume that James took to the life of a student, assuming a normal course or period of study. On the contrary, despite his licence to join his sister's retinue being for the purpose of going 'to the sculis and to study, and to do other his lawful business', he is reported as having been back in Scotland in September 1549, and perhaps even as early as April. He was to be found collecting levies in Fife and repelling English raiders under Lord Clinton, and in October of the same year he was doing the duties of the priory in a provincial council held at Edinburgh. In 1550 he was again in France, attending to his sister's affairs and receiving letters of legitimation from her. Despite the nomenclature, these letters did no more than recognise him as her natural brother; historically, they were intended to 'remove bastardy's stigma, enabling illegitimate sons of nobles to have noble status, marriages, inheritance rights and tax exemptions'.[41] By obtaining these letters, James not only won recognition from his sister but secured his future right to enjoy all the perquisites afforded other noblemen. In Scotland that would allow him to marry – which, as we have seen, he had expressed a desire to do – to raise capital, and to have formal conciliar access to his sovereign. The latter was one of the key perks of the 'ancient blood' of Scotland. Via his formal recognition as a natural brother to the queen, James had taken an early step in ensuring his right to be heard. In future he was to jealously guard it.

In 1552, James again visited France, returning this time via England – potentially his first visit to the realm, then ruled by Edward VI (Somerset having tumbled from power and onto the block in 1549), which was to figure so importantly in his later life. It has been suggested that at this early stage he was employed as a spy, reporting on his sister's activities directly to English authorities. However, this is unlikely; although a James Stewart is recorded as having received English payments, the name, as we have seen, was common enough to have referred to any number of men (if the spy in question even used his real name). What James' trip through England can tell us regards his facility with language. He was to be at home in Scotland, France, and England, and thus we can assume that he spoke the languages of all three countries. Here it is necessary to consider a particularly thorny and insoluble question: of whether Scots and English were distinct languages in the period. Frustratingly, accounts from the sixteenth century differ. Certainly, the pro-union tracts by the likes of Henrisoun which abounded in the 1540s stressed the 'one language' shared by the two kingdoms. That later proponent of union, James VI and I, was also to famously write that the realms were of one tongue. Both the treatise writers and James VI had distinct agendas: to downplay or efface Scotland's independent identity. Earlier in the century, however, Don Pedro de Ayala was to say that 'Scots language is as different from English as Aragonese from Castilian' (he drew a distinction, of course, between lowland Scots, the language of the Scottish court, and the Gaelic spoken in the Highlands and islands). On balance, the non-partisan de Ayala is likely correct. Although Scots grew out of the Inglis language which spread northwards during the early medieval period, by the sixteenth century it had become cemented as a language quite distinct from that being spoken in southern England. It is to James Stewart's credit that he had a facility with language (he travelled in England, wrote to English correspondents, and even lived in England briefly in later life) that his sister did not. Mary Queen of Scots quite notoriously did not learn English until her captivity, and even then she appeared to lack the fluency she enjoyed in Scots and French.

What else can James' leapfrogging tell us? Unlike Arran's half-brother, John Hamilton, who had spent significant periods abroad studying whilst his abbacy lay in the hands of a claustral prior, James seems to have regularly attended his seat. In essence, his 'studying abroad' was therefore a training course in diplomacy, which took precedence over traditional study. Whilst Queen Mary was accompanying the French royal family in progresses around her new realm, James was likewise in motion. To be on the move in the early modern period was a virtue, whether from filth-choked palaces in need of sweetening, or from political scandals and crises. At this stage, the young man and the little girl were thus learning a key lesson which was to come into play at moments of difficulty in both their lives: the value of fleetness of foot.

One might also consider what those around James thought of him at this period. If his half-sister appeared to her new countrymen a malleable and effervescent personality to be polished up like a diamond, how did James Stewart present himself? If Antoinette de Bourbon is anything to go by, the answer is 'not especially clean'. This is of course facile. He appeared to others exactly what he was: an attractive, determined young cleric in the mould of David Beaton or Thomas Wolsey. Gifted with royal blood and Stewart charm, and obviously destined for a multi-faceted career, he was an up and coming man of the future. He was increasingly well-connected, well-travelled, and eager to advance in his sister's and his country's service.

Affairs in Scotland during Mary's time in France and her half-brother's time hopping back and forth across the English Channel did not stand still. On the contrary, as the war with England petered out, Mary of Guise was to make her way more fully onto the political stage, and in doing so the cries for reform of the Catholic Church were to grow more voluble. Mary Queen of Scots was not unaware of her mother's struggles at home – but in her letters to her mother, her ultimate concern is that the advice of her uncles be followed, they being political, military and religious experts.

In her daughter's absence, the queen dowager became fixated on ensuring her the future of the northern kingdom, and this meant taking an active role in politics. Her immediate problem was the earl of Arran, who remained as governor of the realm, and would do so until he could be dislodged. This he would not be until he was quite willing, and he could not be made willing until he was assured that his financial exactions had been remitted (since attaining the governorship in 1543, he had been spending treasury money like a drunken sailor) and adequately recompensed with a French dukedom.

As part of her campaign to assume power in Scotland, Mary of Guise followed in the footsteps of her stepson, crossing the sea to visit her son and daughter in 1550, following the Treaty of Boulogne, which saw an official end to the tedious wars begun by Henry VIII in the 1540s. Though she was unable to see her father, old Duke Claude, before he died, the sight of her children must have been a great recompense for the stoic Frenchwoman who had arrived in Scotland in 1538 an inexperienced girl, and just left it a rising politician.

Mary of Guise brought with her to France almost the entire complement of the Scottish nobility. In doing so, she sought to win over to her side – and her political goals – those lords who had been enamoured of England during the Rough Wooing. She was to be aided not only by generous bribes from Henry II, but by the glitz and glamour of France, which she hoped would excite the avarice of her greedier nobles. In the pursuit of power in Scotland, Mary of Guise was not ambitious; rather, she was simply pursuing what had been the right of her predecessors. When James IV had died, his widow had attained the regency. When James III had died, Mary of Guelders had had it. It was not ambition that drove the dowager, but a sense of having been cheated of what should, by rights, have been hers from the moment her husband died.

During the dowager's joyful reunion with her daughter, one of the most spectacular pieces of royal pageantry in European history took place: the entry of Henry II into Rouen. Such royal entries were part and parcel of the performance of monarchy in the early modern period, taking place when a newly-anointed monarch first entered an important town or city. The theme of the spectacle was the civilising of savages, with a Brazilian village constructed on the banks of the Seine, complete with three-hundred naked 'savages', fifty of whom were genuine imported Brazilians. From a specially erected spectator scaffold, Mary of Guise could watch the villagers hunt, caper, and descend to the river. The salacious pastoral was broken by the drumbeats of war, as the Brazilians turned on one another. Thereafter, a mock sea battle was fought on the river between French and ostensibly Portuguese ships. Tragedy struck when an excess of gunpowder resulted in two of the ships descending to the riverbed with the losses of all aboard, but the visual impact cannot be denied. Throughout all, the role of Scotland as an ally of France was trumpeted.

What Henry, Mary of Guise, and the Scottish lords who accompanied her witnessed over the course of the Rouen festivities (which ran over several days) was a grand celebration of the cessation of war and the victory of France and Scotland. Consequently, Mary Queen of Scots – the office as well as the little girl inhabiting it – played a central role. To all present, the message was clear: Scotland would become a part of France, in its culture, in its monarchy, and in its military. This can have seemed no bad thing to young Mary, but it cannot have done other than struck fear and distrust into the Scottish lords in her mother's retinue. What James Stewart made of it – his sister to be a French queen, with her mother governing Scotland as a semi-colony – makes for intriguing speculation. With a mind being then actively trained to question, he must certainly have wondered at his own future. Rouen opened up two distinct paths. He might enjoy a comfortable living in what would become a French outpost, or he might alternatively join the resistance to French hegemony as he had eagerly joined the resistance to English overlordship.

In 1553 a fascinating rumour reached Emperor Charles V from the imperial ambassador to England, Jean Scheyfve, who reported having heard that Mary of Guise planned to make James regent of Scotland in place of Arran; however, this is unlikely. The raison d'etre of her 1550-1 mission to the French court was to secure the regency for herself. Nevertheless, the rumour is useful in that it reveals that her trust in her stepson, and her belief that he was a good Catholic and faithful to her unwavering pro-French policy, was reasonably believed as late as 1553.

Mary of Guise stayed on in France for a year, during which she was assiduous in petitioning Henry II to support her in her bid to oust Arran from the governorship and install her instead. Throughout, she was supported by her brothers. Full of spite at the thought of Scotland and France uniting in strength, an English emissary was to write of the Guises, 'Monsieur de Guise and Monsieur d'Aumale and the Cardinal of Lorraine partly at her egging and partly upon an ambitious desire to make their house great, be no hindrance to her malicious desire'. Misogyny compelled the emissary to lay the blame at the dowager's door, but the truth is that Guise ambitions were all-encompassing. When a plot to poison her daughter was uncovered, Mary of Guise elected to extend her stay in the country, leading the English ambassador to sourly claim that 'the dowager of Scotland makes all this court weary of her, from the high to the low, such an importunate beggar is she for herself and her chosen friends'. Although one suspects this was wishful thinking on the ambassador's part, it is clear that Mary of Guise was in France to beg, borrow, and steal favours. Her goal was not to secure power for power's sake, but to ensure that her daughter's native kingdom remained secure and free from English incursions. She only left the country after her son, Mary's half-brother, the duke of Longueville, took ill and died in her arms.

Mary of Guise parted from her daughter in autumn 1551. In returning to Scotland, she pre-empted by some months the path to be trod by her stepson James, passing through Edward VI's England. Debarking at Rye, she was conveyed to London where she was treated with all courtesy and thereafter given lodgings at Warblington Castle as the guest of Sir Richard Cotton. She left the English court with the present of two cups and a diamond, and thereafter rode northwards, where her standing had been improved by her travels.

Left behind during Mary of Guise's visit to France had been Governor Arran and the French ambassador, Monsieur d'Oysel (presumably to keep an eye on him). Whilst the dowager had sought to woo the majority of Scotland's political elite with French money and majesty, Arran had remained at home to wonder at what he was missing. The answer was a lucrative position in the French nobility. Though he would not retire in favour of the dowager immediately, he gained his prize in 1554, being elevated to the dukedom of Châtelherault. His elevation and resignation from the governorship coincided with the eleven-year-old Mary's ascent – engineered by her Guise uncles – to full authority as an ostensibly mature queen of Scots.

The war with England was over. Mary Queen of Scots was safe in France, learning her lessons and charming her peers and elders alike. The stage was set for her to live out the rest of her life in her adoptive country, with her mother governing her former home, and her future as France's queen all but secured. James Stewart was rapidly developing a talent for moving back and forward between his home and his sister's, in the process learning the ways of the genteel continental diplomat. Such training was to outfit him as a future leader, requiring as that position would a healthy measure of natural charm and an ability to manage difficult and often competing factions and personalities. For his support of his stepmother, he was even granted further benefices: the priories of Pittenweem in Scotland and Mâcon in France.[42] His contemporaries now looked upon him, whether standing on the deck of a ship, striding from a lecture at the Sorbonne, or taking his chair as prior of St Andrews in ecclesiastical meetings, as an up and comer. The future must have seemed clear: Mary Queen of Scots would become queen of France. With her husband, they would gently nudge Scotland into satellite status, with her mother and useful Catholic brother attending to the affairs of what would simply be a quaint region.

Yet in a decade, Mary of Guise had been driven to her grave by Protestant insurgents armed with English gold and English support. Mary Queen of Scots would have seen the end of her life of luxury in the gentle swell of the French lowlands. James would have turned his back on the faith of his childhood and become one of the leading adherents of his stepmother's rag-tag band of noble enemies. Scotland itself would be turned almost overnight from a Catholic nation to a Protestant one. Brother and sister would find themselves on opposite sides of an unbridgeable divide, with Mary retaining the lessons of her Guise uncles, and James under the sway of an even more powerful personality.

The Preacher and the Cardinal

In 1554, the year of her elevation to the regency of Scotland, Mary of Guise's position must have looked secure. Her daughter was safely ensconced in unparalleled French luxury; she had assumed the regency of Scotland with French aid; and in 1553 the Protestant boy king Edward VI had succumbed to a horrifying pulmonary illness, leaving the Catholic Mary Tudor to inherit the English throne (which circumstance deprived Scottish Protestants of a royal ally south of the border). Her struggles, however, were only just beginning.

Protestantism had been difficult to seed in Scotland as long as it had been the religion of the auld enemy, of the aggressive Henry VIII, the duke of Somerset, and Edward VI. The fact that the religion went hand in glove with a desire for unity between the realms was a difficult sell with memories of the burning of Edinburgh, the battle of Pinkie, and innumerable smaller English atrocities fresh in Scottish minds. With the accession of Mary Tudor and her re-establishment of Catholicism in England, the link between pro-Englishness and Protestantism was weakened. To be a Scottish Protestant was no longer to hold out the hand of friendship to men who returned a dagger thrust or a flaming torch.

Yet this is not the only explanation for the growth in Protestantism which was to plague Mary of Guise and turn Scotland quickly from a Catholic to a Protestant country which sought friendship with its aggressive and historically hostile neighbour. For one thing, it was generally believed that amity with England could keep Scotland independent, putting an end to the chance of a successful conquest from the south. The more far-sighted might also have recognised (as did Henry VII) that any monarchical union resulting from the thistle and rose marriage (in the event of the extinction of the Tudors) might be made on Scotland's terms. Amity could also open up trade with England, and lucrative relations with the Lutheran Denmark-Norway and Holstein could only be improved if Scotland joined them in rejecting the papacy.

In order to make sense of what seems – and was – a *volte-face* in Scotland's history, it is important to understand that the reformation and its coeval development of peace with England was a spiritual, political, dynastic, and economic force. From a modern perspective, it is easy to see secular reasons as having paramount importance, but to do so is to force an unfair degree of cynicism on early modern thought patterns. To many people in the period, God was as real a figure in their daily lives as their monarch - mostly unseen, yet present in the governmental system under which they lived. The promise of immortality to lives which were short and often harsh was tempting, and whether Catholic or Protestant, finding the true faith mattered.

As has been noted, the Catholic Church in Scotland was riddled with corruption: James' own advancement to the priory of St Andrews at seven years old stands testament to it. Complaints were also rife about the parish churches which were 'rent or falling down': a serious problem for a faith which was predicated on visual splendour and mystery rather than pure scripture.[43] Reformers sought not only a spiritual revolution, but a social one, expounding on the improvements that could be made to ordinary Scots' lives in the event of reformation. Additionally, a new breed of preachers was to be born in Scotland, seizing not only upon the neglected laity but carefully wooing the nobility. The inhabitants of those areas who had been worst stung by the Rough Wooing had, as well, an understandable desire to ensure the safety of their immortal souls – and fearful people were ripe for being cautioned of the dangers of idolatry, and a susceptibility to the promises of redemption through evangelicalism.

The Regent Mary would pursue a tolerant course, but in hindsight likely came to see that this did little but nurture her enemies, who had in her a ready-made figure of hatred: a woman and a foreigner. Her response to unfolding crises was uncharacteristically blind. With an unwavering desire to ensure French hegemony over Scotland in the name of her daughter, Mary gave lucrative positions to Frenchmen and encouraged the enlistment of French soldiers on Scottish soil. In this she was inadvertently undermining what Scottish resistance to Henry VIII's marriage proposal had been founded on: the country's independence from foreign rule. It is likely that the dowager understood Scottish independence only insofar as it had been marked by anti-Englishness; she could not see that swapping England for France did not erase the Scottish political community's desire to run their own affairs.

In the middle of the 1550s, the most famous and vociferous advocate of religious reform was to step back onto Scottish soil. John Knox, freed from the servitude he had been forced into in the French galleys after the Castilians had lost St Andrews Castle, returned full of fire and fury in 1555.

Knox had initially been ordained a deacon in the Catholic faith but had begun to doubt his calling in 1543. Thereafter he had begun to dissent, persuaded ultimately by the execution of his friend, the Protestant martyr George Wishart, who had been burnt spectacularly in the forecourt of St Andrews castle in the last months of Cardinal Beaton's life.

Sentenced to eighteen months in the French galleys for joining the Castilian band who had subsequently murdered Beaton, Knox took refuge in England after his release. His hands were still scarred by the arduous and agonising toil. There he had won a fan in the shape of the duke of Somerset, who had advanced him to a position in the garrison town of Berwick. Although he likely met his future wife, Marjorie Bowes, in Berwick, Knox was unable to marry due to the girl's father's opposition; instead he took up a new position in Newcastle. In the following year he was appointed one of six chaplains to Edward VI. After Somerset's fall, the new protector, the duke of Northumberland, continued to prefer Knox, and he continued in England, contributing to the *Book of Common Prayer*, until the boy-king's death. With the accession of Mary Tudor, England became a dangerous place for men like Knox, and he wisely fled to the continent.

In Geneva Knox found kindred spirits. The spiritual home of the Reformation, and the physical home of John Calvin, it was whilst there that the Scottish preacher was offered a willing and open congregation in Frankfurt. There he might have stayed, had not an influx of English Protestant exiles brought contention. The brotherhood of Protestants was not, as Knox might have hoped, one of unity, but fraught with its own schisms. To negotiate these troubled waters required patience, compromise, and skill in politicking. If there was one talent the Scottish preacher lacked, it was how to finesse, how to give way, as a politician or statesman might do. He was thus bested by the more politically-astute and subtle rivals he locked horns with in the English Protestant contingent. Where they had subtle tongues and artfully-wagging fingers, he had an iron tongue and clunking fist: his milieu was the pulpit rather than the debating chamber. Bowing to pressure, Knox reluctantly packed up and returned to Scotland, where the lessons he was to impart were to be predominantly spiritual.

Since leaving the country in chains in 1547, Knox had learnt some valuable lessons, chief amongst which was the importance of winning aristocratic support to the cause of reform (or, indeed, to any cause). Amongst his targets was the young James Stewart. By now a man of the world himself, and legitimised brother to the absent queen, he would prove an invaluable tool if only he could be won around.

As part of a deliberate and careful tour of his home nation, Knox records that he met with James in the home of the laird James Sandilands of Calder. In the wind- and snow-blasted Calder House near Livingston, the two men first came to exchange ideas. We have no clear idea of what James saw when his gaze met the man who would make him a proselyte, but we can discount the idea of a wild-eyed, ranting despot. The classic image of Knox, which still frowns down from a plinth outside St Giles Cathedral in Edinburgh and glares out from the much-copied engraving in Theodore de Beza's *Icones*, is disputed. Yet there must have been something magnetic and impressive about him. Much has been written on the famous preacher's political and religious arguments. It is verging on understatement to claim that he did not approve of the recent accession of Mary Tudor; in fact, her reign was to inspire his most famous and misogynistic writing, *The First Blast of the Trumpet Against the Monstrous Regiment of Women*. That lay in his future. At the time he met James Stewart, however, he had penned *A Godly Letter of Warning to the Faithfull in London, Newcastle and Berwick*, which set forth his opinion of rulers. 'For all those', he wrote 'that would draw us from God (be they kings or queens), being of the devil's nature, are enemies unto God, and therefore God wills that in such cases we declare ourselves enemies unto them'.[44] This was heady stuff. Although the tenor of his argument – the idea that unjust, ungodly, or unlawful rulers might be resisted or deposed – was not new, the idea of popular or elective sovereignty was in general decline in Europe in

61

the early modern period. Instead, the trend was towards absolutism and centralised control, of political communities which obeyed rather than took part in decision-making. What did this mean for James Stewart? In essence, it indicated that he might resist his sister and stepmother if occasion called for it. If it also inspired thoughts that he might seize the crown for himself, this would have been understandable, but unlikely. For that to be the case, James would have had to support an absolute overturning of the long-standing Scottish affection for hereditary rule and the laws of primogeniture, swept aside his sister, his own elder brother or brothers, and the Hamilton and Lennox Stewart branches of the family. This would have been far too dangerous a course to pursue and was one unlikely to be followed by even the most ardent of reformers. It would have meant destroying the crown he is popularly said to have coveted and instead setting up an elective monarchy.

Knox's return to Scotland was short-lived (he left in July 1556) but impactful. By the time he departed he had won to his cause a significant number of disgruntled lords and gentry. One of these was the enigmatic William Maitland of Lethington, a secretary of Mary of Guise who, alongside James, sat on her privy council. The two men were to become fast friends, sharing as they did a belief in the reformed faith and a commitment to achieving some kind of lasting amity with England.

The band of converted men and women Knox left behind after his whirlwind tour did not immediately unseat the newly-installed regent. Mary of Guise continued to pursue her tolerant course. In her July 1555 parliament, she even made some tentative steps in conciliating those who had turned against the louche practices of Catholicism. The eating of flesh during Lent was cracked down on; traditional May Day revels were curtailed; and, quaintly, 'women or others about summer trees singing' were outlawed. Although she could not have known it, she was setting the tone for a Calvinist Scotland. She was, indeed, so conciliatory that James and a number of other high-ranking Scotsmen felt comfortable enough to send a letter to Knox in Geneva in March 1557, inviting their idol to return. This is critical. Believing that the regent was either soft or open-minded, James and his friends clearly saw their cause as one which could be achieved within the system rather than one requiring its overthrow. Knox was not convinced. From Dieppe he wrote encouraging them to rebel against the French presence in Scotland and overthrow the Catholic Church by force.

It was to be the action of Mary Tudor in England that was to cause crisis in Scotland. The pitiable English queen had married Philip of Spain, eleven years her junior, and had accordingly allowed her country to join his in a renewed Habsburg-Valois war. The Valois king Henry II naturally leant on his advisors, the Guise brothers, to demand Scottish aid. The Guise brothers in turn leant on Mary of Guise and her daughter. To the regent's shock, her nobility simply refused to do other than defend their country in the event of invasion; they would not invade England at France's command. This refusal was not along religious lines. Even the Catholic earl of Huntly, the most powerful magnate in Scotland, thumbed his nose at Regent Mary, who saw it as her mission to bring what she oddly thought of as a 'young' nation 'to a state of perfection and to an unwonted subservience to those who wish to see justice reign'. Mary of Guise can have had no great love for Scotland or its people. It was, after all, the country into which policy had deposited her. However, she did have a tremendous sense of duty, no doubt bolstered by religious conviction. It was her duty to preserve her daughter's realm as a Catholic country, and to make it conformable to union with cultured and centralised France. Now her nobility was frustrating her at every turn. Noble as her sentiments undoubtedly were, the Scots themselves likely did not see their future as being subservient to France or a Frenchwoman.

It was the Protestants, still fired up by Knox's visit (and the stream of letters he was producing), whose reaction was most significant. At the end of 1557, a number of them banded together to form an alternative government, known as the First Band of the Lords of the Congregation. Jettisoning even the pretence of wishing for what they called 'true religion' to be achieved by peaceful means, they declared all-out revolution. It was a warning, and a stark one. The Protestants meant business.

At this stage, James Stewart remained an adherent of his stepmother. He even became involved in a raid into Northumberland in August 1557. However, his adherence to the new faith had become a complication, and potentially a hazardous one. James, his mind already open to the possibility of reform, seems to have been one of those people who becomes attached to a new ideology and pursues it with the much-attested zeal of the convert. Overnight he was transformed into a committed reformer and staunch critic of the faith in which he had been raised. Yet he was not ready to turn his back entirely on the woman whom he had called his stepmother. Ideally, he might have converted the regent, but Mary of Guise was not for turning; indeed, she laughed out loud at Knox's ham-fisted attempts by letter to harangue her into giving up Catholicism.[45] The problem thus remained. To James, the solution seems to have been to wait for his stepmother to retire or die, and then reinstall Arran (or Châtelherault, as he was now known), who could be depended upon for his lack of dependability. He might, it was supposed, be bought into supporting Protestant government. The idea was a dead letter. In effect, James and his friends were hamstrung. They knew what they wanted – a reformed Scotland – but had no means of getting it as long as Mary of Guise gave them no excuse to rebel openly, and Mary Tudor in counter-reformation England would offer no ground support to anti-Catholic insurgents. The result was stalemate, and it is testament to James' political nous that he accepted it. He also accepted that his sister, growing up happily in France, would marry the French dauphin, and likely never return to Scotland. His eyes were turned to the future. For now, immediately acting on his mentor's creed was both foolish and dangerous.

Whilst Knox won James to the Protestant cause, his sister was undergoing her own period of indoctrination. In the absence of her mother, this was conducted by her uncle, the cardinal of Lorraine. This sinister figure has been the subject of much debate. Born in 1524, Charles of Lorraine had become archbishop of Reims (the crowning place of French kings) in 1538, and a cardinal in 1547. He succeeded his uncle as cardinal of Lorraine in 1550, the older gentleman having been one of the richest prelates and pluralists in the country. A great artistic patron, Charles was to patronise the poet Ronsard and the famed humanist scholar Rabelais. Naturally he provided a useful bogeyman for Protestant polemicists. Two years after Charles' death, Huguenot writer Louis Regnier de la Planche published his *Legende de Charles Cardinal de Lorraine et de ses freres*, which charged the Guises' with, amongst other things, 'ambition … being accompanied with covetousness, cruelty, ungodliness, and manifest villainy'.[46]

The more scandalous-minded of historians and novelists have even gone as far as to suggest that he embarked upon an incestuous affair with his young niece. Originally, this seems to have stemmed from words attributed to Mary's future husband, the earl of Bothwell, who reputedly called her 'the cardinal's whore' prior to their marriage. The scandal seems to have been exacerbated by contemporary French politics, with the anonymous author of the 1574 pamphlet *Le Reveille-Matin de Francois* describing how the cardinal accepted a painting in which he, Mary, Catherine de Medici, and his sister-in-law the duchess of Guise (Anne d'Este, Duke Francis's wife) were depicted nude, entwined in one another's arms.[47] This particular piece of gossip can be – and should be – assigned to the rubbish heap.

Equally shamefully, Planche's tract picked up the same story to accuse Charles of prostituting his niece in a bid for power:

Also through their earnest desire that their Niece might have issue, and yet knowing King Frauncis but simply disposed thereunto, in that his generative partes were altogither dulled and hindred; they permitted many courtiers to have her companie, who did their endevours to make her very fruitfull: yet am I ashamed to know that in a certayne table [painting] which an Italian of Laques found meanes to get ... conveyed unto the Cardinall of Lorraines chamber, with certeyne letters from the Pope in steade of our Ladie of Grace, wherein were the sayde Cardinall of Lorraine, the Queene his Niece, the Queene mother, and the Duchesse of Guise most lively set out, their bodyes naked, their armes one about an others necke, and all their legges enterlaced togither.[48]

The theme is very much the same: scandal was attached to Mary as an adjunct of attacks on her family. The reference to secret letters from the pope combined with lascivious images of Catholic women and their relative was simply a potent mix for achieving a lasting and explosive slander.

The goal of the entire Guise brood – particularly Mary's uncles – was to advance the power of their family. This meant ensuring that their niece toed the family line, did as she was told, and wherever possible made the case for Guises to be preferred to plum positions of authority. Mary appears to have been willing to do as she was told. Once a month the cardinal swept into her household, at whichever palace it happened to be lodged, his deep-set eyes swivelling hither and yon. Servants backed against walls or strove to appear busy as the red robes swirled and the tread of velvet slippers marked his inspection. His mission was to ensure that all was running not just smoothly but grandly. If the Cardinal was far more political than religious, he understood the power of visual display. His ostensible reason for these visits was that his niece's household had never quite recovered from the scandal of her Scottish governess Lady Fleming's affair with Henry II. What might have been an indiscretion was blown into a scandal by the lady's pregnancy and delivery of a royal bastard, Henri d'Angoulême, the bastard of Valois. The replacement of Lady Fleming was to give rise to one of the most infamous episodes in Mary's adolescence: the dismissal of Madame de Parois.

The tale is briefly told. Since Lady Fleming has been an incorrigible flirt and by all accounts an irresistible beauty, she had represented a threat to Catherine de Medici and the king's accepted mistress, Diane de Poitiers. She had to go. In her place was substituted a devout old woman, Madame de Parois, whom Mary found to be intolerably pernickety. The cardinal found no fault with the old woman, extolling her virtues. When the dauphin was moved to his own household, however, having reached the appropriate age, things got tricky. Mary's uncle was insistent that his niece be accorded all appropriate estate. As an independent queen, and a member of the Guise family, it was crucial that she be seen to live in splendour. This she could scarcely do without money, and on the subject of financing his niece's lifestyle the cardinal was silent. Madame de Parois complained bitterly about the ludicrousness of the situation, making cuts where she could but achieving little; Mary was at this stage a spender. Matters boiled over, with open warfare declared between queen and governess. In April 1556 the cardinal himself deigned to get involved, writing to his sister that Parois was no longer suitable and ought to be cast off. She was still there a year later, however, and so Mary herself took up her pen and wrote to her mother. In this letter she laid out her passionate hatred of the elderly woman in no uncertain terms, hinting rather sneakily at fears that Parois would come between mother and daughter. Madame de Parois diplomatically resigned from service.

This incident, silly though it might seem to the modern reader, is useful for a number of reasons. Firstly, it illustrates just how far Mary was willing to follow her uncle's advice, even when it was demonstrably problematic. Secondly, it shows the young queen beginning to exert herself at a time when she was under the thumb of her uncle: an ultra-Catholic member of the family. Thirdly, it has been used to besmirch the queen, with biographer Roderick Graham condemning her actions as an early display of a cruel temper. Antonia Fraser is rather fairer, but given to another kind of romanticism, noting that Mary displayed a 'feminine and perfectly understandable sensitivity to the onslaughts of criticism which she had good reason to believe were unfair'.[49] Both readings can be dismissed, but only to a degree. Mary's manner was high-handed and imperious, but the episode was a clash of wills that got out of hand. Mary's will here, as it was to be in future, was guided by her uncle. The attitude expressed in the letter to Mary of Guise, though – particularly the insinuation that Parois was likely to try and come between mother and child – smacks of a fox-like teenage attempt to wring a doting mother's heart. Mary Queen of Scots was learning how to get what she wanted at the red-robed knees of her uncle Charles.

At roughly the same time, then, both Mary and James Stewart were undergoing remarkably similar experiences. Both were sought out, wooed, and utterly convinced by the arguments and attitudes of older men: one an ultra-Protestant preaching religious reform and iconoclasm, the other an ultra-Catholic preaching orthodoxy, statecraft, and the importance of display. The cardinal and the preacher had begun digging a trench between brother and sister, which was difficult to cross. That trench was to become a gorge, and that gorge a chasm. For the moment, though, both Knox and the cardinal of Lorraine had got what they wanted: a small band of highly-placed converts, including the queen's brother; and Guises as Scotland's regent and France's future queen.

It was in an atmosphere of strained frivolity that negotiations began in earnest for the queen's marriage to the dauphin. This was to involve both brother and sister – the one, naturally, as the putative bride, and the other as a commissioner, his recognition as a player in the affairs of Scotland now absolute.

Commissioner and Queen

On an icy December day in 1557, a group of men huddled around the document to which they had just put their names. It was a petition, intended for the eyes of their Catholic regent, Mary of Guise. It contained five requests:

1.   The right to assemble publicly or privately, to read prayers in their native tongue.

2.   That 'any qualified person in the knowledge' should be free to discuss difficult aspects of the Scripture.

3.   That baptism should be administered in the vernacular.

4.   That the Lord's supper should be administered likewise.

5.   That the scandalous lives of the clergy should be reformed, according to the precepts of the New Testament.

These men were of James Stewart's new party – the Protestant party, which was rapidly setting itself up as an opposition party. When she read it, Mary of Guise must have rolled her eyes, as a modern Prime Minister might at a set of demands from a group of rebellious backbenchers. Yet she needed these men of the new faith. She needed their acquiescence to her daughter's marriage. She could only hope, as winter tightened its grip and Christmas beckoned, that once the marriage between her daughter and the future king of France was solemnised, she could finally stop having to bow to the demands of an assertive group of nobles and gentry who had suddenly decided that her way of worship – and the way that her and their ancestors had worshipped since the birth of western Christianity – was wrong. She returned a vague answer, seeking time to consider the request without saying either no or yes, but allowing Protestant worship to continue in secret as long as it did not touch Edinburgh. As usual, she sought a middle road, the better to ensure that open rebellion could avoided. More pressing still was that the three estates which comprised the parliament of Scotland, two of which – the nobility and the commons – were now riddled with reformers, would allow smooth passage of Mary Queen of Scots' French match.[50]

As the year of France's – and Mary of Guise's – victory dawned, the Protestants were still hamstrung by the fact that the regent refused to give them cause to rebel against her authority, and England still choked under the fumes of their burning coreligionists. The Guise star was to gain further glister at the end of January 1558. In the course of the interminable Franco-Spanish war, England was to lose Calais, its foothold on the continent, during a siege led by Mary Queen of Scots' uncle, the duke of Guise. Mary Tudor was rapidly approaching the nadir of her reign, sorrow compounded upon misery. Her husband, the handsome young Philip II, had abandoned her, citing the need to tend to his own countries' affairs, having acceded to Spain's throne in 1556 (and having been king of Naples and Sicily from 1554). She was down, but not yet out; Scottish Protestants could still expect no support from England.

The petition, and the Band of the Congregation which bonded the men behind it, was the work of the more militant members of the Protestant party. James was as yet a moderate, even a conservative, voice. Still, the picture it paints of the state of the realm during his sister's years in France in an interesting one. Disharmony and disunity abounded, and the prospect of the queen's marriage to the fourteen-

71

year-old dauphin could have meant either continued French and Catholic fiefdom, or the opportunity for a strong leader to wait out the regent and institute a peaceful course of reform. James Stewart was still a believer in the latter. To accordion history, it is probably fair to say he hoped in time to replace the prime minister rather than blow up the houses of parliament. This, at least, is the cynical, political view of James' attitude. While it is probably the correct one, in fairness it is also likely that he retained a measure of respect and admiration for the stepmother who had shown no inclination to persecute him or his, and thus had no desire to join an open revolt against her governance.

Despite his new faith, James Stewart thus supported his sister's marriage to the dauphin as a *fait accompli* (much to John Knox's chagrin). With Mary Tudor and Philip ruling England, it certainly made political sense. Under these circumstances, a Franco-Scottish match would be a boon to both countries, forming as it would a bulwark to the military juggernaut of the Anglo-Spanish union. Scotland was, after all, a European country with a role to play – and interests to protect – on that colourful, blood-soaked stage.

Like his fellow members of the Scottish parliament, James also accepted that Scotland needed a man in charge rather than a woman – even if that man was a weak French child – if only to counter the duo of Mary Tudor and Philip in England.[51] Nevertheless, all early modern royal matches were things to be fought over, even when they seemed inevitable (and already enemies of the Guises had voiced opposition). Though these marriages were meant to be joyous occasions, they were in reality business arrangements, and they required teams of negotiators to iron out the details of the transaction. A total of eight commissioners were decided upon by the Scottish parliament, James Stewart amongst them. Two other notable Protestants were with him: the earl of Cassillis and John Erskine of Dun (who, along with Sandilands of Calder, had hosted Knox during his visit). He left for France with his fellows in February 1558 amidst apparently inclement weather, the accoutrements of his passage provided for by his mother.[52] After receiving the formal invitation to act on his sister's behalf in the matter of her marriage, he and the other commissioners were ready to join the formal process of negotiation. Their destination was the chateau of Fontainebleau, where the court was in residence. Up the famous horseshoe staircase the Scotsmen trooped, to encounter – though they did not know it – one of the most duplicitous interludes in Franco-Scottish history.

James found Mary in her element in the great royal palace. Aged fifteen, she was by now a remarkably attractive girl, well-dressed, well-coiffed, and well advised in the most polished of manners. As Diane de Poitiers was to comment, she handled herself well. Henry II's mistress was to write, 'she spoke to the Scottish deputies not as an inexperienced child, but as a woman of age and knowledge'.[53] At home in her opulent surroundings, she gave her brother and his friends what they wanted: solemn, signed oaths that she would protect her native country's rights, liberties, and privileges. The date was the 15th of April. Four days later, her betrothed husband would join her; the dauphin, round-faced and awkward, pledged that if Mary should die without issue, the throne of Scotland would be unmolested by France. It would revert to the nearest in blood – recognised in 1543 as Châtelherault. If Mary and Francis should produce a male heir, he would become joint sovereign of an independent Scotland and France; but if only girls arrived, the eldest should become queen of Scots, but not France (where Salic law held sway).[54] The contract also stipulated that Francis might be offered the crown matrimonial – the commissioners were not empowered to give it, that requiring a further decision by the Scottish parliament – but, in the event of Mary's death, his rights in Scotland and any future remarriage affecting Scotland's throne would require the assent of the

Scottish parliament. On this matter the commissioners were 'respectful but firm … consenting to nothing that tended to introduce any alteration in the order of succession to the crown'.[55] Satisfied that they had done their duty in protecting their country's liberty, the commissioners signed.

The entire thing – contract, pledges, and declarations – had been a farce. On the 4th of April, Mary had signed three secret contracts which pledged that, should she die childless, the realm of Scotland would legally become the property of Henry II and his male heirs. Further, she promised that no fewer than one million crowns should be extracted from her native country to pay retroactively for her education and the money expended by France in repelling English invaders. The final document stated that any future documents – that is, those that she was to sign on the 15th and 19th – were null and void. She had willingly tricked her brother and his fellow commissioners, who were naturally unaware that they were ascribing their names – in the name of their country – to useless paper.

Much has been said about Mary's role here. Her supporters claim that, at the age of fifteen, she could not have understood the import of effectively signing away her country. Her detractors prefer to see her acting either out of stupidity, in calculated malice, or with a complete disregard for Scotland, a country which she could barely remember and cared nothing for. None of these explanations is likely. The queen, at this stage, was certainly old enough and independent enough to know what she was doing, but so too was she doing what she thought was best: and what she thought was best was what her uncles advised her was best. That is not to say she was merely their puppet; however, Henry II and the Guise brothers had nurtured her to believe that absorption into France was no bad thing for her native country and its inhabitants, which, as her mother's struggles illustrated, required to be brought into better subjection. In this she was little different from those politicians and monarchs centuries later who would strive for Scotland to be joined with England into a single state (indeed, even James VI and I was far more eager to eradicate the independence of Scotland than ever his mother was in these secret documents). It was duplicity, to be sure, and an extremely wily example of statecraft, but understandable given her belief in it being for the best of reasons. Putting aside the questionable morality of backstabbing her brother and his fellow Scottish deputies, it was a neat way of ensuring what she wanted, and what she had been led to believe was right for her native realm: unity with France. Whatever affection she might have felt for her brother she put aside: he was there as a commissioner, and the commissioners were to be misled.

With James and his friends fooled, and the official documents signed, the marriage could go ahead. It was to be one of the happiest days of Mary's life, and it was certainly one of the most extravagant displays Paris had ever witnessed. On Sunday 24th April, the city's citizens gathered into the Place du Parvis in front of Notre-Dame cathedral. It was standing room only. The duke of Guise, that liberator of Calais, had orchestrated the event, having a special raised walkway built so that everyone could have a clear view of proceedings. The walkway ran from the archbishop's palace to the cathedral itself, and it was along this route that Mary and her husband strode to adoring cheers. To ensure maximum public spectacle, the marriage ceremony itself was to take place outside, on a temporary stage that had also been erected. Seating was provided on the stage for honoured guests – including James and his colleagues.

A hush descended at 10am, when elaborately-dressed Swiss halberdiers began proceedings, marching from the palace to musical accompaniment. Their turn over, the duke of Guise appeared on the stage; it would not do for anyone to forget that the day was a victory for France's most powerful clan. The duke signalled the appearance of more musicians and, as they played, the members of the royal household and senior churchmen processed along the walkway. This was all only a prelude to the moment of maximum excitement: the appearance of the royal family.

The squat dauphin, who had been preened to what was hoped by his father to be an impressive state, was flanked by his younger brothers. Then came the bride, escorted by Henry II and her cousin, the duke of Lorraine. As with modern weddings, she was what the crowd had been waiting for, and she did not disappoint. Her dress caught the eye first. She had chosen to wear white, which caught and reflected the sun. Traditionally the colour of French mourning, it provided a daring touch, its train running along the walkway to where Catherine de Medici and an assemblage of brightly-dressed court ladies brought up the rear, like the glittering trail of a comet. On her head sat a heavy gold crown, studded with precious stones, and on her breast flashed the 'Great Harry', a pendant featuring a diamond so great it made its way into the Scottish crown jewels.

For Mary, this was a moment of ultimate triumph. It was the reason she had been taken from her home and her mother in 1548; it was the assurance of her future; it was what her uncles had groomed her for since she had been given her own household. Charmingly, we have a pleasant insight into the bride's feelings in the form of a note written to her mother on the morning of the festivities. She believed herself, she gushed, to be 'one of the happiest women in the world'.[56]

But what did James make of his sister's elevation to dauphiness, in the midst of all this pageantry? John Guy suggests that 'he disliked everything he saw, partly from jealousy, partly because many of his friends came from the close circle of English Protestant exiles in Paris who hated the idea that there were still French (Catholic) troops in Scotland and determined to expel them if they could'.[57] This is probably unfair. Undoubtedly James had made the acquaintance of English exiles – under Mary Tudor, it was safer for them to take refuge with the Huguenot communities – but there is no evidence that he exhibited any particular jealousy, and it must be remembered that he favoured the match as a means of keeping Mary out of Scotland. As long as she was happy and secure in her magnificent surroundings, he and his religious confederates could work towards instituting a pro-Protestant government at home. He had, further, supported the granting of the crown matrimonial, though he was deaf – as the Scottish parliament turned out to be – on the subject of sending over the physical Scottish crown for tenancy in the abbey of Saint Denis.

The morning passed in appropriate splendour, the crowd showered with largesse, before an official state banquet, to which James was invited, took place at the Paris Palais. Taking up a number of rooms in the palace, the guests were treated to the sight of mechanical ships sailed on artificial waves. The theme of the day was an emerging French empire, which, with Mary's marriage, would encompass the British Isles. As a token of honour, the earl of Cassillis did duty as the bride's carver, and the earl of Rothes held her cup.[58] Dancing and song went on until midnight, long after the newlyweds had been 'put to thair beddis', and the jollity continued for six days, with jousting, tournaments, and archery contests.[59] In all of this revelry, neither James nor Mary could have seriously considered that she would ever return to Scotland to govern in person.

The mission of commissioners and Scottish queen had almost been accomplished, save for lingering months of negotiations over the granting of the crown. The agreement of the Scottish parliament to give Mary of Guise's new son-in-law the crown matrimonial was not given until the three estates sat in November, and even then it was a fudge. Predictably, there was a backlash from the Hamilton family; the crown matrimonial in theory allowed Francis to establish his own dynasty even if Mary died without issue by him. However, the Scottish parliament and the commissioners thought they had signed sufficient safeguards, including native parliamentary approval of any future tinkering with the throne. The parliament, on Châtelherault's cavilling, insisted afresh that even with the granting of the crown to Francis, there would be no prejudice to the Hamilton right of succession. As noted, James Stewart appears to have supported this, joining with those who agreed in principle to Francis being their king, but refusing utterly to subvert the succession (or to allow the physical crown to leave Scotland).

A story often repeated is that tragedy struck when five of the party (Cassillis, Orkney, Rothes, Fleming, and the mysterious laird of Easter Wemyss, who seems to have been attached to the group of Scottish commissioners) died. The chronicler Pitscottie attributes their deaths to poisoning from eating meat laced with an 'Italian posset' at a banquet. The only one who ate the poisoned meat but did not die was, apparently, James, 'the quenis broder'. According to Pitscottie, he escaped death by being hung from his heels by mediciners, which caused the poison to 'drop out', but which nevertheless resulted in him requiring medicine for the rest of his life.[60] As colourful as this story is, it is almost certainly a fabrication. Probably the commissioners succumbed to plague. At any rate their deaths took place at different times, and only months after the wedding.[61] In order for the tale to have a kernel of truth, it would have to be that they were murdered not for their refusal to grant the crown matrimonial ahead of the wedding, but for their refusal to agree to it later in the year, when the Scottish parliament did grant the crown – not in its physical manifestation, but in its office – to the dauphin. At any rate, the whole story, with its deliberate kaleidoscoping of history to overlay marriage, deaths, and negotiations, smacks of anti-French propaganda.

Missing the festivities in France was Mary of Guise, who had her hands full in Scotland. With the Guise ascendancy heralded by her daughter's marriage, the regent must have felt emboldened.[62]

However, even before the November parliament and almost concomitant with her daughter's marriage, a gruesome event took place which was to be so beneficial to the Protestant cause that it might almost have been desired: the cause was given a martyr. Whilst bonfires were lit and toasts drunk in Scotland's major cities in celebration of the wedding of two remote figures, one old man was in hiding in a poor woman's cottage in Dysart, where he had been quietly instructing her and her children in the ways of the reformed faith. Their peaceful life was shattered by a knock at the door. Two priests entered and dragged the old man from his students. His name was Walter Mill (or Milne) and he had once been a parish priest in Lunan, in Angus. Disgusted by what he saw as error and corruption, he embraced reform, turning his back, like Knox, on the old faith. Mill was hustled to the castle at St Andrews, where a host of Catholic clergymen converged on the 25th of April. He put up a good defence against the accusations levelled at him, but the sentence was a fearful one, and one unusual in Scotland: he was to be burnt. Ominously, none of the town's temporal authorities would consent to deliver such a sentence, and it fell to one of the archbishop's servants to assume the role. Mill was therefore taken out and 'presenttit' to the fire, where he died in agony. He was over eighty years old.

Overnight the case became a sensational one, with the townspeople of St Andrews attempting to build of a cairn of stones as a memorial. As quickly as the archbishop could have them dismantled, more appeared. Quite why such a pitiable, low-key figure was chosen to be burnt is a mystery. Mary of Guise denied knowledge of it, casting blame on John Hamilton, the archbishop (who was half-brother to Châtelherault). On the one hand, it seems wildly out of character for her, even if her daughter's marriage had buoyed her against the Protestants. On the other, if she did know nothing, it suggests that her political power was already on the wane. At any rate, the Protestants had their martyr. Following Mill's execution, anti-Catholic preachers ramped up their rhetoric, flouting the regent's authority and speaking openly about the parishes. When summoned to answer for their behaviour, a significant number of the gentry rallied to their defence in force of arms (the gentry, it will be recalled, being longer inclined to reform than the nobility). Rather than force a confrontation, Mary of Guise rescinded the summons. Nor did she accept open warfare when, at the beginning of September, the traditional St Giles Day festivities were broken up by Protestant rioters who thronged the streets of Edinburgh. From the jaws of her daughter's victory abroad, the burning of Walter Mill, whether the regent's decision or not, meant that only defeat was likely to be snatched.

Of course, that other great challenge of Scottish Protestants remained: they could expect no support from England and would thus be making Scotland a reformed country with a hostile Catholic neighbour on its doorstep. As 1558 drew to a close, however, it became obvious to everyone that Mary Tudor was dying. When she finally slipped out of the world, crying piteously about seeing visions of angels 'like little children' frolicking around her deathbed, the days of Catholic England went with her.[63] The stars were aligning for those who hoped for a future of Protestant amity across mainland Britain.

Two new figures were to emerge, one male and one female, who were to have a greater impact on the relationship between Mary and James Stewart than even Knox or the cardinal of Lorraine had done. In fact, this pair was to outlive both, and in different ways drive brother and sister into early graves.

.

Enter Elizabeth

There was always a wild rush to be the first to deliver news of the death of the old sovereign to the new. Those who galloped from St James' Palace to Hatfield House must have had in the backs of their minds the rewards that might flow from the twenty-five-year-old woman that legend states they found sitting beneath an oak tree in the grounds, a book of Psalms in her hand. Their new queen was a pretty woman, her skin sallower than contemporary standards of beauty required, but her strawberry-blonde hair long and lustrous. She is said to have turned her dark, almost black eyes heavenward and cried out, 'a Domino factum est ilud et est mirabile in oculis nostris!' – 'this is the Lord's doing and it is marvellous in our eyes!'

Elizabeth Tudor was the daughter of Henry VIII by his second wife, Anne Boleyn. It is often stated that, in Catholic eyes, she was a bastard.[64] This is highly misleading. Henry had had Anne executed on trumped-up charges of treason, incest, and witchcraft, after she had foolishly tried to win back his lost affections by flirting in a courtly manner with the men of the royal court. Just before her death, Thomas Cranmer, the reformist archbishop of Canterbury, had declared the marriage null and void. In both Catholic and Protestant eyes, then, Elizabeth had been bastardised. Unlike her sister, she was never to try and undo her father's annulment; instead, she simply ignored the fact of her legal illegitimacy. What she did have in her favour was that the English parliament had ratified Henry VIII's will, which declared the succession in favour of his son, Edward VI, to be followed (in the event of a lack of issue) by his daughters, first Mary and then Elizabeth. On Mary Tudor's death she had become England's lawful queen, but not a legitimate child. It is incorrect to state that she was legitimate to Protestants but illegitimate to Catholics. She was an illegitimate child to both, but lawful queen to both; the danger from Catholics was that they might be more apt to try and make something of her legal bastardy whilst Protestants were content to let sleeping dogs lie. It is testament to Elizabeth's tact and skill that this Achilles heel was never successfully shot at. Part of her strategy was to toe a middle line in religion, not satisfying ardent Catholics or zealous reformers, but not totally alienating those of either faith. Her 1559 settlement was anti-papal, certainly, but it retained enough custom, colour and creed to satisfy those whose beliefs were more in line with traditional Catholicism. As a measure of her success, her Protestant subjects were not only content to refrain from acknowledging her bastardy, but willing play up Anne Boleyn's status as an anointed queen (ignoring the ultimate annulment) and portray her death as a martyrdom

For the first time in James Stewart's life, an irrefutable but legally sanctioned bastard sat on a British throne, and she was a cousin to both him and his sister. Although Scotland was a different country, and he knew all too well that they did things differently there, the rise of his cousin Elizabeth must have given him more reason for envy - if envy he ever felt - than the crowns his sister wore.

One of the new queen's first actions was to appoint her secretary of state. The office fell to the thirty-eight-year-old Sir William Cecil, a veteran who had worked under two protectors and the boy king, before prudently retiring to a quiet life under Queen Mary. Elizabeth was ready to put him back in harness, and the miffed Spanish ambassador reported at the end of 1558 that 'he [Cecil] is the man who does everything'.

Elizabeth and her new master secretary had to contend not only with the problem of Mary Tudor and her Spanish husband's war against France, but with Scotland too. Coyly, Elizabeth was to state that it was not she who had been at war with the French, but her late sister. Cecil set to work hammering out peace, with Elizabeth demanding (as she was quixotically to do for many years) the restitution of Calais. The peace of Cateau-Cambrésis was the result of a European treaty, but it was to have direct implications for the British nations. The Spanish Habsburgs and the French Valois, who had fought on and off for decades over territory in Italy, finally concluded their belligerence, and England was to win a guarantee (never fulfilled) that Calais would be restored after eight years of French governance. In turn, France agreed not to support Mary Queen of Scots' claim to the English throne (she being a legitimately-born cousin of Elizabeth as granddaughter of Henry VIII's sister, Margaret Tudor). With this uneasy peace, Cecil was able to set out in writing his opinions on Scotland:

The best felicity that Scotland can have is either to continue in a perpetual peace with the kingdom of England, or to be made one monarchy with England, as they both make but one isle, divided from the rest of the world.

If the first is sought ... then must it necessarily be provided, that Scotland be not so subject to the appointments of France, as is presently, which being an ancient enemy to England, seeketh always to make Scotland an instrument to exercise thereby their malice upon England, and to make a footstool thereof to look over England as they may. Therefore, when Scotland shall come into the hands of a mere Scottish man in blood, then may be there hope of such accord; but as long as it is at the commandment of the French there is no hope to have accord long betwixt these two realms.[65]

This attitude was music to the ears of the Protestant faction north of the border, who must have thought that all their Christmases had come at once (not that they believed in celebrating Christmas). Indeed, the elevation of Elizabeth to the throne, though she and Cecil had wisely sailed with the prevailing religious wind during Mary Tudor's reign, acted as a catalyst to a wave of more visible activity. Even before Cecil was to set down his opinions on Scotland in April 1559, the Scottish reformers were out in force. Whilst Englishmen were already turning their minds to their new queen's marriage and the men who would rule in her name, those increasingly Calvinist members of the Scottish nobility were hoping that her religion would ensure friendship and her purse would be deep. When the money started flowing northwards, vindication must have seemed almost heaven-sent.

To understand the seemingly odd relationship that was to blossom between James, Mary, Cecil, and Elizabeth, it must be understood that Cecil was a devout Protestant by inclination, but like Elizabeth, he had trimmed his sails during Mary Tudor's reign. However, unlike the more ardent Scottish Calvinists, who were Protestants before they were Scotsmen, Cecil was an Englishman first. During the course of what would become a friendship, James was to attempt to juggle religion and nationalism, never quite conceding the latter in order to promote the former. His sister was to embark on a similar juggling act, albeit with a different religion.

In the early hours of the 1st of January 1559, less than two months after Elizabeth had succeeded to England's throne and before she had been crowned, someone was sneaking through the dark streets of Edinburgh. In their hand was a sheaf of papers. Glancing around, the furtive agent stopped before the wooden doors of the Blackfriars.

Tapping a nail as gently as possible, they succeeded in pinning up one of the papers. At the top, black ink rendered the following in old Scots:

In the name of the blind, crooked, bedridden, widows, orphans and all other poor who are by the hand of God unable to work, to the flocks of friars within this realm, we wish the restitution of wrongs by-past, and reformation in time coming.

A warning followed: if the friars did not return church property and wealth to the people, then with God's help the people would eject the friars. The note was signed 'from all the cities, towns, and villages of Scotland'.

Once the notice was erected, the anonymous libeller hurried on. He had a number of friaries whose doors had to be decorated that night. His peers in the extreme wing of the Protestant faction were likewise at work across the country, their combined effort signalling that the signature was accurate. It was not. It was the work of the those emboldened by the twin boons of Walter Mill's martyrdom and Elizabeth I's accession.

Still, James Stewart refused to abandon his stepmother. The regent did what she could to stem the sudden outpouring of anti-Catholic and anti-French activity. In May 1559, when reformers flocked into the town of Perth (then called St Johnstoun) as a display of their numbers, she postponed a summons she had issued to recalcitrant preachers. When the preachers did not turn up to the summons, she then 'put them to the horn', or outlawed them. This, at least, is the version of the story given by John Knox, as a display of female and Catholic duplicity. The preacher himself had returned to Scotland at the beginning of May, and the Protestants had their prophet back. Only a day after he and his fellow had been outlawed, he was to be found encouraging violence and the destruction of popish churches, friaries, and monastic houses. War had broken out.

Mary of Guise appeared at Perth towards the end of Mary, the town having essentially been seized and occupied by rebellious Protestants. The regent had little choice but to negotiate with her rebels, and in doing so she selected as spokesmen James, his friend the earl of Argyll, and Lord Sempill. This was a wise move. The three were themselves Protestant sympathisers and Scotsmen.

To James' credit, he appears to have tried sincerely to stem what had blown up into rebellion, assured by his stepmother that she desired peace and accord. He met with hard-headed refusal to accept anything other than state acceptance of the Protestant faith. Mary of Guise would likely have preferred to reduce the rebels to obedience, but the numbers were against her – and the Protestant ranks swelled still further when the rabid earl of Glencairn, an early convert, arrived with reinforcements. Instead she agreed to all that the Protestants wanted.

James was in an unenviable position. He was acting on his stepmother's orders, but assailed by condemnation from Knox, his religious leader and the architect of his conversion. On the 31st of May he agreed in principle to join the Congregation, as the increasing band of rebels was still known, on the condition that it would require his stepmother to abandon her promises of full toleration. Although she did not do so, she did use French money to garrison Perth with Scottish soldiers still loyal to her almost as soon as the rebels had left. On the 1st June, James and Argyll, evidently seeing that the regent's days were numbered, used this as an excuse to come out openly against her.

James' decision cannot have been an easy one, torn as he was between a real respect for Mary of Guise and the haranguing of the man who had instructed him in the new faith. Ultimately, he chose to break with Mary of Guise – and therefore his own sister – because he had to.

Tolerance in the sixteenth century could never be more than a temporary expedient, as he well knew. The tolerant would only ever be waiting for a chance to crush those they put up with; the tolerated would only ever be waiting to overthrow those they saw as persecutors. This was certainly the attitude of Knox, who openly demanded the criminalisation of the mass, in all its broken Latin, with which Scots had been familiar for centuries. Mary of Guise's course may have lasted for a shorter period than James Stewart would have liked, but breaking point came when it came, and he was constrained to choose the party of his faith, which stood those who had come to be seen as foreign invaders. According to his mentor he was immediately active in pulling down images in Perth's religious houses. The image, if true, is a powerful one, displaying the depth and sincerity of his conversion. Knox must have been proud. From almost the moment of his break with the regent, we find James noted in the Calendar of State papers with increasing frequency. One can trace him coming into his own as an active player at the heart of Scottish affairs. His sister, meanwhile, was simply the French queen, remote and aloof.

Opposition to the regent was, as the reformers constantly attested, a religious rather than a political one. It is possible that a few even believed this. It was, however, nonsense. As long as Catholicism was supported by French power and money and Protestantism was begging for English aid, religion and politics were inextricably linked. Further, the nobility of Scotland retained – and jealously guarded – their right to be heard in the political sphere. It was a right which they felt their regent was not respecting. At the time, though, it is clear that James' actions in particular were considered to have sinister overtones. James Melville, who was in the employ of the constable of France, was even sent to Scotland in June to find out if the queen's brother aimed at taking the crown for himself. For all the reasons that have been discussed, this was not his intent, nor a realistic proposition (though it is interesting that the constable, no friend to the Guises, considered it a possibility). What James and his fellows needed was the duke of Châtelherault, by now a seasoned veteran of intrigue and still the man who would inherit the throne in the event of anything happening to Mary Queen of Scots. Now in his mid-forties, the duke had gained weight, but no sense of loyalty nor any other sense save self-preservation. The last he had honed to perfection. Coupled with the entitlement he had always felt, he was as personally unattractive as ever. It did not matter. What mattered was that he was next in line to Scotland's throne, and commanded swaths of territorial followers. For the moment, the regent was canny enough to keep him close.

In the perfumed galleries and clipped gardens of France's royal palaces, the struggles of her mother and even the loss of her brother to the insurgent Lords of the Congregation must have felt a world away to the dauphiness. When news of Elizabeth's accession had reached Paris, Mary Queen of Scots had been plunged into ostentatious mourning for the late English queen.[66] Around her were those who absolutely decried what they regarded as a bastard's seizure of the throne (and it is possible that the accession of Elizabeth is what motivated the constable of France to suspect James Stewart of doing likewise the following year). Mary's uncle, the cardinal, sought to take maximum advantage of his niece's place in the English succession. Her silver plate was engraved with the royal arms of England quartered with Scotland, Ireland, and France – an insult to Elizabeth which was to rankle for years. As Antonia Fraser notes, 'even while the treaty of Cateau-Cambrésis was being negotiated the cardinal and others made it their business to say that they doubted whether they should treat with any of England, save the dauphin and his wife'.[67] These were deliberately provocative gestures.

Whether Mary was an active agent in declaring herself rightful queen of England or whether the title was appropriated by the older men around her can never be known for certainty (although she did later quip that she knew no other queen of England save herself, as well as casting blame for the 1558-9 use of England's arms on her father-in-law). However, at the time of Elizabeth's accession it was a point worth making. No one could have foreseen that the bastard daughter of Anne Boleyn would last on England's throne. Fewer still could have imagined that she would remain single. As a married queen with a claim to England's throne, the open declaration of Mary's assured queenship was probably worth the gamble – should Elizabeth have been deposed or died or otherwise lost power in those first shaky months and years, Mary would have been a ready-made substitute.

With civil war in Scotland looming, the new dauphiness could do little more than hope that her father-in-law would provide her mother with enough money and arms to defeat the Protestant threat. The loss of her brother to Congregation at the start of June was irksome, but he was, after all, only a noble-born cleric. The rest of that month, in France, was one of joy and sorrow of a more personal nature. Mary's sister-in-law, the Princess Elisabeth, who had been more like a sibling than James had ever been, was married by proxy to the widowed Philip II (he was to find more satisfaction in Elisabeth than he had in Mary Tudor). Her surrogate family was fragmenting. Not long after this celebration, which must have brought back memories of her own wedding the previous year, a further marriage was contracted between Henry II's sister, Margaret, and the duke of Savoy. The royal family again gathered in splendour to mark the occasion.

King Henry himself took to the jousting field, resplendent in Diane de Poitier's colours of black and white. Still in his prime, the forty-year-old monarch drew the cheers of the crowd which had gathered around the Place de Vosges. Galloping with all the skill of long practice and natural ability, he broke the lances of his new brother-in-law, the duke of Savoy, Mary's uncle, the duke of Guise, and the count of Montgomery, the captain of his Scots Guard.

After these easy victories, the king demanded a final joust with Montgomery. The captain made excuses, but there was no resisting the royal will. Catherine de Medici joined with Montgomery in entreating her husband to give up for the day, but she was equally ineffectual, with Henry quipping that the final lance would be broken in her honour. Off rode king and captain for one last tilt. Their lances met, cracked, and splintered. But as the crowd gasped in excitement, it quickly became clear that something had gone badly wrong. The king sat rigid in his saddle before slumping to the ground. Looking down in horror, Montgomery saw that two sharp, thin spikes of broken wood had impaled his king: one had gone in through his right eye, another through his throat. It was a freak accident, hideous and lethal. Although Henry II lingered on for nine days, drifting in and out of consciousness as pain dictated, he expired on the 10th of July. The fifteen-year-old dauphin and his sixteen-year-old wife were now king and queen of France.

Mary's accession as queen consort of France meant that she was now in a position to send greater aid to her mother. That meant, of course, sending money and troops over to fight against her brother. It was, however, not that easy. The France the young couple inherited was to be dominated by Mary's Guise uncles and was suffering under inflation caused by the recently-concluded Italian wars.[68] King Francis II, as the dauphin had become, was largely powerless, by dint of his age and inclination. A thumbnail sketch of him from the English ambassador is useful in clarifying the problem: 'the king is wont to go abroad very often to amuse himself for several days without transacting business'.[69] On the one hand, this is entirely understandable – any fifteen-year-old might share the same desire to pursue pleasure if it is on offer rather than duty. On the other, it will be remembered that kings of comparable ages had been similarly thrust into positions of power in the period and had – remarkably – been able to exercise it. Whether he pursued pleasure in his married life is unknown; opinions varied as to the consummation of Mary's first marriage. It hardly matters. Francis was not to live long enough to produce issue.

In November, Francis and Mary did make a clear attempt to assist the beleaguered regent in Scotland. In a clever move, they sent Jacques de la Brosse, a veteran captain of the French troops stationed in Scotland, along with a number of theologians from the Sorbonne to debate religion with the insurgent lords of the Congregation. Nevertheless, the means by which the French monarchs sought to help Scotland's regent – however much Mary of Guise complained about the paucity of support versus need – were ironically giving the rebels what they wanted: cause for grievance about foreigners bullying and harassing native Scots. In retaliation, the Protestants redoubled their efforts to seek aid from England – aid which had hitherto been disappointingly slow in coming from the still-cautious Elizabeth and Cecil. All pretence of the conflict being purely religious was dead.

The first official appeal for aid from the Congregation to Elizabeth I had come in July 1559. Cecil, however, had then been careful, asking exactly 'to what end they mean to direct their actions, and how they will be able to accomplish the same ... also if support should be sent hence, what manner an amity might ensure between these two realms'.[70] By openly conferring with a foreign power to bring down the legitimate authority put in place by their sovereign, James and his fellow members of the Congregation had turned traitor. To them, of course, this was excusable; they were the coming government engaging in foreign policy, and what they were doing was no worse than what Mary of Guise had been doing for years.

More concrete support was to come from Elizabeth via Cecil in August. Sent north again was that stalwart of Anglo-Scottish affairs, Ralph Sadler (the same Sadler who had inspected the baby Mary Queen of Scots in 1543 and found her as 'goodly a child' as he had ever seen). Cecil's instructions to Sadler are instructive, not only for revealing Elizabethan policy towards Mary Queen of Scots' native kingdom, but for for what they reveal to us about contemporary suspicions about James Stewart. Primarily, Cecil states that 'the principal scope shall be to nourish the faction between the Scots and the French, so that the French may be more occupied with them and less busy with England'. In other words, it was Elizabeth's desire to extricate Scotsmen from Frenchmen by means of sowing discord. After expressing further anxiety about Mary's pretended title of queen of England and enquiries about Châtelherault, he exhorted Sadler to 'explore whether Lord James means any enterprise towards the crown of Scotland for himself or no; and if he do, and the duke [Châtelherault] be found very cold in his own causes, it shall not be amiss to let Lord James follow his own device therein, without dissuading or persuading him anything therein'.

Once again, we see that non-Scottish commentators (and meddlers) were apt to ascribe to James Stewart a desire for the throne. Even James' biographer - who otherwise accuses him of seeking the crown - absolves him of the charge at this stage.[71] The break with Mary of Guise and subsequent outpouring of friendship to England was not, as Cecil suspected, a bid for Scotland's crown. It was a politico-religious move aimed at establishing Protestantism (and James Stewart had lost none of his reforming zeal) and removing the French, who had succeeded in governing Scotland to an extent that generations of marauding English armies had failed to manage.

At the same time, Mary of Guise was also busy in seeking amity with England. Elizabeth's reply is useful in illustrating what was to be part of her policy towards Scotland throughout her reign: fair words and duplicitous actions.

Touching what the dowager [Mary of Guise] has written respecting the conservation of amity between the two realms (certain rebellars having avaunted that they have received, or hope to receive, support against her), she [Elizabeth] thinks it much that no surer account is made of her honour in this case, and wishes that before any doubt is conceived in this point she would most certainly understand not what men report but how truly. Her doings shall always be constant and agreeable to honour; and as for her mind to peace, she affirms that she is as well inclined to keep it as ever she was and will be most sorry to see any occasion given her by the dowager to the contrary.[72]

This in November 1559, after Elizabeth's secretary and the lords of the Congregation – James highly-placed amongst them – had been labouring tirelessly to ensure that the regent's pro-French policy was destroyed. So much for Elizabeth's honour. The best that can be said of Cecil is that he was doing what he always did – seeking as sly a means as possible of getting what he felt was best for England. In this case, that was a solidly Protestant, independent neighbour. Where Henry VIII had tried and failed to bring Scotland under his direct rule, Cecil and Elizabeth would be content to make of it a junior partner in a league of friendly, reformed British states.

More problematically for Mary of Guise, the duke of Châtelherault had followed James and Argyll in abandoning her cause and declaring for the Congregation in August. The importance of this cannot be overstated. Although he was as unimpressive and shifty as ever, he was nevertheless still heir presumptive to the Scottish throne, and England had been instrumental in working with the Congregational lords to get his son Arran – who had been resident in France and a staunch reformer – home to work on the old duke. As ever, persuasion worked, and Arran was able to convince his father that the future belonged to the Congregation, not the ailing regent. An equally important deserter from the dwindling ranks of the dowager was Maitland of Lethington, her secretary who had been converted to the cause of reform at the same time as James. The guiding principal of this most slippery of statesmen (known as Michael or Muckle Wily – a very wily Machiavelli – to caustic Scots) was his dedication to union between England and Scotland. In this he was swiftly joined by James and later by his sister – indeed, Maitland's unionism was, as will be seen, the glue which held together brother and sister for the first years of her personal reign.

For the present, the Protestants thus had a political glister to their rebellion, and further victory was to come in the spring of 1560. Having announced in October 1559 that Mary of Guise had been lawfully suspended as regent owing to having brought foreign troops to subdue Scots on their own soil, James' ebullient party succeeded in wringing foreign troops from Elizabeth to counter them.

Prior to January 1560, money had been all Elizabeth and Cecil had been willing to part with in their pursuit of a friendly, Protestant Scotland. With the provision of armed aid and hard cash, and the desertion of much of the regent's support (what remained to her being either French troops or disunited Scots), the end was inevitable. In her absence, Mary Queen of Scots' home country was on the path to reformation, due in no small part to her brother who, along with Maitland, was to form the nexus of the victorious Protestant faction. A Guise to her bones, the dowager fought on, but it was a losing battle.

Throughout what was now a civil war, James Stewart played a major – those with Protestant sympathies should say a heroic – role. Now openly treating with England, which was no longer an enemy but a liberator from French tyranny, he took charge of negotiating a formal agreement with the country which had been, for centuries, Scotland's most hostile aggressor. The reasons why James was chosen were manifold. As the late king's acknowledged son, he lent an air of admittedly tarnished majesty to proceedings. From the diplomatic and clerical service he had engaged in under first Châtelherault's regency and then his stepmother's he was a seasoned negotiator. Above all, he could boast a personable charm and love of order, coupled with genuine religious faith fostered by Knox, that was unusual in Calvinist converts, some of whom were in it for political reasons and others being utterly charmless.

The Treaty of Berwick was signed at the end of February 1560 – a coup for its twenty-nine-year-old negotiator. Across the Channel, his sister and her husband were to respond by requesting their French captains in Scotland conciliate the Protestants, making overtures to the English queen if necessary in the pursuit of winning back the Scots. Otherwise, the pair were somewhat hamstrung by Mary's Guise uncles, who were still the power behind the dual thrones, albeit consumed by their own struggles as the popularity of their assumption of government fell steeply. Although the queen wept bitterly to the cardinal of Lorraine, lamenting that his inaction and political machinations had caused her to lose her native realm, she was to find that the man whose advice she had always taken was disinterested in realistic action in Scotland. The scales were falling from her eyes.

The royal couple were also occupied by affairs in France. In March a rebellion was launched by French Huguenots against the Guise faction, known to history as the Tumult of Amboise. It failed, and thereafter mass executions were carried out before the king and queen. Known for her later aversion to bloodshed and her generally pacific disposition, Mary Queen of Scots was at this time prepared – or forced – to be an active spectator in the deaths of hundreds of people. The chilling justice meted out against the Huguenots can have done little to endear her to her Protestant subjects in Scotland. Yet it had another effect on Mary. Hitherto she had led a cosseted life, free of insecurity and rich in leisure. Protestantism was, to her, a nuisance her mother was dealing with in Scotland, and an distasteful plague on France. Now it had become a real, physical threat. Its proponents were not tiresome cranks shouting blasphemy in the streets, but violent men with a distinct political agenda. And her brother had joined their ranks. He was even now harassing her beloved mother. The solemn commissioner she had fooled two year previously had taken on a sinister complexion.

At this time, Mary continued to send letters to her mother begging her to look after her health. Her tone is as it always was to her mother: loving, slightly-hysterical, and still with the traces of childishness which were so conspicuously absent in her dealings with her inferiors. Her entreaties were to no avail. In June, Mary of Guise, worn out, swollen by dropsy, her beauty long-gone but her charm undiminished, called her rebels to her presence. She was dying, and she knew it. She was then in the castle at Edinburgh and, in a display of respect, those who had been fighting her left the sides of the English soldiers who had joined them and slipped inside. James Stewart was amongst them, and, in fact, she asked that he and the Earl Marischal be present when she made her will. James was still with her when, in the early hours of the 11th of June she died.

The passing of Mary of Guise, who had been part of his life whether directly or indirectly since 1538, must have been a sad occasion, for all that he had come to deplore her religion and the French troops with which she flooded Scotland. It is significant too that the dying dowager chose him from amongst friends and rebels to be with her at the end. The regent's biographer, Rosalind Marshall, suggests that he was 'hard and cold, as he always was now' at the time of her death, but this is a touch of the romantic. It is hardly likely she would have tolerated his company nor accepted his presence until the end came if he were such a personally unpleasant figure.

If her death was a sad moment for James, it was to come as an horrific blow to his sister. When the news reached France, it was withheld from Mary for some days until finally the cardinal of Lorraine was selected to break it. Her response was a total physical and emotional collapse. Despite having departed from her mother at the age of five, and only having spent that enjoyable year with her in 1550-1, the Venetian ambassador was to say that 'she loved her mother ... much more than daughters usually love their mothers'.

The precarious health of the Scottish queen, exhibited here and to resurface at various points, has given rise to all manner of conjectures; indeed, seldom has the health of any historical figure been so well documented and debated. It is hazardous to make retroactive diagnoses based on contemporary reports, but a number have been advanced to explain the queen's medical history and behaviour, none wholly convincingly. From anorexia nervosa to acute intermittent porphyria, her ailments have exercised the pens of scholars for centuries.[73] Like her father, she seems to have suffered from what modern doctors might diagnose as a form of bipolar disorder, or manic depression. Her moods were reported as shifting from frenetic high spirits to extended periods of total collapse, and in moments of crisis she was as apt to display extreme courage and quick-thinking as she was to collapse for days. At various points (such as after the Bothwell marriage) she was heard to express suicidal thoughts, and her letters during her English captivity were occasionally, as Philip II's advisor was to complain, chaotic and contradictory.[74] Many who dealt with her, from her brother to Darnley to Thomas Randolph to the pope, were to profess themselves at various times baffled by her mind or actions. Sudden episodes of impulsiveness and frustrated anger, manifested, as we have already seen in the case of Madame de Parois, as deviousness in dealing with those she loved, are also symptomatic of bipolar disorder.

On learning of her mother's death, the collapse was total. The famous deuil blanc portrait of the queen, now in the royal collection, dates from this time. Either by or following a sketch by Clouet, the portrait depicts the young queen in stilted majesty, her eyes tilted, and eyebrows arched. There is very little sense of her legendary beauty present in it: a forerunner, perhaps, of just how much this woman's emotional state showed in her outward appearance (later, ambassadors were to make catty remarks about her beauty being 'other than it was' during moments of emotional excitement). Mary herself seems to have been acutely aware of this alteration. At the time of the painting, she signalled her intention to send a portrait to Elizabeth. The English ambassador reported her as stating, 'I perceive you like me better when I look sadly than when I look merrily, for it is told me that you desired to have me pictured when I wore the deuil'.

The departure of the regent from Scotland's political scene did provide an opportunity for James and his friends. Working hand in glove with Maitland of Lethington and Cecil, who travelled up from London, the emerging leader of the Congregation was to negotiate a new treaty with the French: the Treaty of Edinburgh.[75] What the trio made of each other makes for interesting speculation. Their correspondence indicates a relationship in which Cecil, as the man who had been providing the money (and the power behind Elizabeth's throne) found James and Maitland to be reliable fellows. 'Surely,'

Elizabeth's secretary of state was to write, 'the Lord James is a gentleman of great worthiness!' It is notable that one of Cecil's favourite maxims was, 'gentility is nothing else but ancient riches'. In this James Stewart was to be in full agreement, seeking to enlarge his estates assiduously throughout his lifetime. This was a meeting of minds.

The French negotiators conceded on virtually everything, allowing a total triumph for Protestantism and Anglo-Scottish amity. By the terms of the treaty, Scotland was to be free from foreign domination, its important offices held by native Scots. Elizabeth was to be recognised as England's lawful queen, with Mary and Francis ceasing to claim sovereignty over the country symbolically or otherwise. Both English and French troops were to leave Scotland with the declaration of peace. French domination was not, crucially, simply to be swapped for English. Rather, Scotland's 'ancient liberties' were to be codified: the French were to be expelled whilst England was to be accepted as no more than a friendly neighbour, joined in the same war against Catholic dominance. A comparison might here be made between James and his friends' settlement and the attitude of Protestant rebels during the English government's next foray into another country's internal politics: the Dutch provinces' rebellion against the authority of their monarch, Philip II, in 1585. Almost as soon as English troops arrived to support the rebels, the Dutch estates general invited the earl of Leicester, the English commander, to be their governor, with all the subservience to Elizabeth's rule that that implied. In 1560, the Scots made no such entreaties to English suzerainty; they simply accepted English arms in resisting their Franco-Scottish monarchs' stream of French soldiers and politicians.

More importantly, perhaps, the Congregation flexed its muscle by summoning a parliament. The makeup of the queen's privy council was to be circumscribed, with both parliament and queen choosing its members. More worryingly for Mary, to the Treaty of Edinburgh was added also a demand that she and Francis ratify its terms, failing which English troops might again legally enter Scotland to uphold Protestant power and keep the French out. If James felt a stab of sorrow watching the death of the stepmother he had abandoned, the ultimate outcome must have blotted it out entirely.

In their first foray into Scottish politics, Elizabeth and Cecil had won, and James Stewart shared in their victory, for it was as much his. Whether his sister would ever agree to recognise it would be another matter. To him, she had become an absentee queen – and in her absence she would simply have to accept what the political community had decided upon. Scotland had once again become an orderly world of men, and now it was to be a Protestant world. His faith – the faith that he had only just embraced five years before, when it had seemed like the religion of a noisy minority – was about to emerge in glory. It was hard not to imagine the hand of God in it. On a less divine plane, James had signalled that he was quite willing to sacrifice his sister's temporal authority on the altar of his and his Kirk's spiritual authority. He could not have foreseen that, within a year, his Catholic queen would be back.

Reformation and Reconciliation

The Scottish parliament – the three estates – gathered in August 1560. No summons had gone out to clergy, nobility, or commons from either a regent or the monarchs. An English agent, Thomas Randolph, who had come north with the earl of Arran when that young man left France to convince his father to embrace Protestantism the previous year, was avidly watching events unfold. He was to describe a picture of Protestant harmony.[76] He was either wilfully blind or deliberately misleading.

What has become known to Scottish history as the Reformation Parliament sat illegally. It had received no support or acceptance from the country's sovereign, and thus the legislation it passed was of equally dubious weight. Even its composition was suspect, with Protestant lairds pouring into the capital to take part (this class of landowner having no right to sit in parliament under the institution's traditional constitutional makeup).[77] This was gerrymandering of the most egregious kind. The majority of the country, if not the political community, was still Catholic in belief and practice, even if few were willing to take up arms in defence of Rome.

To James Stewart and his friends, though, legal niceties were less important than realpolitik. What the parliament was to do, though it is possible few realised it at the time, was to set up a semi-autonomous institution in the form of the Scottish Kirk. Though it was never a rival to the Scottish parliament, it nevertheless was to have an indistinct and problematic relationship with the crown, precisely because neither crown nor legally-constituted parliament would delineate its power. This explains why later Mary Queen of Scots was to querulously, but not inaccurately, remark to John Knox, 'I perceive that my subjects shall obey you, and not me; and shall do what they list and not what I command, and so must I be subject to them and not they to me'. The 1560 parliament was to change the face not only of the Scottish form of worship, but of Scottish and English politics. The ancient 'auld alliance' with France was torn up. On the one hand, the northern kingdom had visibly declined absorption into Catholic France. On the other, it had boxed itself into an alliance with another small nation on the fringes of Europe. Henceforth, England and Scotland would be united in turning their backs on the major powers of Europe, the smaller of the two nations relying on the larger in leading resistance against potential continental aggression. The future of Scotland, James now believed, was friendship with England, former friends in Europe becoming stiff-necked Catholic strangers.

An elephant remained in the room. For all its demands that Mary and Francis ratify the Treaty of Edinburgh, thus giving a veneer of respectability to what James and the Congregation had achieved in the queen's absence, or risk English retribution, the queen of Scots was made of sterner stuff. She was quite entitled, as she well knew, to reject out of hand what she viewed as rebellion against her lawful authority. Whilst the cat had been away, the mice had been playing; but the cat had no intention of condoning them. In one important sense, however, she was to be in lock-step with her brother. In her meeting with the English ambassador, Throckmorton, she expressed a desire for Anglo-Scottish amity, noting that she and Elizabeth were 'of one blood, of one country, and in one island'. Charm was her chief weapon. To her credit, Mary had read the political situation and was quite willing to dissimulate, just as Elizabeth had done in her dealings with the regent.

She would commit to nothing and promise much – this was the safe course, given that she could not simply overturn what had happened in her native country from the airy palaces of France. However, she would not agree to ratify anything that had been done illegally – to do so would be to admit that her subjects and the English queen ruled her. Instead, she forestalled the threat of English Protestant invasion by offering up lavish promises of friendship – which she truly desired – and maintained a regal disregard for the political machinations of her rebels. If Elizabeth were to send troops north again in the name of the Treaty of Edinburgh, it would be, in the eyes of the world, an aggressive invasion against a friendly neighbour.

James Stewart could scarcely have been pleased by his sister's show of authority, nor by her outflanking him as a friend to England. He might have been more worried still when news reached Scotland that Mary was pregnant. A child born of his sister and Francis would be Scotland's future king, reared undoubtedly in Catholic France and potentially willing to embark on a counter reformation in Scotland. Briefly, it must have appeared that the Protestant victory newly achieved was a temporary affair – a shaky thing indeed. The rumours, though, were false. The August parliament thus rumbled on, trying as best it could to cement its achievements. Papal authority was declared null. The mass was outlawed, with the death penalty instituted for those found to have celebrated it three times. An anti-Catholic petition penned by Knox was read out. To quell potential parliamentary rebels who might fear that their profitable feuing of ecclesiastical lands might be compromised, discussion was formally confined to doctrinal issues. Lawful authorities were, interestingly, to be obeyed – but only if they were not 'idolaters'.[78] In the end, the latter demand was to make it into a parliamentary Act annulling all previous Acts which did not accord with 'God's holy word'. This was all fairly revolutionary stuff. The

Protestant leaders, James amongst them, were making hay whilst the sun shone. They knew full well that their victory might be short-lived and were already turning their minds to how they might ensure that their legislation would be lasting. The ingenious solution was a marriage to solidify English support against the Catholics, who might one day manage to put aside their own differences and fight back against the new regime. Arran, the Protestant son of Châtelherault, they decided, might marry Elizabeth.

This had been an idea of the Congregation's since at least June 1559.[79] The earls of Glencairn and Morton, and that smooth operator Maitland of Lethington, reluctant though he was (as he could almost always smell failure before he saw it), were duly dispatched southwards to formally request the English queen's long-fingered hand. The Arranists even sent to Mary a formal request to approve the match. She can only have been nonplussed at what must have looked like – and has been read by some historians – as an attempt to usurp the Scottish throne by the backdoor. If those in favour of the marriage succeeded, they would have an alternative king and queen of Scots should Francis and Mary fail to produce issue. In the shorter term, they would bind England – and its Protestant troops – to Scotland as insurance against native Catholics. It is likely that as much as half of the country remained Catholic in their beliefs, and although the majority would no doubt accept or even welcome listening to reformist ministers preach fire and brimstone as an alternative to Catholic priests demanding continual payments for mumbled Latin orisons, there was always the possibility that the leaders of the Catholic regions would mount an opposition to the new regime, as the new regime had formed the Congregation to oppose the late regent.

According to Randolph, still spying, James was 'marvellous earnest' at the prospect of the match. Biographer Maurice Lee ascribes this to his belief that Mary was likely to die, rumours having circulated about the poor state of her health throughout her marriage to Francis. This is problematic. Mary's health was not strong, certainly, and death in the sixteenth-century was never far away. Yet rumours had been swirling since the death of Henry II that she was pregnant, and two months after succeeding as queen of France, she had even appeared publicly in loose-fitting gowns. Thus, a pregnancy was, as far as James knew, as likely as a death. More likely than his anticipating her imminent demise is that he suspected his sister's future was in France. Arran, if he married Elizabeth, would find his future in England. In either case, newly-Protestant Scotland would be free both of its legitimate monarch, absent for life in France, and the Hamilton line which stood as the second family in the realm. Under such circumstances, he could achieve what he wanted; and what he wanted was finally becoming apparent: power quite distinct from a crown.

With the possibility of a pregnant Mary as likely as a dead one, James' support for the Arran match makes sense. A marriage between Arran and Elizabeth (and their heirs) would provide a counterbalance to Mary and Francis (and their heirs). The English-based, Protestant couple might thus balance out the French-based, Catholic couple. In the middle would be James himself, tending to Scotland – which had just been confirmed in its liberties – as a land-rich steward. He might, he must have calculated, be doubly assured of the acquiescence of both royal couples: those in England would acquiesce due to shared religion, and those in France would acquiesce out of loyalties of kinship. If Elizabeth accepted Arran and Mary stayed in France, James would be in a plum position in Scotland. It was a risky and not particularly coherent plan, but he was never to show himself a great or even a particularly interested thinker in terms of foreign policy.

As a prelude to the proposal, the hereditary claim of the Hamilton line was again underscored in the Scottish parliament. This was with James' eager support, and once more suggests his disinclination to secure the crown for himself. Thereafter those in favour were free to meet with the English queen. As Randolph succinctly put it, they were off on 'as mad a journey as any that ever was made'. Scottish zeal met with English indifference. South of the border, the enthusiasm that had been generated in Scotland by the reformation parliament had not excited much interest in England. To Cecil and Elizabeth, the Scots were simply a people who had now been quietened. Now that France was no longer using Scotland as a postern gate, there was little reason to entertain the fancies of Scotland's new ruling class.

Elizabeth, as she was always to do, gave evasive answers, pushing Arran away with honeyed words. At the time she was far too busy consorting with Robert Dudley, her handsome horse master. Cecil, too, despite his wife sharing James' eagerness that Elizabeth should marry Arran, remained opposed. The futility of the scheme rested on a rather simple problem: James had become a unionist, eager to safeguard English support in the Protestant cause by finding a lasting method of uniting the two realms. He was later to make plain how he viewed matters in a letter to his friend Robert Dudley:

these twa nations joinit in one ysland and separated from the rest of the world, quha being sturred oup in times past by the craft of Sathan to shed one ane otheris blood, God haith wonderfully I say bestowed his blessing upon us, overthrowing the work of the adversary quhill he hes convertit the unquenchable inimity to the judgement of man in ane mutual reciproque luif and benevolence betwixt the twa nations.[80]

His was a religious view of the situation, which accounted for everything from geography and geology to human events. Union, for James, was a hopelessly idealistic system of give and take, one country helping and supporting the other. Elizabeth, however, was not a unionist.[81] Though Cecil would have liked nothing more than for his sovereign to marry and produce heirs, she was disinclined to anything other than prolonged negotiations.[82] As for ideological projects involving the amalgamation of nations, the English queen wanted nothing more than to keep her own throne secure, and throughout her life she appeared more annoyed than anything by the importunities of Scottish Protestants and the troubles of other realms. The entire episode, as amusing as it is in light of Elizabeth's perpetual virginity and Arran's eventual insanity, is useful primarily in exposing the trajectory of James Stewart's career and the ramifications that his newly-formed desire for – or rather feeling of entitlement to – power had on his relationship with his sovereign sister.

It was not until December that Elizabeth gave a firm no to the Arran match. By that time, her reputed lover Robert Dudley's wife had been found dead at the foot of a flight of stairs in her home of Cumnor Place. The ensuing scandal had threatened to envelope the queen. Was it murder? Was Dudley the killer, ridding himself of an inconvenient wife so that he might marry Elizabeth? Or was it all a tragic accident? In the wake of it, the English queen was forced to remain as aloof and princely as she could. Her reign was too new, and her bastardy too real, to weather active involvement in such an ugly and sordid affair. For the moment, playful flirtations were to be toned down. Arran would have to look elsewhere for a bride. Maitland and his fellow ambassadors returned home in defeat, to inform James that the plan of which he was a chief proponent was in tatters. He was to be more worried, however, by a death in December which left the death of the Arran match and the mysterious demise of Amy Robsart in the shade.

Throughout November, the health of Mary's husband had deteriorated. Francis II had never been of a strong constitution. At their wedding, spectators must have looked askew at the dumpling-faced boy, inches shorter than his glamourous wife and dwarfed by his elaborate finery. The acquisition of a crown had done little to provide any more than a symbolic air of majesty. As he sat in church, a sudden buzzing cut off the sound of the priest. It was followed by a pain so sharp that the boy collapsed, the congregation gasping as their king was hastily carried out and put to bed. As he lay there, insensible, his little body was convulsed again and again by violent seizures. The protestations of Mary's uncles – that it was only a minor cold, a temporary ear infection – were disbelieved. As Mary and her mother-in-law fought over the right to nurse the obviously dying king, the physicians were called in to deliver their own brand of brutal treatment. Francis was bled. He was given enemas. A hole was bored into his skull to relieve the pressure on his brain. It was all to no avail. On the 5th of December, the boy died in the Hôtel Groslot, and instantaneously Mary's tenure as queen of France was over. She was now, as her mother had been, a widowed dowager queen. She was only a few days shy of her eighteenth birthday.

With the death of Francis, the Guise ascendancy was over. By the following Spring the various branches of the family would all have retired from court to their vast estates in provincial France, there to plot in safety. The dead king's brother succeeded him as Charles IX, and although Mary's uncles tried to marry him to Mary, Catherine de Medici vetoed the idea. The queen mother of France was finally coming into her own, and she was free now to rid herself of the family which had dominated her son. It is often said that she harboured a hatred of

Mary Queen of Scots, but probably this is an exaggeration. The story that Mary had scorned her mother-in-law as a 'shopkeeper's daughter' is apocryphal. Rather it is likely that Catherine's dislike of Mary was predicated on her having long been a Guise mouthpiece – it was political, not personal. Nevertheless, there was no longer a place for Mary at the French court and she played no role in Catherine de Medici's plans for the future of the monarchy.

Mary surrendered her jewels to her mother-in-law with great dignity, and immediately went into the seclusion of her mourning chamber, there to observe the customary forty days. Catherine de Medici was under no illusions about where her daughter-in-law's future lay; in December, she had glibly told Throckmorton that 'it was now in the queen of Scotland to make answers for the matters of Scotland'.[83] It would be a bleak Christmas indeed for the pretty young dowager, who had lost not only her mother but her husband within the space of a year. Mary has been criticised for extending her stay in France after Francis' death into an 'unnatural limbo', with the implication being that she was casting about for some means of avoiding a return to her rebellious homeland. This is nonsense. As she stared into the void of her future, her mind was working rapidly, and it was focused on Scotland.

When Mary emerged in January, her mind was made up. She immediately embarked on what would now be called a 'fact-finding' mission, or a crash course in her country's polity. She sought out those who had been her mother's advisers. The memoirist Sir James Melville furnishes us with the name of those she consulted: D'Oysel, de la Brosse, the bishop of Amiens, De Rubay, and de Martegnes. From her uncles, she drew advice about the religious change in Scotland, with the cardinal advising her to make no alteration if she planned to return to assume the reins of government (a remarkably wise piece of advice from a man whose family were noted for action). Nor was the interest in Scotland she had developed during her mourning period confined to what the French thought of the country. Thomas Randolph, ever the spy, was to report to Cecil in February that the Scottish queen had sent no fewer than three-hundred letters of introduction to men of consequence in her native kingdom, the names presumably culled from the experiences of her mother's advisers. Here was no dithering girl, but an accomplished and determined one. More personal engagement was to come in April, and it was between brother and sister.

The death of Francis had meant, to James and his friends, a sudden and unwelcome shift in what had seemed a clear policy for Scotland's future. It did, however, lessen the import of Elizabeth's refusal to marry Arran. With Mary husbandless, the need for a counterbalance in the form of Elizabeth and one of Scotland's hereditary heirs vanished. However, it also might mean Mary's return to assume the levers of power she had thus far left in the hands of others. This prospect must have filled him – and all in the Congregation – with trepidation. Her attitude to what had happened in her absence was a worrisome unknown. Her widowhood meant also that she would be free to marry again. That was an even greater and potentially threatening possibility. A dispatch of Throckmorton to the English council is worth considering not only for the fears it raises about Mary's next marriage, but for illustrating what her next husband was to expect – and what she was to resist.

Now that … the Scottish queen is left a widow, one of the things your lordships have to consider, and to have an eye to, is the marriage of that queen. During her husband's life there was no great account made of her, for that, being under band of marriage and subjection of her husband (who carried the burden and care of all her matters), there was offered no great occasion to know what was in her.[84]

What Throckmorton alleged to find in Mary was 'great wisdom for her years, modesty, and also … great judgement'. The idea that Francis had carried the burden and care of her was the idealised thinking of a patriarchal society. However, it was the dominant ideology of the period with regard to marriage. James would have feared what man next might, through marriage, take on the cares and burden of governing Scotland. He did not know that his sister had learned from her first husband that the mirage of male ability trouncing that of a female was just that: an illusion. Just as James was developing a taste for exercising power behind the scenes, his sister had discovered that a husband did not mean giving it up.

Whilst Mary was composing her letters to the Scottish political community, the ruling Congregation had their heads together in Edinburgh. The estates met to discuss what was to be done, and the conclusion reached was that James should pay a visit to his sister in person, to play on family loyalty. He had good cause to believe that this would be a winning strategy. Throckmorton reported that he found the queen much disposed towards him and all Stewarts, distrusting only the Hamilton clan and those who favoured it. In April he travelled to France and she received him cordially.

Throughout all of the troubles in Scotland, there had never been a decisive breakdown in the relationship between brother and sister. Despite Mary's genuine love of her mother and dislike of those who rebelled against her authority, she was far too canny to let her heart rule her head. She knew that James now commanded a significant degree of respect and power in Scotland and had the measure of his greed for wealth. In the previous November he had appealed to her and Francis for 2,500 crowns to be paid out of a French abbey and bishopric of which he had been given the benefices. Mary answered that if he behaved himself – 'accomplished her favour according to the trust she has of him' – he would regain the revenue. Thus, the man shown into her presence in April 1561 was not an enemy, but neither was he a friend. He was, however, her brother.

The weight of all that happened in the previous year must have hung between them as they stared at one another across the chamber in the chateau at St Dizier. He was by now a man of proven political skill; he even looked it, with his neat beard, Stewart eyes, and the hawk-like nose of their father. Despite his role of prior of St Andrews, he eschewed clerical dress, preferring instead the chic black style of the committed Protestant, which had the twin benefits of being expensive and sedate-looking. The eighteen-year-old Mary looked like what she was: a queen of two realms, studied in decorum, her power manifested in the elaborate dress and jewellery she wore.

The meeting had been a long time coming. Although James had been charged to 'fully grope' his sister's mind in January, Mary herself had delayed. Not only was she awaiting a favourable response to her letters to Scotland's men of politics, but she had organised commissioners to return ahead of her, to sound out the possibility of renewing the French alliance. It was worth the gamble. As her subjects were eager to find out her attitude, she was equally eager to test Scottish waters. Her French commissioners were fobbed off with delays, and so she had bowed to the inevitable and agreed to meet with her brother. What neither Stewart sibling knew as James made obeisance to his sister, though, was that each had recently held meetings aimed at dividing them.

On the day before the meeting at St Dizier, Mary had received a man in his mid-thirties, who had declared himself a good Catholic Scotsman. His name was John Leslie, and in time he was to become one of her most ardent supporters. His purpose in visiting her, which just managed to steal a march on her brother, was unequivocal. James Stewart, he insisted, was not to be trusted, and nor were any of the leaders of the Congregation, which was itself fracturing. The earl of Huntly, who Mary remembered with anger had turned his back on her mother, would lead the nobility against the new religion if only she would leave France and land at Aberdeen in northern Scotland. The offer looked, on the face of it, attractive. But Mary was no fool. Beginning her personal reign in blood and war would not only set a bad precedent, it would encourage the enmity of Elizabeth. And at present, she still neither knew nor trusted the promises of men like Huntly, who had done little in her absence to prove themselves. Leslie, for the moment, was brushed off.

James himself had travelled to France via England, where he too had had meetings behind his sibling's back. His, however, were of a more illustrious nature. Stopping in London, he had again met William Cecil, and had been shown into the presence of his cousin Queen Elizabeth. There he would have seen a young woman of twenty-six, fair-lashed and long-faced. England's queen was all business. She insisted that James carry with him demands that Mary ratify the Treaty of Edinburgh, which amongst its various clauses called for the Scottish queen to cease using the arms of England in her heraldry. As minor as this may seem, it would mean Mary compromising her claims to England's throne – and neither James nor his sister quite wanted that. What James made of Elizabeth – a lawful queen and a bastard – is not recorded, but we do know that he stood his ground, insisting that his mission to France was unofficial.

Both having engaged in secret meetings, neither Mary nor James could claim moral high ground. However, both were showing themselves to be astute politicians. Over five days they discussed her return to Scotland, James insisting that her newly-reformed subjects were loyal but adding that that loyalty was contingent upon peace and her willingness to accept the religious settlement that had been drawn up without her consent. He added also that she might continue the practice of her own religion privately – and he meant it. Although as committed as ever in his own beliefs, he had exasperated Knox by quipping that if his sister wanted her masses, 'who could stop her'? For her part, Mary temporised, stating that she could not consider Scottish affairs fully until her return – and certainly she could not ratify a treaty affecting a country she was as yet unfamiliar with. Privately she might have hoped that buying time might encourage her French commissioners to produce something in her favour. The subject of Mary's next marriage also came up, and in this she was on no surer ground – although in politics, as Elizabeth well knew, ambiguity in the marriage game could prove useful. Diplomatic to a tee, she informed her brother that she would seek the approval of the Scottish estates, as per the Treaty of Haddington.

The five-day meeting foundered in a sea of platitudes and carefully-designed double-speak. Mary refused her brother's company on her subsequent visit to Nancy (having hidden from him her desire to seek a match with the Spanish infante, Don Carlos). She also told him that she intended to return to Scotland by sea (which, at that time, she did not). On one point, though, she was in earnest: she cared, she claimed, no more for the friendship of France than England. This was neither flummery nor a heated blast of spite against the country of her mother-in-law. France had become a country in which, at eighteen, she was a dowager: she could draw her pension, of course, and hope for a resurrection in the Guise fortunes, but there was no immediate prospect of a future there for her. That lay in Scotland, or Spain, or – and she might well have had intelligence of her brother's English leanings if not his meeting with Elizabeth – England.

In English affairs, James held the whip hand over his sister. In Maurice Lee's pithy phrasing, the approach of both James and Maitland to Mary Queen of Scots was, 'adopt our program, and we shall get England for you'.[85] This, Lee claims, was Mary's overriding desire. 'All of Mary's subsequent policy', he argues, 'turned on this point: she wanted the English throne. This was her end. The problem lay in her choice of means'.[86] This is a criticism often levelled at Queen Mary, but it is deeply unfair. What she wanted was her place in the succession recognised – for what she perceived as an historical injustice on the part of her uncle, Henry VIII, rectified.

The queen of Scots did see herself as entitled to the English throne: it was, in her eyes, usurped by a bastard who had been elevated to it by a dexterous display of pseudo-republicanism by an overreaching king and parliament. Understanding this is the key to understanding the Scottish queen. In her eyes, Elizabeth had managed something quite against the laws of primogeniture, and although she was too wise a politician to seek violent remedy, Mary would occasionally give leave to her exasperation over the puzzle of England. Yet she made no attempt to have Elizabeth deposed or killed. For the present, she was content to accept the realities of the situation and seek only to be recognised as England's heir. The difficulties in achieving that should have been non-existent. It was, after all, accepted practice that the heir was the eldest living child of the eldest branch of the family. As granddaughter of Henry's VII's eldest child, this was her. Even that, though, had been obfuscated by Henry VIII's will and the parliament that supported it. The succession plans drawn up by the old king and rubber-stamped by his parliament explicitly snubbed his elder sister and her descendants. As frustrating as it would be, Mary would have to be named heir by Elizabeth simply to get assurance of what was quite clearly hers. For that she needed her half-brother, who was thick with the English queen and her chief secretary. Brother and sister, sharing a goal of uniting the Scottish and English thrones (albeit for different reasons and to different ends) would simply have to rub along together.

A story emerges from John Leslie's pen, much later, but presumably based on Mary's recollections of her meeting with James at St Dizier. In it, the covetous bastard entreats her to grant him the earldom of Moray. She refuses, however, encouraging him instead to follow his clerical calling. The story might be apocryphal. It might even be that, decades later, Mary confused her meeting at St Dizier with the correspondence she had with her brother in November 1560 (when she had pled for his loyalty and suggested that reward would follow if he finally settled on a clerical or temporal life). Nevertheless, the tale has an element of truth in that it captures James' character well, illustrating his desire for earthly possessions – mainly in the form of land. His greed for land and wealth is beyond doubt. This may seem odd in a man whose religious beliefs were sincere. But however zealous his Protestant beliefs, which upheld Christ's teaching denouncing covetousness, he need not have felt the need to live by them. That made him no less a faithful Protestant than those ardent Catholics - such as Cardinal Beaton - who kept wives, nor even less a Protestant than his friend Cecil, who amassed considerable wealth over his long lifetime. It is also suggested that James sought the temporary regency of Scotland from his sister – power, in other words – but was refused due to his own refusal to renounce his religion and his tendency to share state secrets with England.[87] This also rings true.

The meeting over, brother and sister parted to again engage in a spot of duplicity. James went straight to Throckmorton, revealing all that had passed in his discussions with Mary.[88] After cooling his heels for ten days – perhaps hoping to find out more of his sister's secret negotiations with Spain, or even that the regency of Scotland would somehow eventuate – he left for home. *En route*, he visited Elizabeth again, despite his sister's orders. If this looks like the rankest treachery, it should be remembered that cultivating England and its ruler was James' means of ensuring what he and his sister wanted: a smooth, bloodless recognition of the Stewart place in the English succession. As Mary herself had to begrudgingly admit, this was Elizabeth's game, and for now she and her brother had to play it.

Rumours have flown since that during his interview with Queen Elizabeth, James requested that the English queen intercept Mary's ships, preventing her return to Scotland. This seems unlikely. Not only would it have achieved nothing but ill-will on Mary's part – and on the part of her subjects – but that ill-will would have compromised his policy of Anglo-Scottish amity. Thomas Randolph, however, was busily writing to Cecil from Scotland about local gossip, which held that both James and Maitland were hoping that Mary's return from France might be delayed. If true, this is also puzzling, and can only be explained by the Congregation members hoping to further cement their anti-Catholic stance by refusing Mary's proposed renewal of the French alliance. This they did in late May. In June and July, James embarked on a mission to subdue Catholicism in the north of Scotland. It is thus possible that he hoped to ensure that when Mary did return, she would find a country whitewashed entirely by Protestantism rather than one in which patches of the old faith shone through. Likely we will never know if James wanted Mary back in Scotland immediately, later, or never – certainly his contemporaries did not, with Randolph thinking one thing and Throckmorton another.[89] It is possible that James himself did not know which the best outcome would be, as the potential outcomes of each cycled through his mind. Although historians have expended a great deal of ink attempting to square the contradictory rumours as to whether he desired Mary's return or not, they have been wasting effort.

118

Neither body of evidence might be wrong. There is no more reason to assume that sixteenth-century politicians always pursued unwavering policies than do politicians today (a fact that should be remembered when considering Elizabeth's later behaviour). Ultimately, Mary's homecoming became inevitable, and James reasoned that if a sovereign authority was to be present in Scotland, his best hopes for exercising power lay in one who was pliant and who shared his pro-English goals.

When James left her side, Mary had her own bit of secret business to attend to. She travelled to Nancy, ostensibly to visit her uncle Charles and stop off at her mother's burial place (the body of the former regent having been interred at St Pierre). However, she wanted to hide from the Congregation that she was making progress in her negotiations for a match with Don Carlos. There she fell ill with a tertian ague. It may be that, however, this was a recurrence of her tendency to collapse at times of stress or emotional strain. The foundering Spanish match coupled with the reminder of her mother's death might well have contributed to her illness. Nevertheless, positivity appeared over the summer in the form of an outpouring of support from her Protestant subjects. James, she must have reasoned, had been as good as his word. From Maitland came a pledge of fealty and an attractive alternative to the Treaty of Edinburgh (with all its threatening rhetoric), which recognised Elizabeth as England's lawful monarch whilst asking the English to allow Mary the position Châtelherault had long held in Scotland: heir presumptive. From the sinister earl of Morton, a disagreeable Protestant with a dark reputation, came a messenger, Archibald Douglas, who tried to weasel his master's way out of accusations of rebellion. From James himself came an extraordinary letter, which Mary read carefully.

In writing to his sister, James set out his desire for her presence in Scotland, it being 'necessary for the quieting of your realm and weal of your whole affairs'. There is no reason disbelieve him. To James, Mary was safer under his brotherly gaze than abroad seeking independent alliances with Catholic princes. He begged for a regency to be put in place if she decided against returning immediately, and a note of hysteria crept in as he stated, 'for the love of God, press no matters of religion, not for any man's advice'. Presumably he did not include his own. His pleas that Mary should make no alteration in the settled religion of her people were well-meant as well as self-righteous and self-serving. Indeed, Mary's uncles would advise her similarly, and she would tell Throckmorton herself that although she would remain a Catholic even if she were the only one in Scotland, she would not constrain her subjects.

His sister was not the only queen to whom James was writing. In reply to a tetchy – and sabre-rattling – letter from Elizabeth telling the Congregation to compel Mary to ratify the Treaty of Edinburgh or face the consequences, James picked up his pen. Beginning with a typically Calvinist exhortation to God, he wrote, 'You are two young and excellent queens, whose sex will not permit you to advance your glory by war and bloodshedding. You ought to love each other'.[90] This was wishful thinking, but it was the kind of diplomacy in which he excelled. On his sister's behalf he excused her usage of England's arms on her heraldry – which Mary herself was to do, blaming her late father-in-law – and made a special plea. 'The law of all nations,' he stated, sailing close to the wind, '[is that she is] next in lawful descent of the right line of King Henry the Seventh'. In closing, he made a renewed appeal for perpetual friendship. James was keeping up his end of the bargain. Elizabeth, however, would refuse to recognise Mary's obvious claim to the English throne until Mary ratified the treaty; Mary, in turn, would refuse to ratify the treaty until her claim was recognised. Perpetual friendship was more difficult to achieve than mutual suspicion.

Maitland and James' solution – a renewed treaty by which each queen recognised the rights of the other, Elizabeth as lawful queen until her death and Mary as lawful heir – could not blossom in a stalemate.

Wrangling with Elizabeth would lead Mary to request – and be denied – a safe conduct (an early modern passport) through England. This was a fit of pique on Elizabeth's part, born of Mary's refusal to ratify the Treaty of Edinburgh until she returned to Scotland. The treaty was to remain a major stumbling block in Anglo-Scottish relations for years. It thus serves as a potent reminded of how shaky the Anglo-Scottish amity was, how tentative was the Protestant reformation in Scotland, and how much Mary's sovereign power had survived despite the troubles it had faced during her absence. Rising above the English queen's petty behaviour, Mary decided to make a sea voyage, the reverse of that which had first carried her to France.

On the 14th of August, a flotilla of galleys packed with costumes, furniture, hangings, horses, jewels, and money, embarked from the formerly English port of Calais. Three of her uncles went with her: Claude, the duke of Aumale, Rene, the marquis of Elbeuf, and Francis, the grand prior. A quiver of other high-ranking Frenchman accompanied her, comprising military men and poets. With her too went her four Marys, Beaton, Seton, Fleming, and Livingston, who had first come with her out of Scotland. Mary had organised, in this fleet, all the trappings of a flat-pack royal court. Scotland had not seen one since before the death of her mother. It would up to her to build it. The next time brother and sister would come face to face would be on his home ground: her realm.

Welcome, illustrat Lady, and our Queen!

An interested observer on the east coast of England might, in August 1561, have spotted an unusual sight. A fleet of boats, the largest galley painted white, were speeding their way through the slate waters of the North Sea. Aboard was the eighteen-year-old Mary Queen of Scots, returning to the country she had been carried away from as a five-year-old.

When her galley docked at Leith, John Knox informs us that the weather was dreadful, a sea mist cloaking the town like a warning from God. The weather does not seem to have bothered the queen very much. Neither does the muted reception, which was lacklustre due to the early and unexpected arrival of the returning royal. The ship carrying the queen's horses had been captured by an English patrol ship, supposedly on the lookout for pirates. Thus, Mary Queen of Scots had to enter into the company of her subjects on a borrowed mule, which she did with good graces. Tradition has it that she dined at the home of a local merchant, Andrew Lamb, where she and her party could shake off their sea legs before the short trip to Holyroodhouse. Probably the Lamb story is apocryphal, the house which stands to this day being from a later period, but the tenor of her reception – good cheer amongst welcoming people – is right.

Travelling through her capital and coming upon the palace at its eastern edge, Mary must have been struck by the difference in scale of almost everything, from the number of people to the size of buildings. However, Scotland was not, as is often suggested, a rural backwater.

Even Mary's mother had voiced pleasant surprise about the condition of the country and its people when she had arrived in 1538.[91] What the queen found, then, was likely no different to France save in scale. Medieval squalor lurked beneath renaissance splendour. Grinding poverty and filthy people slopped shoeless through muck, whilst nobles on horseback, their noses in the air, trotted beside them.

The palace of Holyroodhouse, set in extensive parklands, had been remodelled by James V, its architecture and floorplan designed along the lines of Valois royal palaces. The size, of course, was different. The palace's rooms were smaller and more cramped than those to which Mary had become accustomed. Partly this was due to practicality. Scotland was a colder country than temperate France; the soaring ceilings and airy rooms of a French chateau would have been impossible to heat. In time, the queen would nevertheless unpack all the accoutrements of a royal court in her bid to re-establish Stewart authority in the country. In her antechamber she would hang portraits of her royal predecessors, so that those visiting her would be awed by the prestige of her lineage. Everywhere the arms of Scotland and France would be proudly displayed, to remind all that she was both a dowager queen of the latter and sovereign of the former. Honoured guests she would receive in her ceremonial bedchamber (this according to Valois practice; her cousin Elizabeth made of her bedchamber a female-only space) where the great state bed proclaimed her status.

As word of her arrival spread through the town, people flocked to pay their respects, although a sour note was struck when a party of Calvinists appeared below her chamber windows chanting Psalms. Mary responded diplomatically, despite the disgust of her French attendants, inviting them to sing for her again. However, the hotter Protestants would soon show themselves invulnerable to charm.

On the first Sunday after Mary's return, a much-discussed disturbance took place. In the little chapel at Holyroodhouse, Mary was listening to her priest celebrate the mass. Doing so had been a fixture of her life from as early as she could remember. In France, the monarch's daily mass had been part of the court's schedule, with the royal couple processing to and from the service accompanied by their household. A sudden noise interrupted the Latin. The palace had been infiltrated by an angry mob, intent on seizing the priest. According to Knox's history, they instead came upon her brother, who was barring the door of the chapel, keeping his promise that Mary might celebrate her religion in private. In an attempt at mollification, he informed the mob that he was standing guard not to protect the priest, but to prevent any man sneaking in to listen to corrupt Catholic idolatry. The story is an interesting one, illustrating as it does James' commitment to keeping his promise to his sister. He could not have had a more flagrant opportunity to display that commitment had he staged the entire thing. At any rate, it motivated the queen to publicly proclaim her unwillingness to alter the state of religion she had found on her arrival. The sting in the tail was that the estates should settle the question: the implication here was that they had not already done so. Tacitly, Mary was able to suggest her disapproval of 1560's parliament.

Mary was to make her state entry in Edinburgh on the 2nd of September. This was to be her equivalent of what Henry II had organised at Rouen, although there were to be no naked Brazilians tamed by the forces of civilisation on the banks of the Water of Leith. Instead, the royal party was met by 'Moors' – townspeople in black masks – who led the queen through a series of orchestrated processions. A vernacular Bible was handed to her by a child, in a mirror image of what had happened at the coronation procession of Queen Elizabeth. It was less to Mary's taste than it had been to the English queen's. A flaming dragon was burnt whilst a Psalm was sung, and the earl of Huntly had to intervene to stop an effigy of a Catholic priest being torched. Although Mary smiled throughout, the blatant attempt to force anti-Catholic propaganda down her throat cannot have been welcome. It all came on the back, moreover, of a fiery sermon by Knox in which the preacher claimed that one mass was more fearful than ten-thousand armed enemies.[92] The appropriation of Mary's state entry, whilst it might have seemed like a show of Protestant unity, was anything but. In fact, it coincided with a fracturing of the movement. Now that Mary was back, there was an inevitable split between those whose only aims were religious, and those who were willing to accept their queen's compromise and take up posts in governments. In short, zealots were to find themselves abandoned by realists. James, to his credit, was one of the latter and this time Knox's criticisms were to lack potency.

A particularly awkward moment for the queen's brother came on the 4th of September. For the first time, his mentor and his sister came face to face. In what would be one of a series of meetings between the preacher and his sovereign, James Stewart stood at his sister's right hand. Eighteen-year-old Mary took the upper hand with forty-seven-year-old Knox, revealing that she thought much as her mother had done: that the Congregation's aims were more political than religious. The gist of the debate, as Knox portrays it, is that the queen expounded against his *First Blast of the Trumpet* and appealed to the value of individual conscience, handling herself well in debate until she was bested by his oratorical skills. Although Mary's appeal to conscience has a pleasantly modern ring (and Elizabeth was admired even in her day for her desire to leave men's consciences alone), Knox countered it with a quip that conscience required knowledge, of which she had none.

The omnipresent Thomas Randolph's account of the meeting is somewhat different; in his version, Knox simply reduced the queen to tears.[93] Whatever the truth of what passed, Mary won a short-term victory. Throughout, her brother remained her confederate. He was, however, to hedge his bets and keep the ultra-Protestants happy by insisting that, when Mary travelled on her first progress around her kingdom a few days later, she must be denied her mass. His promise was, after all, that she might have it privately in the chapel at Holyroodhouse, not at every palace and in every lodging place in Scotland.[94] If her brother's tightrope walking bothered the queen, she was likely more concerned by the danger to her life she also faced: as she lay in her chamber at Stirling, a lit candle set light to the bedcurtains. Mary woke up in time to avoid being either burnt or asphyxiated, but 'the populace said at the time that this was the fulfilment of a very old prophecy – that a queen should be burnt at Stirling'. Mary Queen of Scots' belief in prophecy was to become more directly relevant later.

The first order of business was for the queen to select her council, and in doing so she accepted only four Catholic magnates, who were dwarfed by the members of the Congregation she retained. James Stewart and Maitland of Lethington were given leading roles in her government, with the message going out that she intended to make no great alterations in the realm. Instead, she was quite willing to form a ruling triumvirate with her half-brother and his capable friend. This was a wise move. Her policy was one of conciliation. From the outset of her personal reign, she was to tread a careful path, accepting the dominance of the Protestant faction which had come to pass in her absence, whilst allowing Catholics central roles in her household staff. Her aim was to win Scots of all faiths and all political classes over. As she gained in confidence, she would thus honour her lairds (that class of landowners who had no parliamentary voice constitutionally but had nevertheless flooded the illegal 1560 parliament) and attempt to convince Catholic and Protestant subjects to work together.

From James' perspective, Mary's acquiescence to his dominance in her councils was entirely right and proper. The presence of a sovereign in Scotland meant a jostling for influence amongst the nobility, accustomed as its members were to acting as hereditary counsellors to their monarch. By dint of his Stewart blood and legitimation, Lord James, as he was known, was chief amongst them. This was no attempt to usurp his sister's throne or authority but the accepted system of Scottish monarchy. The sovereign made decisions, but those decisions must be informed by the counsel of leading noblemen. If Mary was first amongst equals, her brother was a close second. No matter what Cecil might have suspected – or hoped – James Stewart did not want to sit on the Scottish throne. He wanted to be the power behind it. In that desire he was no different from his peers. He was simply more successful.

In the first year of Mary's personal reign, James was the prime motivator of domestic policy. After all, he knew the players, knew the issues, and, along with Maitland, understood the laws of the realm. His sister, as anyone might, needed an anchor in unfamiliar waters. In November he was given a commission to settle the Borders, where he went in person to oversee a brutal regime of rough justice which would have made his royal father proud. He began also to settle the issue of ecclesiastical finance, and in a way that would not harm him or his fellow nobles. In the convention of estates (of lesser weight than a parliament) called for December, Mary even accepted the right to confirm feu charters – a right which had hitherto been the privilege of the pope (albeit it had long been exercised by Scottish monarchs in practice). For a fee, he and Mary were willing to settle lands on the nobility – a move that both enriched the treasury's coffers and firmly committed nobles to Protestantism.[95] This was what he had wanted: this was the raw exercise of power. Yet we should not assume too readily that he turned his sister into a mindless puppet-queen. On the contrary, she was to write, 'my brother the prior and [Maitland of] Lethington show themselves well affected … except for the difficulty about religion, [they] conform in the rest to what I want'.[96] Her strategy was one of divide and rule. As long as she had the most respected politicians in the Congregation leading her government and supporting her, those who attacked her could only look like what they were: hard-line extremists.

Whilst her minsters enacted policy, Mary was busily decorating her apartments and restoring the prestige of a tarnished monarchy. This was not a frivolous sideshow, nor an unwillingness to grapple with serious policy: it was serious policy. As her father and grandfather had done, Mary was eager to stress the outward trappings of sovereignty. This meant putting up tapestries and material objects such as cloths of state, certainly, but it required a great deal more. She had to be seen – as she had been on her first royal progress in September. She had to foster good relationships between the crown and the political community. She had to institute a schedule of engagement with her councillors, those denied access to the council, and the wives and sisters of important men. As a female monarch, Mary had to carve out a self-image and sell it. Hers was that of an open and friendly sovereign, who would dine in public at noon, read Livy with the scholar George Buchanan or attend council meetings in the afternoons, and invite courtiers to dance or play dice and cards in her apartments in the evenings. With the deposition of her mother and the rise of the Congregation, the Scottish crown had fallen further than it had in centuries. It was up to Mary to polish it back up.

The queen, at this stage, was more interested in two succession questions: her own right to succeed in England, which was still being ignored by Elizabeth, and the future succession of Scotland, which certainly hinged on her own marriage. Her half-brother was too busy administering Scotland – this was his real love – and so the member of the triumvirate charged with advancing foreign policy was Maitland.

Maitland of Lethington, as is well attested, was a committed unionist. His overriding goal, however quixotic, was to join Scotland to England in an equal union through peaceful means. His attempts to renegotiate the Treaty of Edinburgh had failed. Although she had agreed in principle to renegotiation, Elizabeth had typically changed her mind afterwards. Maitland had another card left to play. That was a proposed meeting between the queens. A diplomatic dance ensued, with neither Maitland nor Cecil willing to officially propose the idea. With masterful falsity, Queen Mary's secretary was to imply to Queen Elizabeth's that his mistress might be won over to Protestantism in the course of a face-to-face meeting. It is possible he really believed that this would be achievable; Mary had certainly gulled James into thinking so. But Mary was resolute in her personal faith, however much it suited her for others to believe otherwise. Cecil was not gulled. He ignored Maitland's overtures. Mary herself then stepped into the breach, writing to Elizabeth directly with the proposal. It must have seemed at first that the English queen had snubbed her; a proper reply took until March. In the meantime, relations between brother and sister were at an all-time high.

James had long desired the vacant earldom of Moray. At the end of January, Mary awarded it to him, though the grant was made in secrecy so as not to offend the Catholic earl of Huntly, who had been administering what was a neighbouring region. In February he was, as a stopgap, publicly ennobled as the earl of Mar. These titles were a further insurance policy for James. As has been noted, the Scottish nobility – the 'ancient blood' – enjoyed special access to the monarch and the right to counsel him or her. If anything should happen to Mary,

James was now an irrefutable royal councillor, who might rightly claim the right to influence and guide her successor.

Mary was not only showering honours on her brother; she was to indulge in a favourite activity – matchmaking. The bride she provided for her brother was Agnes Keith, a daughter of the fourth Earl Marischal and hereditary lord high constable of Scotland. A portrait of Agnes by Hans Eworth exists from about the time of her wedding. [97] She stares out primly, but the eye is drawn more to her costume than her face. If her portrait is any indication, Agnes had a love of fashion and display. Her headdress and jewels are fine, her sleeves latticed, and her collar finely detailed with thread-work. By all accounts the pair were a love match – an unusual thing for people of their rank in the period. They had as homes James' priory in St Andrews, and a smaller hunting lodge at Pitlethie in Fife. If George Buchanan is to believed, she provided her husband a domestic refuge: 'his house, like a holy temple, was not only free from impiety, but free from improper conversation'.[98]

It will be recalled that James had long been notionally contracted to Christian Stewart, daughter of the master of Buchan. Evidently this had never been intended as anything more than a property transaction. The unfortunate Christian, who had been living for years with James' mother at Lochleven, was then claimed as bride by his brother. As Lang notes, James was to write home in high dudgeon, 'complaining of this marriage as an act of treachery,' and speaking of Christian as 'that innocent'.[99] As ever, his concern was over the apportioning of the young woman's estates, which he demanded remain his under the contract he had nullified by marrying Agnes Keith. In the glare of Mary's favour, James was at this point enriching his coffers as nobles always did.

With her brother marrying a rich heiress to whom he seems to have genuinely been attached, Mary spared no expense. Knox was to write in condemnatory tones, warning his acolyte not to let marriage dull his faith, or 'it will be said your wife hath changed your nature'.[100] This, though, was possibly Mary's strategy: divorcing her brother from the hated cleric by marrying him to a woman he loved, and all with his sister's blessing and goodwill. The queen of Scots had her own methods of binding men to her side. The wedding was an event of some splendour, confirming the queen in her munificent role and demonstrating that her brother was her creature, not Knox's. Her provision of a bride reveals also a subtler shift in their relationship. By now she had clearly accepted that he was not going to be a clerical adviser, but a temporal one. By endowing him with land, title, and a wife, she was buying his loyalty and revealing her acceptance of his Protestantism. It might also have been that she wished to keep alive his hope that she might be converted. If so, it worked. He was to write eagerly southwards about the possibility of converting his sister and tried directly by handing her a pamphlet on the Colloquy at Poissy.[101] This ambivalence in Catholicism was purely political and Mary was to more definitely demonstrate it during her later captivity in England.

The 'joyousity' continued, allowing the Scottish queen to move forward her domestic campaign of aggrandisement and turn her mind to that other succession question: the getting of an heir for Scotland's – and perhaps England's – throne. In the spring, Mary ordered dug an artificial lake in the park at Holyrood to celebrate another wedding, that of Lord Fleming and Elizabeth Ross.[102] Pitscottie informs us that 'thair was maid wpon the locht of Airthour Saitt [the artificial 'loch of Arthur's seat'] gaillayis and ane castle maid alsua thair of tymmer and greit artaillze schot in everie syde, the quens grace and the nobolietie present'.[103] Present also was the Swedish ambassador, pressing his suit for his master's marriage to the queen. This was Mary at her best: the country's sovereign lady had returned, and with her festival, spectacle, and pleasure. Small wonder that Knox was to comment sourly, "thair began the masking, which from year to year hath continewed since'. His blandishments fell on both Stewart siblings' deaf ears. Mary was simply immune to his desire that prodigality be wiped from Scotland, and her brother was not immune to the pleasures of cultural pursuits.

It was not all fun and games. One rather odd cloud did appear on the horizon that spring, but it was to be lined with silver in the eyes of Mary and James. Since Francis had died and Queen Elizabeth had rejected him in December 1560, the earl of Arran had grown steadily more unhinged. There had long been bad blood between Châtelherault's unpredictable son and the earl of Bothwell, but in March the two appeared to have become friends. Later in the month, Knox was sitting at his desk, probably penning one of his acidic letters, when the door burst open. In strode Arran, claiming that Bothwell had betrayed him. Knox, understandably, was confused. He asked Arran to tell him the whole story. What poured forth was bizarre.

A scheme, allegedly, had been concocted, whereby the duo of Arran and Bothwell would abduct the queen and imprison her. The pair would then slay James and Maitland, taking their places in the ruling triumvirate. Sensing that Arran was either delusional or mad, Knox advised him to forget the whole thing. Instead, the earl wrote to Mary and James, repeating the story. The queen and her brother went into action immediately. Bothwell – probably unfairly, if the story was a complete invention – was imprisoned in Edinburgh Castle, but managed a daring escape down the sheer rock walls. Arran was confined as a madman. He was to live until 1609, but never to regain his liberty.

The entire episode is fishy. Lee suggests that both Mary and James were keen to 'break the power of the Hamiltons'.[104] However, Châtelherault was still alive, and he had other sons. If the aim was to discredit the Hamilton branch of the family, declaring Arran insane and locking him up (and many witnesses attest to his insane ravings beyond Knox) it was a weak plan. If Mary should die before having issue, the throne would fall to Châtelherault and, after his death, his mad son would likely be a nominal king ruled by his younger brother (who was to become the 1st marquis of Hamilton in 1599). The affair did, to an extent, make the Hamilton name and those associated with it a laughing stock in terms of their political aspirations, but this was more likely a fringe benefit than the result of any deliberate policy on the part of the queen and her brother. Like most successful politicians, James was adept at turning unusual events to his advantage rather than causing those events in the first place. In this his sister was to be less successful – but then, her position was more visible.

With Elizabeth's tentative agreement to a meeting sent in late March, preparation was able to go ahead for a summit between the two queens. The queen of Scots and her brother were united in excitement about the possibilities it would offer. Hand in hand, they were marching towards that shared goal: a recognition of the Stewart right to the succession, and with it a perpetual amity between the two ancient enemies. Maitland earned his stripes in negotiating directly with the English queen and August or September were chosen as favoured months, York to be the venue. Mary was jubilant. She even received a portrait of the English queen, enquiring of Randolph – whom she had by now raised up from nosy spy to formal ambassador – whether it was a good likeness. Out went the 'close writings' – those private letters of invitation destined for favoured members of the political community. The only difficulty seemed to be the appearance of Nicholas Gouda, an agent from the pope who sought to elicit from Mary an agreement that she would send Scottish representatives to the Council of Trent. She refused, fully realising, as James did, that if Elizabeth found out, she would use it as an excuse to cancel the summit. For his part, Gouda unfairly put the blame squarely on James.

However, in July Elizabeth sent word that a postponement must take place; she cited the religious troubles in France as an excuse. To meet with the duke of Guise's niece, notwithstanding Mary was her own cousin, would cause the Huguenots to think she had abandoned their cause and faith. This was no more than a specious excuse; she had been perfectly willing for plans to be made after the duke of Guise had massacred dozens of Huguenots at Wassy in March. As was her habit, Elizabeth had reneged on a decision after having thought it through again. She found after all that she had no desire to meet Mary; her curiosity was overcome by her realisation that nothing would come of a meeting that she could not get without one. It might seem naïve of Mary to have trusted her cousin. However, the English queen's mutability and prevarication, whilst well-known to us, were not yet definite aspects of her character in 1562.

Mary was devasted and underwent one of her periods of deep depression. It did not last. With a characteristic volte-face in mood, she adroitly got up and put the close writing summons to good use, changing the planned progress south into a late-summer north-eastern jaunt. The queen had not yet visited the north-east of her kingdom, where the earl of Huntly controlled vast areas of land and people. During the course of this progress, she was to face rebellion and her brother was to take up arms in her defence. In doing so, she was to illustrate her bounty to James Stewart before the world – and let Catholic observers note sourly that she had thrown in her lot with the Protestant heretics.

United they Stand

A royal progress comprised a vast chain of people and animals, winding its way along rutted roads with banners flying and drums beating. Those who lived in Aberdeen would have seen the dust clouds and heard the noise of the approach before they saw its source: in late August, it heralded the arrival of Mary Queen of Scots, her brother, as always, at her side. Along for the journey was the ever-complaining Randolph, grumbling on the journey about the food and the weather, and later about having to share a bed with Maitland.

The purpose of the whole business was, like any royal progress, for the monarch to show herself off to her people. It was particularly important that she make an impression on the gentry and nobility who had not yet attended her court; by visiting them, she could honour them with the role of host to royalty, thereby securing their loyalty. This was not a naturalised Frenchwoman imposing her values on an inferior people, but rather a Scottish monarch employing the tactics of her forebears (James V and James IV had been great progressors). The Scottish nobility, further, were well acquainted with the ancient codes of behaviour, and well attuned to operating a system of hierarchical homage amongst their own tenantry. Chief amongst the nobility of the north was the earl of Huntly, a demi-prince of his vast estates and followers, who had as yet shown no liking for his queen's lukewarm approach to Catholicism or her pro-English policies.

Huntly, it will be remembered, had sent, through John Leslie, a promise to Mary that if she had arrived at Aberdeen the previous year, he would have raised the north against Protestantism in her name. She had not trusted him. That distrust must have seemed justified when the 'Cock o' the North', as the strutting old man was known, arrived in the town at the head of 1500 men. He invited Mary to visit him at his fortress of Strathbogie, but the queen refused, fearing she might be held captive there; the earl, after all, would do what he could to put a stop to her and James' policy of amity with England, even if it meant preventing a future meeting with Elizabeth by means of kidnap. Huntly's bravado was doubly annoying because of the behaviour of his son, John. In June, Sir John had defied royal authority in Edinburgh for some time, relying on his father's power and his apparent charm to keep him above the law. Eventually he had been incarcerated in the town, the sheriffs not displaying the fear of his family name to which he presumably felt entitled. He had apologised for his behaviour but ruined the effect by fleeing his bondage and escaping into what was essentially the earl of Huntly's fiefdom in the north.[105] Incensed by Huntly's effrontery, Mary confirmed James as earl of Moray publicly, replacing his placeholder title of Mar.[106] He was no longer Lord James, or even the second-tier earl of Mar, but Moray: the latest incumbent of an ancient line of powerful northern magnates. With a pen stroke, the queen had gifted her brother the entire revenue of the earldom and the loyalty of its tenantry. We might question the wisdom of her granting power over a place and people that James had no personal connection with. However, at the time no one seems to have criticised what she did and was to do again for other men she favoured. Further, her grandfather James IV had given the same earldom to another James Stewart, one of his own illegitimate sons, who had died in 1544. Mary was simply restoring what had once been in the family.

When the royal cavalcade reached Inverness, Mary found the castle doors barred to her. The captain insisted that he could only admit his queen on the orders of Huntly or his son, Sir John. This was open treachery. It was also incredibly stupid. Mary stayed in the town, no doubt passing a sleepless night, before returning the next day with a number of locals. When the captain finally unbarred and opened the gates, she ordered him hanged, before leading her troupe out of the town. So began a fearful journey, in which the unfamiliar hills on either side of the road might have concealed men of the clan Gordon. At any point these clansmen might have set upon the party, seizing Mary and killing Moray. When they reached Findlater Castle, the found it under the control of the Gordons. As at Inverness, the occupants thumbed their nose at their queen. Insult landing on injury, Mary returned to Aberdeen, and there summoned her brother's more militant friends. The soldiers stormed Strathbogie, demanding the surrender of its cannons. The countess allowed the queen's captain entry towards the end of September and attempted to win her sympathy by showing off the Catholic relics that adorned the little chapel. It was a pathetic move, in the purest sense of the word, and it is difficult not to sympathise with the old woman. However, Mary had discovered something Elizabeth I would not until 1588: that a queen might have the heart and stomach of a king. It was in the midst of this adventure that the Scottish queen made her famous quip about wishing she were a man. As Randolph reported,

I never saw the queen merrier, never dismayed, nor never thought I that stomach in her that I find. She repented nothing but, when the lords and others at Inverness came in the morning from the watch, that she was not a man, to lie all night in the fields, or to walk upon the causeway, with a jack and knapsack, a Glasgow buckler, and a broadsword.[107]

Full of war, Mary expended not a jot of sympathy on the countess or her husband. This was a matter of authority and political resistance to it. Huntly had become a rebel, nothing more. To spare him would have offended her Protestant subjects and sent out a dangerous signal to the Catholic ones that they might do as they pleased, even to the point of flouting her. The earl was put to the horn after he fled Strathbogie by a back door, having ignored a two-day amnesty in which he might have submitted himself to the queen's justice. From the relative safety of Badenoch, he sent his wife to try and intercede with the queen, but it was to no avail. He summoned his clansmen and raised his battle standard, hoping either to seize the queen, eliminate her chief advisers, or both.

About sixteen miles west of Aberdeen lies the Corrichie burn. It was around here that the battle took place on the 28th of October. Mary selected Moray as her general, and this has given rise to the false notion that the entire affair was an attempt on his part to reduce the power of the Catholic Gordons. This is unfair. Throughout, Mary was the driver of events. Her brother was chosen because she trusted him, and his military experience stretched back as far as the 1540s, when he had helped repulse English invaders during the Rough Wooing. The Gordon men were roundly thrashed, and the old earl, corpulent and ill, dropped dead from his horse, likely from a massive stroke or heart attack.

Mary was not thinking in black and white religious terms, but in varicoloured political ones. After confessing treason against the triumvirate, Sir John was executed, and his eldest son, the master of Huntly, was taken in ward (after Moray interceded with Mary to spare his life, if Knox is accurate).[108] The great castle at Strathbogie – an edifice that could rival any other palace in Scotland for size and splendour – was ransacked, brother and sister sharing the spoils. The widowed countess, who was aunt to Moray's wife Agnes, offered no resistance, despite having encouraged her husband's revolt. An educated woman, she and her daughter, Jean Gordon, were welcomed into Mary's court as gentlewomen.

A great deal has been written on the subject of Mary Queen of Scots destroying the most senior Catholic figure in Scotland. Those who support the queen have lamented that she brought down a man – possibly at the connivance of her brother – who might have been a great ally in her later struggles. Those who decry her scorn her for doing the same, suggesting it was an act of foolishness or bloodthirst. The truth, however, is that Mary was acting out of political expediency. Her goal at this point was to enforce Stewart authority, and this was a policy that stood above religious division. She brought down a man who had betrayed her mother, joining the Congregation out of greed and self-preservation before abandoning it too after the regent's downfall. More recently he had shown himself to be a potential troublemaker in her clear policy of amity with England's queen. And on the northern progress, he had defied her authority and allowed his son to harry and threaten her ministers. The sight of the queen destroying the Catholic magnate might have upset continental observers, but in the end, they were to be of little help to Mary Queen of Scots. Further, in the long run, the earl's surviving son, who succeeded as earl of Huntly, was to regain her favour in 1565, making the whole argument moot. The old earl, sick and overweight, likely did not have much longer to live anyway, and his son was a proven liability. The destruction of the Cock o' the North is thus a footnote in her overall history, useful not as evidence of her success or failure as queen, but of her willingness to put politics above religion. She was quite prepared to ruin an overmighty Catholic subject and invest a Protestant one – her brother – with titles, arms, and wealth. If this did not buy his unquestioning loyalty, that is not her fault.

At the conclusion of the northern progress, Moray and Mary were more solidly united than ever. Afterwards, his increased power was to make him reckless and self-important, and she was to develop an independent streak that was incompatible with his desire to govern from behind the throne: but for now they were at their apogee as brother and sister. In a mutually rewarding move, they had chosen one another over Protestant extremists on his side and Catholic rebels on hers. Maitland was promoted, and the role of chancellor, which had nominally been Huntly's, went to the hard-nosed Protestant Morton. Four months later, the corpse of the earl was propped up in its casket and tried, in a grotesque charade in which the queen took part. All might have gone very well in their future, were it not for the problematic fact of Mary's womanhood.

It was a truth universally acknowledged that a queen in possession of a kingdom must be in want of a king. Mary could not, after all, provide an heir to Scotland's throne if she remained single, and one of the measures of a monarch's success was their ability to provide for the future. Since her return to Scotland she had played the role of gracious monarch, Catholic in private, but quite willing to play the Protestant game. This had brought peace and stability, but it had not induced Elizabeth to bow to the reality of the laws of succession and acknowledge that Mary was her heir presumptive. Still she had that other foreign policy card to play: a marriage.

It was both foolish and dangerous to remain single, as Elizabeth had thus far determined to do. Yet it was both foolish and dangerous to hand over power to a husband, unless that husband could be forced to acknowledge his wife as an equal or, better yet, a superior. So began in earnest Mary Queen of Scots' search for a replacement for Francis. The queen's choice was, again, Don Carlos of Spain. Maitland was the vessel chosen to bring it about. One might expect that her desire for a

Catholic match would have raised objection from her brother, bringing as it did the prospect of his sister gaining the backing of the devout – the violently devout – Philip II. His reasons for acquiescing might be many. For one, his sister seemed to want the match, and it was too delicate a time to break with her. For another, she had just broken a Catholic magnate, and it is possible he trusted her not to try and alter Scotland's religion if she were carried abroad to distant Spain. She had, after all, been queen of a powerful Catholic country before and it had helped rather than hindered the Congregation. Further, rumours of Don Carlos' madness were rife, and Mary's plan to marry him had always been a Guise chimera, more likely in the heads of that family than it appeared to the rest of the world. If it did come to pass, of course, Moray knew that Elizabeth had promised to protect Protestantism by force if a Catholic power threatened it in Scotland. Perhaps most likely, however, is this: Moray was as exasperated as his sister with Elizabeth. In January the English queen called a parliament with the leaked purpose of excluding the Stewart line from the English succession. Although Elizabeth tried to excuse it, it was a snub to all that Mary and her brother had been working so diligently towards.

The siblings had done all that they could to foster amity, each banking heavily on this policy winning recognition of the Stewart right to succeed in England. This had failed, and Mary began to suspect that her recently-ennobled brother might not have the superhuman abilities she had at first hoped. It was time to up the ante, and Moray had to go along with it, given that Mary might be starting to doubt him. Might Elizabeth not finally be compelled into making a counteroffer by the prospect of a Spanish match?[109] It is possible that Moray hoped so. Whatever the explanation for his apparent acceptance of the marriage proposal, the fact is that Moray had no desire to entangle himself in foreign policy. This he was content to leave to the trusted Maitland. His passion, and the sum total of his sense of duty and entitlement, was to manage domestic affairs as any chief minister might. Thus, instructions in his diplomatic mailbag, Maitland was off to London to negotiate with Quadra, the Spanish ambassador, in February of 1563. This at least indicates that there was an interest in having the English queen fully appraised – and hopefully fearful – of a match between Scotland's queen and Spain's infante. In the same month, an episode occurred that was to drive home the dangers attendant on and the vulnerability of a single female monarch.

Pierre de Bocosel de Chastelard strikes the modern reader as something of a stereotype: a simpering, lovelorn French poet. He had come to Scotland in November 1562 and immediately attached himself to the royal court. He wrote poems of love to the Scottish queen, and she responded in kind. There was nothing particularly remarkable in this. The game of courtly love was one which had been being played in European courts for decades. It involved the male poet or petitioner turning his hand to conventional verses of amour which he would circulate or send directly to the lady from whom he wanted something. She, in turn, would quite publicly acknowledge his suit and compose her own verses in reply. It was a game of wit, of literary showmanship, and of political exchange. Mary of Guise had played it when she encouraged the attentions of the 3rd earl of Bothwell and the 4th earl of Lennox in the 1540s, and so Scotland was not unfamiliar with it. There were rules to the game; it should not, for example, exceed propriety. Chastelard was to do just that. On the night before Maitland left for London, the amorous poet hid under Mary's bed, his sword and dagger still on him. This was not difficult to do: the state bed was an enormous edifice, and access to Mary's bedchamber was, as has been noted, as free as any Valois monarch. It was only when her ladies did their night-time search that he was discovered. He had conceived, he claimed, a real passion for the queen far beyond anything acceptable to the rules of courtly love. Mary was having none of it, and the poet was banished from court. All might have been well, had Chastelard not been a fool.

By Valentine's Day, Mary had taken the court on another short progress, this time to the Fife coast. She lodged in Rossend Castle, a pretty whitewashed building in Burntisland. The queen was being disrobed in her bedchamber, her ladies unclasping her hair, loosening her laces, and detaching the myriad pins that held together her dress. The door flew open and Chastelard entered the room to a chorus of affronted screams, Mary's women hurrying to cover her *déshabillé*. Real fear must have passed through the queen – not only was her honour at stake, but her personal safety. As Knox tells it, Mary fell into an hysterical panic, screaming for help, which swiftly arrived in the form of her brother. She allegedly cried for Moray to stab the poet to death immediately, only for his cooler head to prevail, the need for due process outweighing arbitrary justice. Knox, of course, had a vested interest in portraying Mary as a tyrannical, hysterical woman in contradistinction to the masculine clear-headedness of Moray. Whatever the truth of their exchange, however, Chastelard was imprisoned, tried, and sent to the block at St Andrews, where he died on the 22nd of February.

At the time and in ensuring centuries, the Chastelard affair has given rise to a number of theories.[110] Some claim that his intent was to kill the Scottish queen. Others suggest that he was an agent of the Huguenots, tasked with ruining Mary's reputation so that she might lose credit on the international marriage market. Neither is particularly convincing. For one thing, he was a hopeless assassin. For another, he must have known that his actions might – as they did – result in his execution. It is difficult to find anything in his career that suggests the poet was willing to die for the Protestant cause. Far more likely is that Knox's version is accurate in the broad sense, if not in the small details. Chastelard had conceived a passion for the Scottish queen that he felt entitled him to break with all sense of decorum and try and force his attentions, perhaps physically, on her.

In the Chastelard affair, Mary deserves sympathy rather than censure. Even if she encouraged his courtly amour, she can hardly be blamed for his precipitate and importunate attempts to ravish her. Though his execution was inevitably extreme, he ought to have known better. The lovesick poet joined Huntly in a parade of men whose own stupidity brought them down. Unfortunately, Mary has all too often been blamed for the ends they made. Nevertheless, the whole sorry episode was to give John Knox and his fellow Protestants a gleeful opportunity to rail anew against the supposed depravity of the royal court. If Mary wanted to avoid her name being dragged through the mud, as Elizabeth's had been over her flirtation with Robert Dudley, it was time to marry.

Philip II had never been particularly keen on a match between his mentally ill son and the Scottish queen. All that kept him playing along was the belief, encouraged by Mary and Maitland, that she might have a French alternative in readiness if he gave her a firm 'no'. As long as the possibility dangled, Catholics in Scotland took heart. Archbishop Hamilton, half-brother of Châtelherault, went so far as to say mass at Easter, stirring the ire and inkpot of Knox. In April, the preacher again had an interview with Mary. This was their third. They had met in December 1562 in Mary's bedchamber at Holyroodhouse, after Knox had delivered a sermon condemning the dancing that went on at court. Then, they had had a rather spirited and surprisingly amicable discussion, as he defended himself against what he claimed were false rumours about what had been reported of him. The April meeting too was fairly uncontroversial, save that Mary went on to punish Hamilton for infringing on the anti-Catholic proclamations made in 1561. For his part Knox had reason not to stir up too much antagonism. His greatest desire was that the parliament which was to sit in May would settle the religious question once and for all, and in his favour. The queen had, after all, promised that her first parliament would address it.

It was not to be. What was to result was quarrelling between Moray and Knox, and a shade thrown on the relationship between brother and sister. The old preacher was apoplectic about the parliament passing without cementing the Protestant settlement. Moray, however, would not support him in raising a clamour about it, despite his being outfoxed by his sister.[111] Mary had ensured her brother's timidity by making some conciliar changes prior to the sitting of parliament in late-May and early June. In addition to the installation of Morton, she had raised the Catholic earl of Atholl and the Protestant earl of Ruthven (a cadaverous old man she could not stand) to her privy council. In many ways this was an inevitable consequence of James's elevation to the Moray earldom and Huntly's concomitant fall. Mary sought balance in her government, and that could not be achieved if the scales were weighted too heavily in favour of Protestants – even moderate ones like Moray and Maitland, the latter of whom she began to pay more heed to. Nevertheless, the new bodies threatened to outshine her brother. This was exactly her intent. As long as Moray worried that the triumvirate was developing into a proper, full-bodied council of equal voices, he would be tractable. It must have seemed to him that, having given generously with one hand, his sister was taking away with the other. Politics was already fragmenting what had seemed, months before, a solid relationship.

More importantly, from Mary's perspective, she had succeeded in parting her brother from Knox: 'the matter fell so hot betwixt the earl of Moray ... and John Knox, that familiarly after that time they spoke not together more than a year and a half, for the said John by his letter gave a discharge to the said Earl of all further intromission or care with his affairs'.[112] Not only was Knox to vent his spleen at Moray – whom he regarded now as a traitor more concerned with possessions than religion – but at Mary. At their fourth meeting, he would reduce the queen to tears. 'What are ye within this commonwealth?' she famously asked him. 'A subject born within the same, madam,' was his stinging reply. This he followed up with a subtle jab at the queen's brother: 'And albeit I neither be Earl, Lord nor Baron within it, yet has God made me (however abject that ever I be in your eyes) a profitable member within the same'. Revenge for her tears was to come at the end of the year, when Knox, after summoning Protestants across the realm to join him in protest against two of their number who had been arrested for disturbing the peace, was put on trial. His crime was simple: he had illegally summoned armed men in defiance of royal authority.

The queen's council was tasked with hearing the case against the preacher. Moray, understandably, was in a quandary. He had fought with Knox, yes, but he had no desire to see his quondam mentor suffer for religion's sake. He appealed to the preacher to throw himself on the queen's mercy; but submission was never Knox's stance. Instead he took up his own part liberally, in the full knowledge that his followers had assembled in force to frighten the council. He was acquitted, the councillors being unable to condemn him for encouraging Protestant insurrection when many them had done just that at the time of the 1560 parliament. Moray, of course, had a vote on the council; he was amongst those who voted to spare Knox. His sister was not pleased. The venomous preacher had had the last laugh, again.

If Mary wanted to silence Knox, or at least to annoy him, and if she wanted to break free from the triumvirate that had proved so ineffectual in securing recognition of her family's right to succeed to the English throne, she would have to find a suitable husband. After the ominous rumblings of 1563 – especially coming after 1562's high point – her brother must have looked to the future with trepidation. He would have been right to do so.

Brother of the Bride

Towards the end of 1562, at the time when Mary Queen of Scots was hunting down the earl of Huntly, panic flared in the halls at Hampton Court. What a seemed a bad cold had erupted into a fever for the English queen. The physicians gathered, their brows knitted. None wanted to be the one to tell Elizabeth what they all knew: she had contracted smallpox. This virulent disease was one of the deadliest in sixteenth-century Europe, and even those who survived it were often left with disfiguring facial scars. Elizabeth did not look like she would be one of the survivors. As she drifted in and out of consciousness, she gasped out orders for the future of her realm: it was to be governed by none other than Robert Dudley, her horse master and reputed lover. She did, she qualified, love him, but never to the point of impropriety.

Thanks to the ministrations of a disgruntled German physician, Burcot, Elizabeth beat the odds and survived, her complexion clear. The brush with death and her orders on what was to happen in the event of it had, however, sent her government and that in Scotland into apoplexies. Dudley, who was an unpopular man and the son and grandson of traitors, to bear dominion over the English? The Stewart line ignored, again, in favour of an upstart? It would not do. Yet Elizabeth's wishes do reveal the depth of the trust she felt in her master of horse.

As she recovered her health and spirits, Elizabeth was to find her realm again exercised by the succession question, much to her chagrin. She and Cecil were to be vexed also by the ongoing discussions across

Europe about the marriage of Mary Queen of Scots. The English queen's proposed solution was that Mary should wed an Englishman. In reality, it seems clear that she simply did not want Mary to marry at all. She had found the single life to her taste, so why should not her cousin do the same? At her first parliament in 1559 Elizabeth had declared her intention to remain unmarried. The world had chosen to ignore her. Accordingly, she had decided to play on the erstwhile hopes of her parliament and eager foreign princes. However, it is likely that she had already decided that, whatever flirtations she engaged in, diplomatic or private, she would live and die a virgin.

Elizabeth's decision was a dereliction of duty. Her unwillingness to countenance discussion of the succession merely compounded this. However, Mary was to make no such claims; the Scottish queen was deeply invested in providing for the future of her dynasty. In September 1563 Randolph was charged with proposing an English match for Mary Queen of Scots, without any bridegroom being explicitly named. This encouraged Moray to write to Cecil, asking as much as he dared for a name to be thrown into the ring. He could not, after all, hope to continue to push the increasingly independently-minded Mary in the direction of English amity with only vague suggestions. Events were to turn somewhat in his favour with the fizzling out of the Spanish match (it would be completely killed off by Philip II in August 1564). However, when Elizabeth was finally induced to suggest a candidate, it was to everyone's surprise – and not a little scorn – that the name put forward was Robert Dudley.

Mary at first treated the offer with good humour. It must have seemed like an opening gambit – certainly it could not have been serious. Moray must have been similarly bemused. Robert Dudley was not only a man made by Elizabeth, but in the eyes of many he had been her lover. To both siblings' horror, though, the English queen appeared to be in earnest. If they were to entertain even the possibility of such a *mésalliance*, they would only do so if the English queen would sweeten the cheap offer with a legal promise to recognise the Stewart dynasty's English inheritance. It was still not ideal, from either perspective. If Mary married Dudley, she would be giving up the chance of a grander match elsewhere; and for Moray it would mean his political career would be curtailed by the arrival of a man who would have greater influence with his sister and his English cousin than he could ever hope for.

The sincerity of Elizabeth's offer has always been conjectured on. Did she really mean for Mary to accept Robert Dudley? The answer is no. Again, she wanted Mary to remain unmarried. She was thus in the position of offering a gift that the recipient would neither want and could not accept, in order to claim the high ground when the inevitable refusal came. Her stance would be, essentially, 'I made you an offer and you refused it. I need offer you nothing more and will take any attempt on your part to find another offer as a direct insult'. Elizabeth did not want the uneasy relationship she had with Mary complicated by a husband, who would undoubtedly have something to say about politics. A man – any man – might destabilise the seniority she enjoyed as the woman who had in her gift what Mary desired: English recognition of Stewart succession rights. Her strategy of keeping Mary single was incredibly short-sighted and selfish. However, there is no reason to expect Elizabeth to have cared any more about providing for Scotland's succession than she did about providing for England's. In the short-term things were working well for her. She did not want people to discuss the long-term, presumably believing that God would provide.

Mary and her brother were forced to consider an English match by the reality of her situation as well as dynastic considerations. Although she had dreamed of a grand foreign alliance, the sad truth was that

Mary's continental suitors were wholly unsuitable or disinterested.[113] Don Carlos was mad. Eric of Sweden was homicidal (he would go on to personally butcher five noble prisoners whilst in a rage). Archduke Charles of Styria was stable, but he showed no particular desire to marry the queen of Scots, and his brother Maximillian was positively against it. The duke of Ferrara had been married already; no children had been produced, which raised doubts about his fertility, and it was rumoured he had murdered his wife. The prince of Condé, widowed in 1564, would bring difficulties with the French royal family. At home, Mary's suitors had amounted to the mad Arran and the dead Sir John Gordon. As both the queen and Moray were still pursuing Elizabeth's friendship – not for altruistic reasons, of course – an English match would be welcome, as long as a concession could be wrung from Elizabeth with regard to recognising the Stewarts.

There was a far more attractive candidate than Robert Dudley. This was Henry Stewart, Lord Darnley. The son of the earl of Lennox (that rival to Châtelherault in the Scottish succession, who had fled to England after being toyed with by Mary of Guise) and Margaret Douglas, the daughter of Margaret Tudor and the old rogue Angus, Darnley had been invited to Elizabeth's court in 1563. He had remained there ever since, showing himself a model courtier, and attracting not a whisper of scandal. Despite prurient gossip, there is no evidence that Darnley was promiscuous with either men or women – indeed, only later was there gossip that during his time in Scotland he had taken up with an unnamed Douglass woman (a far cry from the amours of Henry VIII or even James V). About the worst that was said of him was that he had shown himself, in either England or France, to be a 'great cock chick'. This should not be taken as a reference to his having indulged in homosexual activities. To be a 'cock' in the period was to swagger, as Huntly, the Cock o' the North, had done. The word did not acquire its phallic denotation until the 1610s. To be a 'chick' was to be, unsurprisingly, young – the meaning in use since the 14th century. Darnley, then, was said to be a very young man who nevertheless swaggered as though he was much older. For this accusation there is plenty of later evidence.

On Michaelmas Day, 1564, Elizabeth ennobled Dudley as the earl of Leicester, ostensibly to make him a more suitable match for her Scottish cousin. Present at the ceremony was Sir James Melville, a Scottish diplomat who was then working in favour of the marriage negotiations with England. At the close of the ceremony, during which the queen had tickled her favourite under the chin in full view of the court, Elizabeth asked Melville what he thought of the new earl. He replied that he thought Leicester lucky to have such a generous and gracious mistress. 'Yet,' she quipped, pointing at Darnley who, as a prince of the blood, was carrying the sword of state, 'you like better of yonder long [tall] lad'.

Melville did prefer a match with Darnley more than one with Leicester, though he was much too clever to say it. Instead, he worked with the entitled Margaret, countess of Lennox, to help bring it about. Elizabeth seems not to have minded. The English queen had written to Mary requesting her permission to allow Lennox back into Scotland, where his lands had been forfeited since he had taken up voluntary English exile in the 1540s. He had done well out of this exile. Henry VIII had greatly favoured the turncoat Scotsman, not least by granting him the hand of his sister's daughter, Margaret Douglas. However, for two decades he had simmered over the loss of his Scottish estates, which he believed he was entitled to by right of blood. A tedious back-and-forth had rumbled on between Mary and Elizabeth, with Mary welcoming the exile home in the spirit of amity, only for Elizabeth to then demur over what she herself had proposed. It had only ended with the departure of Lennox for Scotland a few weeks before Dudley's elevation to the earldom of Leicester. The granting of Lennox's passport northwards marked a run of favour shown to the family by the English queen, which had been prompted by the publication of a troublesome tract by John Hales, titled *A Declaration of the Succession of the Crown Imperial of England*, which declared the Stewart claim invalid, and thereby threatened to undermine Elizabeth's tentative pro-Scottish policy.

In Scotland, Lennox, though he must have been resented and disliked for his years of perfidy, turned the full force of a not inconsiderable personal charm on Mary, attending mass with her before relaxing back into Protestantism. Moray, too, welcomed him, albeit tentatively. Lennox had become a naturalised Englishman. He was, further, a Stewart. In him, the queen's brother must have found a living example of Anglo-Scottish amity. It was not to last. By the following spring, Maitland was reporting to Cecil that all the Protestants of the realm, from the Hamiltons (naturally) to Moray 'in their hearts mislike Lennox'.[114] For the moment, though, his son Darnley was simply another piece on the chessboard, still lodging under the wing of the queen on the opposite side. In the meantime, Melville organised a conference at Berwick to discuss the Leicester match. It took place in November 1564, and Elizabeth's commissioners were to do nothing to progress the marriage. That Mary must marry Leicester was Elizabeth's line, and only after the indissoluble link had been forged would she deign to consider the Stewart's place in England's succession. Moray and Maitland, who had taken part as Mary's commissioners, were furious. Here, again, was a slap in the face from Elizabeth after all their work in favour of amity. When Moray returned to Edinburgh, he found his sister's mood matched his own. All that the Scots could do was to

153

play the game anew: pretend that a grand Catholic match might be forthcoming, and thereby try and force Elizabeth's hand.

Moray, jointly with Maitland, exceeded their authority in promising that Mary would wed Leicester if Elizabeth recognised the Stewarts. Cecil, in his replies, continued to play for time. This went on as December turned to January, and January to February. In February, though, the English queen did something that no one could have seen coming. She gave Darnley leave to join his father in Scotland for a limited time. He was to make no promises, and certainly he was not sent as a suitor, but Elizabeth knew full well that her actions would be viewed as tacitly sending him as a candidate for Mary's hand.

Why did Elizabeth send Darnley north? This is a question which has vexed historians since 1565. Some claim that she knew the handsome young man from Yorkshire to be a violent, drunken youth, and hoped to ruin Mary by him. This is nonsense. There are no reports of bad behaviour on Darnley's part throughout his extended time at Elizabeth's court. Others suggest that she was honest in her stated intentions: Darnley was simply to go north to work with his father on legal issues pertaining to the restitution of his estates. This is equally unconvincing: Elizabeth was no fool. She had been warned by Randolph, who was growing increasingly frantic, fuelled as he was by rumour, that Mary had designs on the Lennox Stewart youth. He was wrong, at this stage; ironically, his fear-mongering probably helped kindle the idea of a match between Mary and Darnley in the heads of both queens.

Surprisingly, there is one possibility that has never been acknowledged. Elizabeth might well have wanted Darnley to marry Mary not because she had some Machiavellian scheme in mind based on knowledge of his hidden depravity, but because any product of the marriage would provide an heir for Scotland and England. The marriage would thus have the benefit of providing for the English succession (as it did) without Elizabeth having to explicitly name the child successor. In the festive period 1564-5, the English queen had again been struck by illness, in the form of a gastric upset, which required her to take to her bed for days. It is possible that this latest brush with illness turned her mind towards the succession.

We are, however, faced with the fact that Elizabeth railed angrily against the marriage when it looked likely and after it had come to pass. This can best be explained by her nature: she was given to tergiversation and had an almost chronic aversion to sticking to a decision. A habitual desire to dissemble then accounts for her apparent outrage at the ultimate marriage between Mary and Darnley. Want it though she might have done, admitting so would have meant revealing her hand. If this was Elizabeth's reasoning, she did not inform Moray of it. However, it might be reasonably suggested that, in February 1565, Elizabeth hoped that a potential Darnley marriage might provide for both kingdoms what she knew she never would: an heir. By publicly opposing it, however, she might allay her Protestant counsellors (who were dead against it) and friends in Scotland and continue to refuse to name her successor more volubly than ever.

The alternative is that the English queen really did oppose the Darnley match, and simply wanted Mary to remain unwed in perpetuity, with no regard for either the English or Scottish successions. By allowing Darnley northwards, she simply hoped to throw a spanner in the works, never suspecting that the Scottish queen would move with the rapidity she did. Certainly, she had previously shown herself inclined to keep Mary single – and her chimeric demands that Darnley return to England when romance blossomed would indicate that this remained her policy. Yet a potential *via media* remains. Elizabeth had proven in the past that she would make decisions and then, once they had been put in motion, she would do everything possible to undo or distance herself from them. So it might have been with Darnley. When she gave him leave to travel to Scotland, she had decided that Mary might have him, thereby giving Scotland and England an heir. By not officially sanctioning him as a suitor, she would retain the power to deny all responsibility, feign outrage, and huffily refuse to name the heir as having any part of England's succession. Once he had gone, though, she changed her mind, and suddenly did not want the Scottish queen and their mutual English cousin to produce a troublesome child. As ever, with Elizabeth, we will never really know what was in her mind. It is possible even she was not sure.

Darnley caught up with Mary at the sandstone Wemyss Castle, where she was on progress. He had first sought her at Holyroodhouse, where he had found only Morton, Randolph, and Robert Stewart (the prior of Holyrood and another illegitimate half-brother to Mary and Moray). There he had made a good, though impecunious, impression on the English ambassador. When she caught sight of him at Wemyss, Mary is said to have been taken with Darnley, declaring that the youth – who was one of the few men taller than herself – was 'the lustiest and best-proportioned long [tall] man she had ever seen'. This was partly flannel. She had met him twice before: his mother had sent him to France to congratulate her on her accession to the French throne after Henry II's death, and again to condole with her on the death of Francis. On neither occasion had she made much account of him – although, in fairness, he would have been little more than a boy. In 1565 he was eighteen or nineteen and, by the standards of the day, a full-grown man.[115] What might have made him more attractive than simply being 'long, small [slim], even and straight' (a boon in a society in which physical impairments were commonplace) was that, until Mary herself produced a child, he was next in line to the English throne if Henry's VIII's will was abrogated and the Stewart line recognised. The fact that he had

156

been born in England was even better: it negated English legal cavilling about inheritance of the throne requiring English birth, like inheritance of any other English property.

Mary welcomed Darnley into her court, and with funds supplied from his father, he began to woo her. She did not immediately accept him. To do so would have been impolitic, when other opportunities existed. When he proposed to her with a diamond ring his mother had given him, she rejected him, taking it 'in evil part'. For Moray, more worrying than the courtship (which Randolph suggests, probably hopefully given he had been tasked with pushing Leicester, had waned in March) was Mary's independent streak. This manifested in religious toleration. In February a Catholic evensong was heard in the capital, and the following month it was said that there were as many masses being attended as Protestant services.[116] The rumour mill was turning. Lennox, it was being whispered, was going to be recognised by the Scottish queen as her heir presumptive, the Protestant Hamiltons denounced as a bastard line. Mary turned a blind eye to the gossip. Desperate to know what on earth was happening, Randolph visited the queen at St Andrews. She was not to be goaded. He was to report to Elizabeth that

she said little to me for that time. The next day she passed wholly in mirth, nor gave any appearance to any of the contrary; nor would not, as she said openly, but be quiet and merry. Her grace lodged in a merchant's house, her train were very few; and there was small repair from any part. Her will was, that for the time that I did tarry, I should dine and sup with her. Your Majesty was aftertimes dranken unto by her, at dinners and suppers.[117]

157

Mary had retired into merriment, living 'like a bourgeois wife' with her modest train. In this she was following the behaviours of both her Valois and Stewart predecessors.

Moray was caught up in the middle of all this, and it is possible to sympathise with his position. If his relationship with his sister was not exactly in the doldrums, it had not recovered to 1562 levels (nor ever would). Elizabeth, too, had shown herself to be anything other than a plain-dealing and honest friend. He was at risk of being left dangerously exposed, caught in the middle between his sister and cousin. He had no alternative if he wanted an English match for Mary than to try and encourage Leicester's half-hearted suit or put the best face on Darnley. He and his sister had dealt as honestly and openly as they could with England's queen. In return they had got vagueness and games. Moray must have been as exasperated as Mary. He was to voice just that to Randolph, who reported his words:

I am known to be a travailer to your effect [the Leicester marriage], which I repent not ... for I do think it the best. If it come well to pass, take the honour who will; it is enough for me to have discharged my duty to God and my country ... if it go otherwise than well, the burden is wholly mine, for that I am the counsellor, the deviser, the persuader – and how well some already like of me, you know, and being ever had in suspicion for England, either I shall be forced to show myself their plain enemy, or every word that I do speak of them ... shall be had in suspicion. If she marry any other, what mind will be bear me, that knoweth how much I do dislike therewith?[118]

Here was Moray's dilemma. It has in it the worry of any politician of any age caught between two competing propositions. His anxieties are all for his own future, having been bounced into a foolish position by

Elizabeth and now caught in its failure. Having committed himself to pressing the Leicester match, which Elizabeth was doing nothing to make attractive, he now faced the possibility of another suitor becoming Mary's husband – and that suitor would know that he, Moray, had not wanted him. Things had begun to look very bleak indeed for this once all-powerful minister.

That exasperation was to climax in March. Elizabeth sent a definitive and hugely provocative message north: she had decided, she intoned, that she would make no pronouncement on the succession – in other words, that she would not accept the Stewart place in it – until she herself had either married or decided for definite that she never would. This was her hardest slap yet, and it struck both Mary and Moray. The Scottish queen collapsed in angry tears. If less prone to depressive moods, Moray must have privately wrung his hands – he was reported as being 'almost stark mad'.[119] His English cousin had played him falsely to, and he must have realised, as Mary did, that a minister who makes the assurances he had but fails to deliver is a worthless commodity. It is no surprise that Randolph found him 'sad and apprehensive' in ensuing months.

Elizabeth had played what seemed an unfair hand – but a trump card all the same. To many contemporaries – to Mary herself – it appeared that the imperious queen of England was meddling directly in Scottish affairs. However, it should be remembered that Elizabeth had her own country to protect. What seems to have bypassed everyone on the Scottish side is that, whether she sought parliamentary recognition of the Stewart claim or not, the English queen was tacitly admitting to favouring it by interfering in the matter of Mary's marriage. If she were to die and Mary succeed, the chosen husband would be England's king, ruling over her people. Not only must that husband not, then, be a menace to the Anglican settlement, he must be acceptable to the nation at large. In this way, Elizabeth's interest in Marys' marriage, however high-handedly she expressed it, was a proxy one, intended to provide for the future. As Moray realised, as long as he and Mary demanded recognition of the Scottish queen as heir presumptive to England, her English counterpart had every right to dictate the course of her future marital path. Neither Moray nor Mary were, however, content for the rights of the Stewart dynasty to be assured by a nod and a wink.

When Mary had recovered from her low mood, she exhibited a renewed determination to pursue the Darnley match (after one last futile stab at Don Carlos).[120] This was good policy. Elizabeth had, after all, been unwise enough to claim that Mary might marry an Englishman. Although her preferred candidate was Leicester, she had not explicitly ruled out Darnley. It is sometimes suggested that the Scottish queen hoped to strengthen her claim to the English throne via marriage to Darnley, as a jab back at Elizabeth's high-handed refusal to recognise the Stewart succession.[121] This is a mistake; on inspection, it falls apart. Older than Darnley and thus an elder grandchild of Margaret Tudor through her son rather than her daughter, Mary's claim was superior. Darnley could neither strengthen nor weaken it. However, as Darnley was male and English-born, he was potentially a rival claimant in the Stewart line. Mary must have calculated that marriage to him would not strengthen her claim but allow her to keep a potential rival in check. Thus, where Mary Tudor had executed her rival, Jane Grey, Mary Stewart married hers. Further, it was clear that any child born of the marriage would unite the rival claims. If Mary married Darnley and produced a child – preferably a son – she would have pulled off the extraordinary coup of turning a rival claimant to England's throne into an ally and delivering a child who united both claims into one.

With this in mind, we should dispense with the often-repeated claim that Mary's marriage to Darnley was rash and born of an excess of sudden passion. It was neither. With no foreign alliances forthcoming and the Leicester marriage deliberately hamstrung by the woman who had first proposed it, Darnley was the wisest possible choice of husband. Though he cannot have been thrilled, knowing Elizabeth would predictably rail against being outfoxed, Moray seems to have tried to make the best of his sister's policy. From the arrival of the 'jolly young man', he had courted him, hoping to sound out his true religious views by taking him to hear Knox preach at St Giles and dining with him afterwards. It was Darnley himself who was to put an end to any prospect of lasting friendship.

Darnley had made a good impression all around, and in March Robert Stewart invited him to view a map of Scotland. The prior of Holyrood pointed out which lands fell under Moray's stewardship. On being shown them, Darnley, not usually noted for his perspicacity, pointed out that his would-be friend's landholdings were too large for any one subject. When word got back to Moray, he was incensed. Here was a clear direction of which way the wind was blowing. His credit with Mary, already shaky, would undoubtedly be wiped out entirely if she took as a husband a man who was suspicious of the extent of the wealth and power he had been amassing. An age-old difficulty between siblings suddenly arose: brother conceived a suspicious hatred of his sister's choice of husband. But this sister was a queen and her brother a subject.

To her credit Mary attempted to conciliate between the man who was likely to become her husband and the brother who had promised much but delivered little. In April, Darnley fell ill with measles, and it is often reported that the queen fell in love with him. This notion appears to be born of some hoary notion that women have an inherent inclination towards nursing, with love for their patients growing out of it. The ridiculousness of this need not be expounded on. As we have seen,

Mary's desire for Darnley was political, not passionate. If she was physically attracted to him – and by all accounts he was an attractive young man – then that was simply the icing on the wedding cake. Mary pressed ahead with her plans for marriage, and her brother was being, as he had feared, left out in the cold.

The prospect of Mary's marriage had realigned Scottish politics. The old triumvirate, already broken, had given way to other influences. The earls of Atholl, Caithness, and Hume had all gained Mary's ear. So too had one of her musicians, an Italian named David Riccio, who had come in the train of the Savoyard ambassador in 1562 and stayed, becoming fast friends with Darnley. Facing ruin, Moray retired to St Andrews. It is doubtful that his sister cared, so intent was she on the world believing that her government was united behind her decision. The course Moray was to pursue was the worst political decision he would ever make, and after he had embarked on it, things would never again be the same between brother and sister.

Breakdown

Before he had retired to St Andrews, Moray had signalled his intentions covertly, writing to his Protestant friend Argyll and the duke of Châtelherault. The duke, whom Moray had long sought to discredit, became a friend of necessity. He was to become involved in a bond of mutual support nominally in the cause of protecting Protestantism. In reality it was the protection of Moray against his sister's marriage to a hostile man. Giving the appropriate religious glean to the enterprise was John Knox. Mary's prospective marriage to Darnley had sufficiently spooked the preacher that he was willing to let bygones be bygones and once again embrace his prodigal son.

Yet, try as he might, Moray could not build up an opposition party to the queen's marriage. Many of his former Protestant allies were on her side; after all, they wanted an English match, and Darnley's religion was sufficiently malleable that rising in arms against the marriage was far too dangerous. In short, they were not convinced by the queen's brother's attempts to create a war of religion. Why should they risk their necks in Moray's fight to retain power?

Mary sent for her brother to attend on her at Stirling, where she Darnley were in residence. She had solid reasoning behind her summons. In March, the earl of Bothwell, last seen escaping from Edinburgh Castle after Arran's madcap accusations had landed him in thrall, had returned to Scotland. He was immediately called to justice, with an appearance in Edinburgh scheduled for the 2nd of May. Moray and Argyll had flooded the capital with 5000 men, the queen's brother realising that Bothwell – who was a bitter opponent of the Anglo-Scottish policy favoured by Moray – must be scared off. The recalcitrant earl was; he slipped away to France on hearing of the mass gathering against him. Mary had been scared too. By showing up in arms, Moray had illustrated that he could command swaths of support. In ordering to him Stirling, she might better have the measure of what he might use it for.

Despite a show of warmth from the queen and her hopeful bridegroom, Moray was unmoveable. He insisted that he could not support any marriage that might disturb the Protestant religion. This was specious. Darnley was, after all, nominally a Protestant, having freshly arrived from England. He did also reveal a truer reason for his opposition. Elizabeth would not be happy with the marriage, and it thus threatened the amity he and Mary had so long fostered. Mary was able to counter that she had dispatched Maitland south to treat with the English queen, with a view to making her more amenable to the match. On this the discussion reached stalemate. Mary, however, was in no mood for stalemate. Having showed a jolt on independence in February, she was now heartily sick of being treated like a wayward child by her English cousin. She was a sovereign queen in her own right: 'she would be fed with yea and nay no longer'. She summoned her nobility to meet at a convention in Perth and approve her marriage plans with or without English consent.

Into this febrile atmosphere Elizabeth finally decided to intrude. That old diplomatic hand, Nicholas Throckmorton (formerly the English ambassador in France) arrived to tell Mary that England's queen was irrevocably opposed to the Darnley match. Whatever had been her reasons for sending the young man to Scotland, she had now thought again. Mary must not marry him. She might take any other English noble, but not Darnley. Elizabeth even tried to fall back on her old promises: if Mary married Leicester, she would think again on the Stewart place in England's succession.

This was too little, too late. Elizabeth was playing an old hand, badly. In a further show of her independence, Mary immediately conferred upon Darnley the earldom of Ross. It was the Scottish queen's turn to be provocative. With another pen stroke, she had ennobled a man – but this man was legally subject to another sovereign. Throckmorton departed, at a loss as to what, other than military intervention, might stop the marriage.

Moray remained with the court at Stirling, hoping that his presence might encourage a Protestant outcry against Darnley. It was to no avail. Even the mooted parliament, which he hoped would finally, with Mary's consent, settle religious question, was not to sit. Yet the breach that had opened up between brother and sister had its effect. At about this time, Randolph reported that the queen's appearance was again affected by events – 'her beauty' was apparently 'another than it was'. The ambassador ascribed what might have been another episode of manic depression to Darnley. This was likely more wishful thinking than anything else, given he was an opponent of the match. Historians since have likewise attributed it to some poor behaviour on the hopeful bridegroom's part. However, it is likely that the desertion of her brother, and his obvious desire to destroy her plans, contributed.

Meanwhile Elizabeth was busily telling all and sundry that the match would invite open hostility between the two realms and demanding the return of both Lennox and Darnley. This was countered, however, by approval pouring in from Catholic France and Spain. Foreign powers at least could see that the English queen was overreaching herself in attempting to dictate what a fellow monarch could and could not do. Amidst the drawing up of battle lines – which were by no means simply Protestant versus Catholic – ridiculous rumours swirled. It was said that

Moray and Argyll planned to kidnap Darnley and send him south. There is no evidence that these rumours had substance, but they do indicate how far Moray's credit had fallen with his sister and in the eyes of the Scottish political community, which had hitherto considered the queen's brother a safe, moderate, reliable pair of hands.

In fact, what Moray was actually up to was much worse. He was planning an action which would not only irreparably harm his relationship with his sister but leave him tainted forever in the eyes of his English cousin. He was trying to organise a rebellion. In doing so, he requested a subsidy of £3000 from Elizabeth on the 1st of July, supposedly to uphold the faith and the English alliance. Maurice Lee suggests that, in doing so, he had not committed to revolt, but wanted simply to frighten Mary into abandoning Darnley via a show of men and arms.[122] However, if he had wished only this, he had no need of a large sum of money; he had only just illustrated his ability to muster men at Bothwell's curtailed arraignment. His subsequent actions, further, indicate that his goal was military revolt from the first.

Mary realised this. Throughout July she canvassed support across the religious divide, and in the middle of the month she issued a summons for all men to prepare to fight. The indication here is obvious: men need only prepare to fight if an enemy were spotted on the horizon. That enemy was her brother and former chief adviser. She had heard that he and Argyll had organised a meeting of their supporters at Glasgow and forbade any man from attending. Instead, they cheekily met at Stirling.

By this time Moray had received warm indications of financial aid against his sovereign. This was high treason. He justified it by, as usual, suggesting that Mary's marriage would threaten Scottish Protestantism and the English alliance which was predicated on it. He could point quite rightly to Mary's courting of Spain and Spanish support for the marriage: did not this imply that her goal was the overthrow of state religion? However, few were willing to embrace rebellion on the basis of threats of what Mary might be planning. Elizabeth, too, despised rebellion and rebels. However, as she had proven in 1559, she was quite prepared to turn a blind eye to, and even aid, those who turned against other princes. Her morality on the issue was therefore somewhat elastic. Nevertheless, she was to remain always overtly critical, and retained a personal distaste for those that engaged in revolt, even if she was the paymistress. It did not matter. What mattered was that hard cash was flowing northwards, through the hands of spy-turned-ambassador Randolph, into the hands of those who opposed the Darnley marriage. Despite Mary having allowed the English ambassador to sit in on her council meetings in the past, he was quite prepared to slip money to the countess of Moray. An astute and loyal woman, Agnes was able to channel it to her husband from their home in Fife.

This cannot have been an easy course of action for Moray. We have seen that he wavered, for example, over abandoning Mary of Guise until he had little other choice. Ironically, history was repeating itself. What gave him an excuse was a suspicion that Mary, as she had indicated in February, might tolerate Catholicism even if she did not re-establish it. Toleration was a dirty word in early modern Europe.[123] It had been a policy of toleration that had allowed insurgent Protestantism to triumph over the old faith. If Mary was to marry Darnley and continue an open policy of conciliation between Catholics and Protestants, the reverse might happen: insurgent Catholicism might triumph over the new faith. Once again, he had been forced to jump by expediency. Mary was intent on marrying hastily to prevent revolt, and he was intent on revolting hastily to prevent her marriage. However, religion was not really the motivating factor for Moray.

Quite why he felt the need to activate a revolt has long exercised historians, given that the queen's brother is generally thought of as a cool, calculating figure. It has been suggested that his aim was to insist Mary break with Darnley and convert, finally ratifying the legislation passed by the 1560 parliament. If she refused, Moray and the rebels would have deposed her, elevating the hapless Châtelherault to the throne of Scotland; thus, Protestantism would have been secure.[124] This is highly unlikely, for a number of reasons. The duke himself might have been encouraged in the belief (hence his desire to join Moray and Argyll in opposing his old enemy, Lennox), but he was not a great thinker or strategist. Moray would never have countenanced deposing a Stewart for a Hamilton. Elizabeth, further, would not approve of her money being used to depose an anointed queen in favour of a rebellious duke and his mad son. The rebellion was born of desperation – the last throw of the dice from a man who had been under severe strain for months, and who saw two options only: do nothing, and be consigned to the wilderness by a young king who distrusted him, or rebel to try and stop it. Either way offered ruin, but the latter gave him a fighting chance to prevent it. There were more personal concerns too. His wife, Agnes Keith, the countess of Moray, was heavily pregnant. The child must be provided for. He would not be able to do so under a King Henry bent on his destruction. He would definitely not be able to do so if the rebellion failed; but if it succeeded, all might be well.

If Moray did not consider, decide upon, and raise revolt in order to depose his sister, neither did he do it for religion or amity with England. These were fig leaves. The whole fiasco was about his right to exercise power, with Argyll a useful friend and Châtelherault a useful idiot. Specifically, it was about the power he believed to be his right slipping away. In a later century he might have been an MP, exiled to the backbenches but stoking up his more disgruntled peers in the hopes of reversing a policy decided upon by his Prime Minister and government.

He was, though, to be hopelessly outclassed by Mary, on this occasion at least.

Moray was not the only one concerned with power at this time. As his slid farther from his grasp, shattering his cool veneer and leading him to the depths of desperate treachery, his sister was continuing to develop a taste for her own. Buoyed by the knowledge that enough of her nobility, Catholic and Protestant, had fallen into line behind her, she sped up her marriage plans. What is immediately noticeable is that, unlike her French match in 1558, marriage to Darnley required no commissioners. It required no prenuptial agreements. It required no give and take. This suited Mary down to the ground. Whereas the French had a strong interest in knowing exactly what Francis would get should Mary predecease him, Darnley and Lennox were inept enough simply to be pleased that the queen was willing to marry a Lennox Stewart. Quite startlingly, Mary was able to secure in Darnley a husband who asked for nothing prior to the marriage, beyond the titles she was willing to give. Whilst she showered the starry-eyed teen with earldoms and a dukedom, conferring royal status upon him by proclamation, he was content to move forward without having his future role codified. In addition to heading off her brother and his friends, then, Mary rushed the marriage to Darnley so as to leave her bridegroom's actual power unwritten. This was a wise move for a woman who wanted to retain her newly-discovered power.

Mary Queen of Scots wanted the independence of action that her cousin Elizabeth enjoyed. However, she wanted to provide for her dynasty's succession too. Whilst the English queen preserved her status by refusing to marry and become subordinate to a husband, the Scottish queen was to attempt to maintain her autonomy despite taking one. As attractive as this might be to modern eyes, however, it was to prove far too audacious a strategy for the sixteenth century.

Mary knew that her brother was still brooding. She knew also that that brooding had turned into plotting. Accordingly, on the 17th of July she summoned him to appear before the council. He wrote back that he would not leave Stirling without assurances of his safety. This was likely done to buy time, and because he was fully aware of the treacherous nature of his dealings. She called his bluff, granting the guarantee and demanding his presence within three days. He did nothing.

The banns of marriage were read out at the Mercat Cross in Edinburgh on the 22th of July. On the 28th she named Darnley king without the interference of Parliament in an act usually criticised as incautious and, again, born of passion. It was anything but. It was a shrewd move which allowed her to trick him into thinking power was his, without having any official body grant him anything or define what political role he might expect to play. In the summer of 1565 it was Moray who was acting with wild imprudence, not his sister. Mary Queen of Scots wanted to exercise power and did not mean to hand it over, even to a husband. The manner of the Darnley marriage in all its hurried freneticism delivered. On the same day the banns were read, Mary reached out again to her brother, inviting him and a train of up to eighty to attend on her. Even now she was hopeful that he might be won round by peaceful means. Again, he ignored her.

The morning after it had been announced that Scotland was to be ruled henceforth by King Henry and Queen Mary, an excited hush fell over Holyroodhouse. Darnley rose early, was dressed by his attendants, and made his way to the chapel. There he found his bride waiting with his father, and on to her finger he slipped three rings, symbolising the Holy Trinity. The deal sealed, the new king slipped off to avoid the mass. This was a politic move, undoubtedly decided upon beforehand. In order to retain Protestant support for the marriage it was important that the new king not be seen to openly endorse the faith that had been conceded only reluctantly to his wife.

Mary Queen of Scots was a married woman once more. She was stripped out of the white French mourning gown in which, as a widow, she had been married, her attendants involving themselves in a delightful custom of each removing a pin from her gown, before she reappeared in more festive attire. Thereafter followed a banquet featuring sixteen courses, with music and dancing to follow. Masques scripted by George Buchanan followed, and the carnival atmosphere went on for three days. In the back of Mary's mind, though, must have lingered two potential dark spots. One was her brother. The other was a lack of definite knowledge that the handsome young man she had married would prove as tractable and mindless as the great doll he so resembled.

Flexing her muscle, Mary and her large council, swollen now with Catholic members, issued a final warning to Moray on August the 1st. Two days later the earl of Huntly, the eldest son who had been imprisoned when his father died and his brother was executed, was released, and restored to favour as a royalist ally. Recalled also was the troublesome earl of Bothwell, who was eager to take up arms for the queen. The message to Moray was clear: you are in a weak position – stop sulking, stop scheming, and come forward to clear the air. Again, he ignored her, and was put to the horn himself on the 6th. This was the ultimate breakdown in their relationship – a thing that no one could have foreseen in the early years of her personal reign.

Now an outlaw, Moray had no choice but to stick to the foolish course on which he had embarked. On his side remained Argyll, Châtelherault, Knox, and a smattering of Protestant gentry. He had been unable to win his old friend Maitland, who, despite his anxieties, had decided that discretion was the better part of valour and remained with the queen.

Even Knox, who had offended the new king, was banned from preaching and skulked off to safety in Ayrshire. Moray's only real hope lay in help from England, and his cousin to the south proved to be utterly unwilling to aid him. All that he had feared had come true. In his last throw of the dice he had lost, and found himself the enemy of a royal sister, and abandoned by the royal cousin in whose interests he had been working for years.

He retired to the west of Scotland and decided that an armed revolt was his only option (the others being capitulation, disgrace and possible execution, or ignominious exile). His sister, however, thrived under conditions of war, as she had demonstrated during her 1562 progress to the north. His property in Moray was seized for the crown, although it would require parliamentary assent to give the confiscation legal weight, and on the 22nd Mary proclaimed her intention of taking to the field against her rebellious brother and his cronies. No proceedings appear to have been taken against the countess of Moray. Simultaneously, Mary reissued her earlier assurances that she and her husband had no intention of altering the state's religion (neatly cutting Moray's spurious religious argument off at the knees). Civil war had broken out.

Mary and Darnley marched west with the royal army, picking up support as they went. She wore a breastplate and carried a pistol at her hip, whilst Darnley glittered in a custom-made suit of golden armour. The symbolism could not have been more striking. In this marriage, the queen was the real power, the spouse who got things done, and the king was a pretty face with a hollow crown. Their destination was Glasgow, where it was rumoured that Moray had been gathering his own forces. He had been, but, when he realised that he was a sitting duck, he effectively managed to give her the slip, avoiding her forces and taking his partisans Châtelherault, Glencairn, Boyd, and Rothes back east, where they rode into Edinburgh itself on the 31st. The downside was that there had not been time to wait for Argyll to meet him in Glasgow with a regiment of his highlanders.

At the royal command, the guns of Edinburgh Castle were trained on the rebels. The keeper of the castle was his maternal kinsman, Lord Erskine. This shows with some gravity just how much the mighty had fallen. His disgrace must have even more keen when the burgesses of the town, those good Protestants who had made Mary's royal entry into the city such a propaganda exercise, refused to have anything to do with him. Why, they surmised, should they take up arms against their queen in the cause of what looked like a glorified family squabble? Friends, and people who had once lived in awe of the mighty minister, now saw him as nothing more than a troublemaker. Even the support of Knox could not buy back what he had lost during the good years: he had, as Knox had cautioned him at the time, sold out the cause of reform for earthly reward, and now he was reaping what he had sown. His tail between his legs, he addressed to his sister a cringing letter in which he warned her against wicked counsel (a tedious platitude common to political discourse in the period) of low-born foreigners and submitting to having his case heard by the counsel. It was Mary's turn to ignore him, and she must have savoured the irony.

By this time Moray's child had been born. It was girl, unsurprisingly named Elizabeth. How he reacted to the news we do not know; his small force was still retreating from the angry vengeance of his sister. Whatever happened, he might have hoped that Mary would look after her new niece. The crime of revolt was his and the queen loved children. For the moment, though, the baby's namesake in England was proving to be less willing to show support than Moray had hoped. Again money was promised, but what he needed was fighting men and these the English council would not provide. Randolph was instructed to break with the rebellious earl and instead treat with Mary; to sweeten this most bitter of pills, the English queen invited her cousin to seek exile in England. By contrast, Mary was busily drawing the gentry and nobility into bonds of support; as she had done in Glasgow, so did she manage in Edinburgh.

On the 19th of September, trapped in Dumfries, the queen's brother turned the letter he had written into a public appeal. Again, he repeated his grievances about the queen's 'evil' councillors, 'strangers [with] neither judgement or experience of the ancient lawes or governance' of Scotland filling the traditional offices of the Scottish nobility. Such men, he alleged, were usurping the hereditary roles belonging to the chief nobility 'who have a speciall care of the publict effaires of [the realm] … by reasoune of our birth and blood'.[125] His long diatribe is revealing. Mary had indeed been giving increasing weight to Riccio, supportive as he was of her marriage. In Moray's case, though, the outrage was more about his own 'birth and blood' entitling him to counsel his queen. Nevertheless, his complaint was to augur ill for Mary. Her attempts to raise up a low-born secretary, coupled with the appointments of new councillors she had been making, were to alienate some of her old guard. A number of her long-standing councillors began to fret, and fume, and eventually to plot, as a consequence of their own declining voices. Their scheming would lead to the securing and slaughtering of a sacrificial lamb the following year.

In early October Elizabeth finally made a decision. She would offer no further tangible help to Moray, secretly or otherwise. She simply, her minister explained, 'cannot in that manner give them the aid they require, without open war, which she means not to do without a just ground and cause given to her by [Mary]'. He was on his own. This should have been predictable: he was her coreligionist, but he was not her equal, whereas Mary was. Still, it was devastating news. His sister was continuing to raise troops and the support on which he had been banking had been withdrawn. With no other choice, he crossed the border at Carlisle on the 6th of October, Châtelherault, Glencairn, Rothes, and Boyd with him. The civil war was over, sister triumphing over brother. For now, they were separated. Neither could have imagined the horrific events which would reunite them.

Separation and Reunion

In the neat gardens at Holyroodhouse, Mary and her new husband met with the French ambassador, Michel de Castelnau, Sieur de la Mauvissière. This was not their first meeting of the summer. The Frenchman had been sent in response to Mary's appeals to the continent for help against her brother's rebellion and aid in restoring Catholicism. John Guy has convincingly argued that the queen had, as a result of Moray's behaviour, come to regard both him and his religion as harbingers of anti-monarchical republicanism.[126] By dint of the deviousness of the man she had trusted, she must now look to Catholic Europe for support. Unfortunately for Mary, France was otherwise occupied by its own wars of religion and could offer little help. The point, however, was that she sought it.

Here something must be said about Mary's attitude towards the religious question. She had, during the brief civil war – which had become known as the 'Chaseabout Raid' – been privately vocal in professing no desire to alter the state's settled Protestantism. Now she appeared to be backtracking. It has been suggested that the events of 1565, from flirtation with Darnley to marriage to war, were part of an elaborate, carefully-laid strategy which was always aimed at the restoration of the old faith. This 'great Catholic design' supposedly involved ruining her brother before restoring Catholicism, tackling Elizabeth with continental help, and then reigning over a united, Catholic Britain.[127] Only Moray had apparently gotten wind of this, and the tragedy was that so few heeded him. The whole idea of this 'grandiose scheme' is deeply problematic.

The queen had, it is true, showed herself lax in condemning Catholicism with the vigour that her more zealous ministers and subjects would have liked. However, this was not part of a deliberate strategy to restore the old faith, but rather a testing of the waters. Her turn towards the continent and its Catholic princes happened as a result of her brother's resistance to her marriage and ultimate revolt. What he had proven was that her Protestant subjects could never be fully trusted, and their loyalty could not be bought, no matter how deep her purse of honours. It is certainly correct that she increased her traffic with the major Catholic powers, telling France and the Vatican that she was intent on restoring the old faith. This was, however, a blind. She could hardly count on their support against rebels, domestic troubles, and Elizabeth's wilfulness, if they thought (as Darnley spitefully wanted them to think from November onwards) that she was lax in the faith. What Mary appreciated, and the Pope and her Guise relations did not, was that restoring the old faith in Scotland could not be done precipitately. If it took dissembling to safeguard against rebellion – and worse, republicanism – she would make all the right noises to guarantee it. But noises were all 'Queen Mary's Catholic interlude' amounted to.[128]

Throughout her personal reign, Mary had accepted an anomalous position. In early modern Europe, the sovereign chose the religion, parliament backed it, and the people did as they were told or were cast as heretics. This was ugly and autocratic, but it was accepted. Mary had instead concealed her religion, hoping that her Protestant brother would work with Elizabeth in codifying her dynasty's place in the English succession. That policy had failed, largely due to the English queen's intransigence. Further, Queen Elizabeth was now openly sheltering

177

rebels against the Scottish crown. Mary now changed tack. Elizabeth, she knew now, would never willingly do or say anything about the succession – not, at least, by a course of amity. Frightening her with the support of mighty Catholic powers might, though, work where diplomacy had not. What she wanted was a change in her foreign policy, not a sweeping religious disturbance.

There was no grand strategy here. To suggest there was is to imagine that both Moray and Mary knew in advance of the extraordinary events of 1565 exactly how they would fall out. In reality, she could never have guessed he would go as far as an armed revolt, still less that it would drive him over the border. He could not have guessed that his protestations that Protestantism were under threat would come true, largely as a result of his making the religion look more rebellious and dangerous than it had at any point during her personal reign. Moray, in short, did not predict Mary's pro-Catholic overtures; he provoked them.

At any rate, Mary had other problems on her mind once her brother had fled. The first was ensuring stability. This meant good governance. As we have seen, Moray had criticised her reliance on David Riccio, the musician-turned-French secretary who had achieved the status of informal adviser. He had used this as an excuse to rebel, revealing his anger at being frozen out of her circle of influence, particularly in relation to her marriage. Riccio was a charming man, of indeterminate age; his company was congenial, and his musical tastes and talent fitted well with the cultured and worldly household the queen had cultivated. He was deeply unpopular, however, mainly because Scottish tradition held that the role of counsellor was, as Moray had stated, the prerogative of the realm's landed nobility. It was inconceivable and unacceptable that a man who had simply replaced her old French secretary, Raulet, was swanning around the court as though he were her chief adviser. Gradually opposition built on the foundations of resentment. Even the dependable Maitland, in whom Mary's trust had been shaken owing to his long-term friendship with her brother, melted away, retiring to his estate and leaving his offices to be administered by Riccio. Conveniently, his seat, Lethington Castle (present day Lennoxlove) was within riding distance of the king's favoured hunting spots.

Why, we might ask, was Mary so intent on undermining her country's long-held tradition? One obvious reason is that so many of her nobility had proven themselves untrustworthy. Further, to pick out one as a chief adviser would be to alienate the rest. What she wanted was a non-partisan figure whose loyalty and subservience were beyond doubt. What she wanted was a William Cecil.

The raising up of new men was a peculiarly Tudor phenomenon. Henry VII had his Empson and Dudley. Henry VIII had his Wolsey and Cromwell. Elizabeth, of course, had her Cecil. These men were all bought by and trained up in the service of the crown. None had been - or were - especially popular. In Scotland, antipathy to new men walking the corridors of power was even greater, and if the upstart was a foreigner, so much the worse. Mary seems not to have greatly concerned herself with this. As Elizabeth had her right-hand man, so would she.

The elephant in the room here was her husband. King Henry he was in name, but not in power. This understandably galled. When Mary had been married previously, it will be recalled, it was accepted that she was 'under band of marriage and subjection of her husband (who carried the burden and care of all her matters)'. This was not to be the case in this marriage.

At first, Darnley seems to have accepted the key role Riccio played in matters of state. The two men had become friends, with the Italian doing everything he could to promote the match. They had even shared a bed after Darnley's arrival in the country – a fact which has given rise to any number of sexually-charged theories (although, strangely, no one has suggested that Maitland and Randolph became lovers during the 1562 progress). However, the new king was showing a worrying desire to be more than just a stud horse. During the visit of Castelnau, he showed an interest in the meeting at Bayonne between the Habsurgs and the Valois. He kept as a servant the lawyer Sir James Balfour, a deeply shifty figure who sat on Mary's council and had been her own favourite. In his inner circle were also Catholic lawyers, and he employed one of his secretaries, Yaxley, on a secret mission to Spain to elicit money from Philip II (the unfortunate Yaxley drowned on the return journey and the money was seized by the English).

All of this was a problem to a queen who wanted to retain her independence after marriage. Her response was to freeze him out of council meetings and recall the coinage which trumpeted his kingly status. It is sometimes claimed that her actions were due to his unwillingness to engage in state affairs, but the opposite is true; he was too willing for her liking. Evidence here can be found in the memoirs of Lord Herries, Mary's partisan, who notes that the famous iron stamp the queen had made of Darnley's signature appeared before he embarked on a lifestyle of hedonistic leisure, not as a result of it.[129] Herries had no reason to sympathise with Darnley, and so his recollections on this point are probably trustworthy. In them, he reveals the source of Mary's dislike of her husband:

The king had done some things and signed papers without the knowledge of the queen … she thought although she had made her husband a partner in the government, she had not given the power absolutely in his hands … [her banished lords] knew [her] spirit would not quit [relinquish] any of her authority, so they addressed themselves to the king ... And then, lest the king should be persuaded to pass gifts or any such thing privately, by himself, she appointed all things in that kind should be sealed with a seal, which she gave her secretary David Riccio ... with express orders not to put the seal to any paper unless it be first signed with her own hand.[130]

So began a period of almost comic one-upmanship, as king and queen fought at every turn to undermine one another. Dangerously, it would spill over into the religious sphere. The only bright spot was the news, which Mary delivered to her frustratingly independent husband at Linlithgow Palace in November, that she was pregnant. This meant, for her, a period of political inactivity; for him, it meant that it was time for him to take his rightful place as her master.

Whilst Mary flirted with the restoration of the old faith and sought to remain independent despite the acquisition of a husband, her brother was in dire straits. After arriving in England in early October, he had determined to go to London to see the queen. It was, as he wrote to Leicester, his desire to 'make an end of these troubles'. Elizabeth's immediate reaction was to refuse him her presence. Unsurprisingly, however, she then changed her mind and invited him to come. No doubt wearily, he travelled from Ware to London. When he was shown into Elizabeth's presence, he was, probably by pre-design, forced to make submission on his knees before the French and Spanish ambassadors. He and one of his Chaseabout accomplices, the Abbot of Kilwinning, begged his cousin to intercede with his sister on his behalf. Elizabeth, playing her role to the hilt, retorted, 'I am astonished that you have dared, without warning, to come before me: are you not branded as rebels to your sovereign? Have you not spurned your summons, and taken arms against her authority? I command you, on the faith of a gentleman, to tell the truth'.

Moray dutifully played his part in this piece of grand comic theatre, declaring that the accusations against him and, crucially, the rumours that Elizabeth had supported him in them, were slanderous. The queen then turned in triumph to the ambassadors before ordering the pair of 'unworthy traitors' from her presence. The whole thing was, of course, designed to be heard in France, in Spain, and in Scotland. By playing along, Moray knew that his cousin would indeed write to Mary seeking his forgiveness and restoration. It is interesting that still he banked on Elizabeth's support; Châtelherault would make his own peace with Mary (accepting a voluntary five-year exile), much to the fury of Darnley and Lennox, inveterate enemies of their rivals the Hamiltons as they were. Argyll, still in Scotland, would also conceive significant suspicions of England and Elizabeth.

However, Mary's favour could not be won in a day, even by Elizabeth I. Her brother therefore travelled north and took up residence in Newcastle, where he would be within easy each of the Scottish border as and when he had safe passage home. The English queen would indeed press for his sister's forgiveness (in November she expressed hopes of resolving 'all things tending to the welfare and tranquillity of both the realms') but Mary was deaf to her pleas. Even Maitland proposed some means of the earl being allowed to live abroad whilst receiving income from his estates. This also went nowhere, and Moray sank into poverty.

His sister, though, did show signs of considering his restoration in January, believing as she did that it might once and for all divorce her Protestant subjects from their treacherous dealings with the English.[131] She had had nothing but fair words from her Catholic friends abroad, and so it seems she was considering again how best to keep her country and her subjects in loyalty: if she could get Moray back on her own terms, there would be no need to follow a dangerous path involving foreign intervention, and she might make as a condition of his return some definite indication of the Stewart succession rights. As a result, she postponed the parliament due to sit in February at which the forfeiture of her brother's estates was to be formally declared. Keeping two irons in the fire, though, she was also writing to the pope at the end of January, expressing her desire to restore the old faith. This was, more than anything, a face-saving exercise. Over the festive period, Darnley had shown her up with his greater display of religious commitment.

By February, the Scottish queen had still given no clear indication that she would accept her brother back. She had, further, antagonised Elizabeth by sending Randolph out of Scotland, having discovered that the ambassador had been active in funding the rebellion against her. His prospects as bleak as ever, Moray wrote to his wife a ruminative letter lamenting his situation. 'I pray you,' he entreated Agnes, 'be blithe and praise God for all that he sends, for it is only he that gives and takes, and it is he only that may and will restore again. And [it] becomes us all in loveliness of heart to await patiently for his leisure … God to comfort you to [until] our meeting. With my commendation to all friends that are friends indeed, the number of which is grown marvellous scant'. If Mary and Elizabeth would not provide, hoped Moray, God, who worked all things, would. All his prayers were for restoration, no matter the cost. His wife was in Scotland. His child was in Scotland. His interests – not in the narrow sense, but in terms of what exercised his mind – were in Scotland. Were it not for the fact that he had brought his troubles on his own head, it would be possible to sympathise with his plight.

Help was to come in the form of a messenger from across the border, who attended on him in at the end of the month. From this man he learned that matters in Scotland had been progressing with deadly speed.

Riccio had continued to be a thorn in the side of the body politic. However, little could be done about him without giving any proposed enterprise against him a veneer of respectability. Those lords and lairds who had grown weary of having their accustomed access to the queen curtailed or managed by a foreigner (who expected bribes for his services) had decided that the route to ridding themselves of him lay in the new king. The earl of Morton was chosen as the representative best placed to win Darnley over, which he did by convincing the young king that it was Riccio who was encouraging the queen to bar him from exercising the power to which a king was entitled. Undermining Mary's skilful handling of Darnley's kingship the previous year, Morton was able to demonstrate to the boy that he had been duped: echoing part of Moray's Dumfries appeal, he pointed out that his kingship, which had seemed so dazzling when Mary had arbitrarily proclaimed it, had no legal weight without parliamentary approval. It is also likely that the black-minded earl, assisted by the more reasonable-seeming Maitland, insinuated that the Italian was bedding Mary, as ridiculous as the rumour was. No matter how personally repulsive Morton might have been – Marjorie Bowen has labelled him 'a man of whom nothing good has ever been said' – Darnley swallowed his overtures.[132] Deprived of power and surrounded by flatterers, amongst them his poisonous father, he was an easy sell. If the rumours put about by his enemies are true, he had sunk into a life of embittered alcoholism. Morton, Maitland, Lennox, and the other conspirators therefore had a remarkably easy job of convincing him to lend his name and title to a political coup.

Without the queen's knowledge, a plot had been hatched whereby Darnley would enter into a bond – which he did willingly – with those who wished to restore the proper order of things. This would involve seizing and hanging Riccio as a traitor, pardoning the exiled Moray and his friends, cancelling the upcoming parliament, and conferring upon

Darnley the crown matrimonial, with which he might take up the reins of power as a king rather than a mere consort. All of this had to be achieved before the parliament scheduled for March sat, as Mary would undoubtedly press for her brother's forfeiture and very possibly make some attempt to undermine Protestantism.

All of this must have seemed like manna from Heaven to Moray. Here was his opportunity to return to Scotland, but more than that it was a chance to make the king whom he had feared would ruin him instead beholden to him and his friends. He had no sympathy for his sister: the fact that he had berated her repeatedly for her promotion of Riccio only proved that she would be the victim of her own folly in not listening to his counsel. The bonds were all drawn up: by them, Darnley would forgive Moray, restore his estates, and cancel the dreaded parliament in favour of a new one which would formally restore the Chaseabout rebels. In return Moray and the other lords implicated in the bond would support him in gaining the crown, and intercede with Elizabeth to free his mother, the countess of Lennox, who had been languishing in the Tower of London since his marriage. No mention was made of the murder of Riccio, of course. Moray was far too canny to sign anything which would leave him open to murder charges.

The plot was known about in England almost from its inception, Moray and many of his fellow Protestant lords never having ceased traffic with the English government. The only people who appeared to suspect nothing were Mary and Riccio. Both went on with life as normal. On March the 7th the parliament met in Edinburgh, with Mary riding at the head of the procession. On Saturday the 9th, before anything against Moray could be passed, the conspirators decided to strike.

Queen Mary was in her closet, a tiny room off her bedchamber, entertaining a small number of her inner circle to supper. The atmosphere was pleasant, lit as it was by candlelight and tinkling with laughter. This stopped when the door connecting Mary's private apartments with Darnley's flew open, and the king strode in. This was unusual. The couple were scarcely on speaking terms. Still, Darnley sat down and put his arm around his wife, who offered him something to eat. He barely had time to demur when Lord Ruthven appeared, his withered, cancer-ridden form encased in armour and, absurdly, a nightgown.

There then flooded into the queen's apartments a small army of men attached to the leaders of the conspiracy, Lennox men amongst them. Darnley held back his wife, who was six months pregnant, as Riccio was dragged from the chamber, pleading for his life in all the languages at his disposal. His entreaties did him no good. The conspirators gave full vent to their bloodlust as they dragged him out of the queen's chambers, throwing his body downstairs after stripping it of its finery and leaving the king's own dagger sticking out of it. When the body was later prepared for burial, Riccio was found to have been stabbed fifty-six times. After Riccio's death, however, all was not quiet. The conspirators had roused those loyal to Mary – including the earls of Bothwell and Huntly – and the place became a virtual warzone, the attention of the townspeople outside drawn to the noise. Eventually, Darnley and Ruthven managed to quieten things down, Bothwell allegedly escaping over the menagerie's lion pit.

Mary, quite naturally, was distraught. Her servant, confidante, and best friend had been brutally murdered. Men of her council had been in on it, and it was clear that they had enlisted her husband. Rather than giving in to panic, however, she immediately started to calculate how she might detach Darnley from his newfound friends, whilst retaining his reputation so as protect her own image and that of her coming child.

Moray knew the date of the assassination of Riccio, electing to leave Berwick, to which he had travelled, on the 10th. He met the Catholic Lord Hume – a side-changer who had been pressed into the job by Darnley – and the pair heard news of the murder whilst at Dunbar. He raced to his sister's side, not with any notion of comforting or protecting her, but of advertising his presence as one which might restore order to a world gone mad in his absence.

Moray took the initiative, meeting with Darnley and affirming that all that had been promised would be put in order if only he could induce his wife to sign documents of indemnity against the conspirators. The sting was that he and Mary were to remain under guard. Mary summoned her brother into her presence as late-morning light fell through the windows of Holyroodhouse, and the pair engaged in a game of display, the sincerity of which we might question on the part of both siblings. On her side, Mary must have known that the appearance of her brother following on the heels of her secretary's assassination was no coincidence. He, further, must have known that she knew this. However, he had at least the alibi of having been absent from the killing itself, and the queen was always to reserve her hatred for those who had wielded the bloody daggers.

'Oh my brother,' she cried. 'If you had been here, they had not used me thus'. In reaction, tears fell from Moray's eyes. Mary knew that she must convince her brother that she was a naïve and helpless woman. But it might also be that she was genuinely pleased to see someone who, though his rebellion was and always would be unforgiveable, had been part of a much happier and more stable period of her life. She was not a woman without feeling. Moray knew that his sister was clever and brave and must be watched like a hawk. But it is also possible that he pitied the sight of her, heavily pregnant, and having just been through an ordeal which, with his fussy nature, he probably had never expected to become so violent. Nor was he a man without feeling.

The reconciliation over, Moray left, and Mary embarked on the first stage of her plan. It had occurred to her immediately after the assassination that her life was in danger. She suspected, understandably but incorrectly, that the conspiracy had been Darnley's, intended to bring about her death and that of her baby. Still she had deep worries about republicanism, believing the conspirators hoped to steal the crown and place it on Darnley's head, making him their puppet instead of hers. It is, however, unlikely that the callow king had any such idea. He must have known – and his father more so – that Mary's and the baby's lives were his safeguard against the legally-recognised Hamilton claim to the throne.

The queen engaged her midwife to put it about that all was not well with the pregnancy, and a move to sweeter airs must be considered. That, she hoped, would give the conspirators pause. She met her brother again in the afternoon. This time Moray appeared on his knees – a familiar pose, he having adopted it before his cousin – alongside Morton, Ruthven, and Darnley. She promised that if they brought her a deed of indemnity she would sign it. She then took her brother's hand in one of hers and her husband's in the other and the trio walked up and down her chamber, a picture of order and goodwill restored. Moray and his friends then went off to supper at Morton's house in the nearby burgh of the Canongate.[133]

Mary now slipped into action. In between embracing her brother and promising to remit the assassination, she had been feigning serious illness and setting to work on Darnley. He was as easy a sell to her as he had been to the conspirators, and it did not take much to convince him that he had, again, been duped by men who would now turn their ire on him. Did not the guards they had posted prove their malicious intent? Darnley, who had been fearful himself since the brutality of the assassination had unfolded, agreed, and played the part she devised for him by assuring his fellow conspirators that he would make sure his wife did not try to escape the palace. With the guards thus dismissed, the royal couple and a pair of servants made a daring midnight escape through a kitchens and wine cellar, and out a service entry at the back of the building. Waiting for them were her captain of the guard, John Traquair, and Sir Arthur Erskine, both with horses.

The royal couple rode for the safety of Dunbar, where Mary remained in action, drawing support, and Darnley remained ineffectual. The conspirators were confounded, and incandescent over their betrayal by the king. Their 'botched putsch' was over.[134] In anger, they sent to Mary a bond signed by the king which revealed that he had been a prime mover in the conspiracy rather than, as he would have had it, a mere figurehead. Moray was to send much the same information to his sister. It is doubtful that Mary was much surprised by this. For now, though, she needed her husband by her side. Her pregnancy was drawing on, and she must make the realm as secure as she could. It must have been some relief that loyal faces mustered to her in the form of Atholl, Fleming, Livingstone, and Seton. Even the ultra-Protestant Glencairn and Argyll were eager to make peace. The conspirators foolish enough to put their names to the actual murder bond, though, knew the jig was up. Morton, and lords Ruthven and Lindsay fled to England, swearing bloody revenge on their turncoat king. Ruthven would succumb to the disease that had been wasting him before he could make good on his promise. Those who had had foreknowledge, but had played no active role, remained. Maitland was one of them, disgraced but not exiled. Moray was another.

As the queen gathered support for a triumphant march on Edinburgh, her brother made one of the most delightful moves of the whole ugly episode. Turning up at the abandoned parliament hall in which he was to be forfeited, he called out to his absent accusers. His voices carried up to the rafters and echoed around the empty chamber. With that, he could declare himself free of all charges, those who were to forfeit him – who were then converging on Dunbar – not having turned up on the appointed day. His separation from his sister had brought him low, but it had not erased his canniness.

He and Argyll were ordered to the west, so as not to engage in any more plotting under the queen's nose at a critical time. He went on the proviso that he was out of his sister's favour but could expect a return if he behaved himself. He felt confident enough to admit to her that he would not abandon the cause of Morton, as long as doing so was consummate with loyalty to the crown. God, after all, was providing, as exactly as he had hoped when he wrote to his countess from Newcastle. Whether he had learned from enforced separation from his sovereign any lessons about how to better conduct resistance remained to be seen.

When, on the 10th of March, Mary and her forces arrived in Edinburgh to a rapturous welcome, her position must have looked – with no pun intended – impregnable. She had managed to restore a show of reunion with her brother. She had even managed to build an uneasy relationship with her wayward young husband – in public at least. By these achievements she proved to Scotland and the world that she was in charge of her family. She could not have foreseen that explosive events would blow apart her relationships with both.

Prince and Prophecy

However it happen for to fall,

The lyon shall be lord of all;

The French quen shal bearre the sonne,

Shal rule all Britainne to the sea;

Ane from the Bruce's blood shal come also,

As neere as the ninth degree.

So runs a popular sixteenth-century Scottish prophecy, that appears to have been altered and refashioned as each royal baby dictated. Victoria Flood suggests it was composed in 1542, for the expected birth of a son to James V and Mary of Guise (which turned out to be Mary, another French queen).[135] It worked equally well for the birth of James VI to his mother, a dowager queen of France.

Prophecies were serious business. To Mary Queen of Scots, the idea that she would produce a child who would unite two thrones was not only a mythic dream, it was a goal that would be fulfilled, and which she must do her part to see to fruition. When, on the 19th of June 1566, her son James came crying into the world, the dowager queen of France exulted. Here was the lion who would be lord of all Britain. When the child's father made his awkward appearance, she was to say as much. To the Englishman, Sir William Stanley, who was present at the audience, she quipped, 'this is the prince whom I hope shall first unite the two kingdoms of England and Scotland'. This confused Stanley, who enquired about Mary and Darnley's right to succeed. The queen sighed, before stage-whispering that her husband had 'broken to' her.

The queen had taken to her confinement chamber, safe behind the stout walls of Edinburgh castle, on the 3rd of June. Prior to this, relations between husband and wife had been coolly polite. They had to be, in order to quell vicious scandal-mongers who hoped to insinuate that the coming child was Riccio's. But Mary did not trust her husband as far as she could throw him. Her brother, too, had remained in a state of glacial tolerance since his return from England. Before she could safely retreat into the feminine cocoon of the birthing chamber, she had sought to achieve a sense of harmony in the political community. This was no easy task given the situation: Protestants hated and distrusted Catholics; men who had been loyal throughout hated and distrusted those who had engaged in conspiracy; those who had engaged in conspiracy returned their feelings; everyone hated the king. Few politicians could forgive a man who shown himself to be a coward under the thumb of his wife. Fewer still wanted to back a lame duck.

In this morass, Mary did what she could. She brought her brother and other Protestants back to court in April and gave Moray back his seat on her Privy Council. Once he had regained it he lost no time in trying to win the restoration of his old friend Maitland and the detestable Morton, still in England and begging the English queen to recognise and help him, just as Moray had once done. With her brother had come his long-time cohort Argyll, but the committed Protestant had undergone a change. It was not a religious but a political one; the earl was now an enemy of England, having decided that Elizabeth, though a fellow Protestant, was an untrustworthy minx. His newfound antipathy manifested in friendship with Shane O'Neill, an Irish king and stalwart enemy of the Englishwoman who professed herself queen of Ireland. As the old Treaty of Berwick had expressly required Argyll, as part of a reciprocal pact of defence with England, to fight against O'Neill, this friendship was a direct attack on English amity. This disturbed Moray, who was as Anglophile as ever, and set him to work recommitting his friend to the cause. The effect was the loss of a potential card that Mary might have played. It did little to convince her that her brother had been sufficiently chastened by his errors that he might ever be her creature.

So it was that when Mary did enter her confinement, she left behind a brother who was restored to something like favour, but nothing like influence. As he was to admit a week after Prince James' birth, he had no credit to work anything. Yet, in the second week of July, he was happily informing Cecil that all had changed: he was *persona grata* again. He was to embark on justice ayres, receive a cringing apology from Darnley after the king insulted him, and even manage in September to get Maitland his office back. The reasons behind Mary's volte-face remain the subject of conjecture. What we can rule out is that Mary had a feminine, psychological need for him, being, 'like women born to the purple, egocentric'.[136] Nor was she 'subconsciously mortifying her flesh'.[137] The answer more likely lies in another campaign she was engaged in at the time: the pacification of the Kirk. By September, this course was set. On the 17th the queen oversaw the beginnings of reform which even Knox would have approved. Moray, who remained the most respected Protestant politician in her employ, was also worth bringing in to play.

The reason for the sudden show of friendliness towards Protestantism and all who professed it lay crying in his cradle. The heir that, as Mary herself said, she hoped would succeed to the throne of England would only have his rights recognised if the pro-Catholic policy she had flirted with for five weeks was countered by a show of amity-building pro-Protestantism. Moray was a useful tool. He was, as he illustrated in the disagreement with Argyll, not just a Protestant but a pro-English one. Mary knew that Elizabeth had fought hard for his restoration at the beginning of the year. Now that she had a healthy male heir, she hoped to display once again that she would accord with Elizabeth's wishes; she did not just accept Moray back into the country, as England's queen had requested, but into full royal favour. It was all for the child, who now represented the lion that might one day rule the entire island: if only the English government would accept the laws of primogeniture.

The queen's brother remained an ideological unionist, committed to that cause by the idea of shared religion. As such, he was the man best placed to wheedle Elizabeth. The idea of forcing the English queen's hand with a show of Catholic strength was, Mary belatedly realised, untenable. The political 'aberration' of her Catholic interlude was well and truly over. Amity must again be tried, the English government won over by the prospect of a male heir raised in a political environment of which they could not disapprove. She intended, of course, that little James would be raised a Catholic, but that desire had to be tempered. The Protestants, her brother especially, had already shown what they might do were they not mollified with influence and concessions; the restoration of the old faith must wait, and in the meantime, queen and prince must be seen to be surrounded by loyal Protestants. She was right to consider them as a potential source of trouble. In August, Moray was cryptically writing to the English diplomat Throckmorton, 'suggesting that either Lord Leicester or Lord Bedforde be sent as Queen Elizabeth's representative at the christening of the prince. Hopes recipient will come too as we will frelie communicat mony thingis with you that we wald be laith to schaw unto ... utheris'.[138] Such dealings needed to be monitored or, better yet, turned to her advantage in the prosecution of the Stewart dynasty's inheritance. Mary's tiresome obsession with her dynastic rights remained undimmed. With a vigour engendered by the birth of her son, her policy over the summer was Amity #2.

The elimination of Riccio had left a gap in the queen's unofficial council. But it had taught her a lesson. Henceforth she would abandon her attempts to ape the Tudor policy of raising up a relative unknown in order to have loyal, non-partisan advice. Instead she sought a man of whom no one could disapprove: a committed Protestant who had, throughout his career, shown loyalty to the Scottish crown. That man was the earl of Bothwell.

Bothwell had had, as we have seen, a chequered career. A border lord of the Hepburn clan, he occupied the hereditary office of Scotland's lord high admiral. His nature is elusive: for every report that he was a brutal thug exists another that his travels in France and Europe had bred in him a taste for high culture and a scholarly bent. In appearance he was squat and hard-faced. During the regency of Mary of Guise, he had remained loyal, and despite his notorious hatred of all things English, he could be relied upon to support the crown. Moray and Randolph had, it is true, induced two of the earl's servants to tell Mary that he had called her a 'cardinal's whore', which had encouraged Mary's distrust of him in the past. However, his loyalty during the Chaseabout Raid and the aftermath of Riccio's murder apparently led her to either forgive him or doubt the claims of his enemies. Indeed, between the two events she had arranged his marriage with the wealthy Jean Gordon, sister of the earl of Huntly.

Bothwell rose in favour in tandem with Moray and Maitland's restoration. To this we need not attribute a wild passion for the border lord – which no one did at the time – but rather an attempt to build a coalition which included two of the old triumvirate, brought in a loyal man, and adhered to the Scottish tradition that those of noble blood were entitled to counsel the monarch. Over the course of the summer and autumn, the queen was to make use of Bothwell, but was careful also to include her brother and his friend the secretary. Her progresses around Scotland – hunting in Alloa in Traquair, and justice ayres in the south – were to include these men. Darnley's counsel was not sought. When he forced himself into his wife's company, as he did at Alloa and Traquair, however, he met with a kind of weary tolerance. Mary neither liked nor trusted her husband, but he had proven himself fertile. Having gotten an heir, a spare must be considered, for reasons of state and duty. She continued to fund him lavishly, as her attitude towards the outward trapping of monarch had not (and never would) falter.

In later life Mary reported an ugly incident during the Traquair hunting trip, which indicated that the king remained impervious to her attempts to conciliate. Allegedly, he demanded she accompany him on a stag hunt the following morning. She attempted to excuse herself, telling him that she suspected she was pregnant (which reveals that, at least years later, she believed herself to have been sleeping with her husband at this time) only for him to retort that 'a mare should be worked when she was in foal' and that 'if we lose this one, we can make another'.[139] There are reasons to doubt this story. For one thing, Mary could not have suspected herself pregnant barely two months after the birth of her child. For another, the queen attributed almost the same exchange ('if you lose this one, we can make another') to Darnley during their escape from Holyroodhouse after Riccio's death. It is possible that the king did make some vulgar or unpleasant claim at some point, but, telling the story decades later, Mary appears to have garbled and confused what was said when. Perhaps this was due to the captain of her guard, John Stewart, the laird of Traquair, being present on both occasions.

In October, the queen was in the Borders town of Jedburgh when news was brought to her that Bothwell had been nearly slain in an affray with his enemies, the Armstrongs. She continued attending to her business – hearing law suits in the town – before riding to the earl's grim fortress at Hermitage to see how he fared. This act was mangled by her former friend and later enemy, Lennox Stewart adherent George Buchanan, into a passionate and precipitate ride to see her wounded lover. It was not, as her delay in going proves. Nevertheless, the hard riding she had been doing throughout the summer had taken a toll. When she returned to Jedburgh from Hermitage Castle, she fell seriously ill with a stomach ulcer. Blood poured out of her mouth, followed by convulsions and the loss of sight and speech. After this gruesomeness, she fell into a coma. So serious was the attack that her servants thought she had died and opened the windows to let her soul fly free. Decades later, in the same narratives (those of her partisans Claude Nau and John Leslie) in which Darnley's ugly words at Traquair appear, a story emerged that, as she lay insensible, her brother set to work gathering up her silver plate and jewels. Again, the sources are so biased as to make the claims questionable (it was after Mary's deposition that Moray did, indeed, gain custody of her jewels); however, they are illustrative of the general belief that the queen's brother was and always had been a covetous man.

Refusing to accept her death, Mary's French physician worked quickly, binding her body in bandages, massaging her limbs, and forcing wine down her throat. The unorthodox treatment worked, and within hours she had recovered enough to speak and see. Word was sent to her husband, who was sulking in Glasgow at the time, and, to his credit, he set out immediately for the borders. What he found, however, was a woman still recovering from illness, who blamed the entire attack on the worry she had endured for months regarding his behaviour. He lodged only one night in the town before leaving, a flea in his ear.

To understand the storm which was brewing, however, we must look to the political rather than the domestic sphere. The queen's brush with death had badly frightened her council and the wider Scottish political community. Part of that fear lay in the existence of Darnley, their nominal king. Had the queen died, what on earth would they have been expected to do with him, or he with them? His anomalous position would have to be addressed – that much was clear. It would, further, have to be addressed quickly. Darnley was at this point just under the age of twenty-one. In 1564, the Scottish parliament had declared that 'the lawful and perfect age of the prince ... be at 21 years complete ... her highness, her predecessors and successors after the said age of 21 years complete might have done and may do all things that thereafter a prince of lawful and perfect age might have done or may do of the law'.[140] If the king of Scots was to continue to pursue parliamentary backing in having his kingship recognised, it would be difficult to argue against it once he had reached the 'perfect age' of a prince. Time was on the young man's side. As worryingly, Darnley had expressed the intent of pressing parliament to grant him the earldom of Angus, which his mother had long claimed as part of the family's inheritance. This was to raise the hackles of Morton, who had been administering the estate (and enjoying its revenue) on behalf of his young nephew from 1558 until his flight into England (Darnley's mother only having reluctantly relinquished her own claim to them in 1564). Powerless in England, Morton knew one thing: Darnley had to go.

The shock of her illness brought about a relapse in Mary's low spirits. Rumours arose that unless she could be rid of her husband – the husband whom she believed had brought on an illness that nearly killed her – she would commit suicide.[141] Yet she knew that marriage was indissoluble, and so the depression persisted. From the borders, she travelled to Craigmillar Castle, outside the capital. It was there that she fell ill again, the sickness this time attributed to deep sorrow (another attack, we can surmise, of severe depression). Fearing for her life, she sent out a politic message, to be delivered southwards, that she wished her 'good sister' Elizabeth to stand as protector of the prince in the event of her death. Her stay at the castle, though, has been overshadowed by what followed, and what cast Mary not as victim, but as scheming murderess. It was to be the site of one of the murkiest chapters in her life: the so-called conference at Craigmillar, wherein the participants (Mary, Moray, Bothwell, Huntly, Maitland, and Argyll) discussed the problem of Darnley.

What was said, and by whom, at this meeting remains controversial. Mary appears to have expressed a desire that her assembled ministers find some honourable means by which she could escape her troubled marriage, which would not compromise the position of her son. Divorce was therefore out of the question. According to Mary's later account, the wily Maitland led discussions, insisting that a means would be found which would be approved by parliament and to which the fussy Moray might 'look through his fingers'. Bonds were allegedly signed to this effect. Moray's version of events is somewhat different. In his own later account – a direct reply to Mary's – he claimed that he had been privy to nothing that smacked of illegality, and that nothing had been signed. The likeliest conclusion we can reach is that the Craigmillar conference had been overstated in its importance. This was a round-table discussion of a vexing problem, that took place during one of the queen's depressive episodes. Certainly, her ministers were united in agreeing that Darnley must be dealt with, but no murder was organised, nor even mooted. Probably the lords present afterwards debated some method of imprisoning or trying the king for treason, or having parliament refuse to acknowledge the queen's conferment of kingly status on him. At any rate, Mary was to continue to express suicidal thoughts as late as December, which rather argues against the idea that she had struck upon a master plan to solve the problem of Darnley towards the end of November.[142]

December 1566 was chosen as the month of Prince James' baptism, and accordingly Mary and her court assembled there at the start of the month, following a stopover in Edinburgh. Mary had always done visual spectacle well – she had always understood the value of it to monarchy – and this was to be her all-time high point. Organisation of the three-day event fell to Bothwell, which might seem odd given Mary had planned a Catholic ceremony for a Catholic prince. Again, this was good policy. Mary was required to provide an extravaganza that would present to the world a united front, whereby the religion of the monarch and heir were carefully balanced against the support and participation of the Protestants in her nobility. Over one-hundred lairds were invited to the celebrations, which affirms the success of the queen's policy of courting this section of the gentry. Elizabeth was chosen as godmother, the earl of Bedford travelling up via Berwick to stand as proxy. As Godfather, the Catholic Charles IX was chosen, the French ambassador standing in for him. Invited to represent the Scottish clergy were the Catholic-disposed archbishop of St Andrews (John Hamilton, half-brother to Châtelherault), who presided, as well as the bishops of Dunkeld and Brechin. Invited also were the Protestant commendators abbots of Newbottle, Glenluce, Kinloss, Kilwinning, Melrose, Dunfermline, Jedburgh, and Holyrood. All was balance.

Fireworks were lit, banquets were prepared in the castle kitchens, and masques were devised. All was splendour, and all was expensive. For the first time, Mary, who had prided herself on her financial prudence (another slap at those who thought female rule was synonymous with spendthrift governance) raised her first tax. £1200 was levied in total, all to be used in turning the Scottish court into a world-class setting for public spectacle. What her brother thought of the visual aspects of this great celebration is not known; with Bothwell, Huntly, and Bedford, however, he refused to enter the chapel royal to witness the actual sacrament being administered by the 'pocky priest', John Hamilton, whom Mary refused to let spit into the baby's mouth (that particular custom being a step too far for her). It did not matter. What mattered was that these staunch Protestants had come and had thus announced to the world their acceptance of their Catholic queen's policy of toleration. It bode well for the amity. So too did Elizabeth's magnificent gift of a solid gold christening font.

Gold also was used in the suit prepared for the king's father to wear. Darnley, however, had gotten wind of the fact that he was to be given no official role, nor was he to be recognised as king of Scots by Bedford. He was, in this festivity, to perform the function Mary had always intended for him to perform: that of an attractive clothes horse. This he would not do, and after having no luck begging the French ambassador to intercede for him, he sulked in his apartments whilst the fireworks exploded in the frosty air above Stirling.

Mary was furious. Bothwell, in his blue suit, was drafted in to perform the ceremonial roles which would have been Darnley's. Here we find evidence that Mary was not, as has been alleged, Bothwell's lover. It is scarcely conceivable that, had she embarked on a torrid affair with the earl, she would have paraded it in front of the eyes of Europe and beneath the nose of her husband. The queen took revenge of a kind on her troublesome spouse by acceding to Bedford's wishes that she pardon the conspirators involved in Riccio's murder. These men, Morton predominantly, were her husband's greatest enemies. In forgiving them, which was against every personal instinct she had, she thus achieved a double-victory in avenging herself on Darnley and his embarrassing refusal to attend his son's christening, and scoring points

201

with Elizabeth, whom she had already sweetened with her request that England's queen become her son's protector in the event of her death.

Darnley, when he heard of the pardon, was understandably terrified. His response was to ride southwest across the snowy plains, to his father's lands in Glasgow. He had turned twenty-one in early December, and both he and his father must have known the knives would be out. In Lennox country he would at least be safe and surrounded by fawning servants. He was right to run.

Mary's policy at this time remained one of balance and conciliation. She did not always get it right. She attempted to reward the archbishop of St Andrews for his work at the baptism by restoring his consistorial jurisdiction; at the outcry from the Kirk and her brother, she rescinded it. This too has been used against her. Critics suggest that her goal was to give the power required to a man who could divorce Bothwell from Jean Gordon (which Hamilton did in 1567), and that the appointment was part of a plot between the lovers to murder Darnley. However, this seems unlikely. Nothing could have been more conducive to undermining everything she had done with care and political diligence than organising and participating in a bizarre murder plot.

In January the earl of Morton was back, and immediately he embarked on drumming up support in prosecuting his blood feud against the king who had thrown him to the wolves. In this he was to find a willing ally in Bothwell, who, buoyed by his credit with the queen, had begun to consider how he might improve his power. His father and grandfather had courted widowed queens of Scotland, and he had no intention of breaking the tradition. But first Mary would have to be made a widow. In the middle of the month Morton met with Bothwell at Whittingham, and it is here, with the endorsement of Maitland, who was also present, that the pair put their heads together and came up with one of the most audaciously stupid plots known to history.

202

In the midst of this, Mary was endeavouring to get her husband back to Edinburgh. Rumours had reached her that the Lennoxes were engaged in schemes of their own, their aim being to seize Prince James, declare Darnley a true king, and rule in the baby's name. These plots, if they existed, were pie-in-the-sky, but they convinced Mary that it would be better to have her husband somewhere where he might be watched. She visited Glasgow in person, and it was during one of their interviews that the young king, who had fallen ill with what appeared to his physicians to be another outbreak of measles or pox, made what seems to have been a genuine speech of remorse:

I confess that I have failed in some things ... I am but young, and you will say you have forgiven me sundry times. May not a man of my age, for lack of counsel, of which I am very destitute, fall twice or thrice, and yet repent himself and be chastised by the experience? If I have made any fail, I crave pardon and protest that I shall never fail again. I desire no other thing but that we may be together as husband and wife, and, if you will not consent hereto, I desire never to rise forth of this bed.[143]

He was probably sincere. Whether Mary believed him or not, she wanted him back in Edinburgh – at any rate, before leaving Glasgow she had poured out her distrust of Darnley to the city's archbishop. However, she managed to convince him that he would be quite safe if he returned with her, and it is probable that she believed this. Throughout her life, the queen held the state of monarchy in high regard, and it is likely that she did not conceive that anyone would kill her husband. The most she wanted was for him to lose all chance of power and, if possible, that he be deposed without actually having been crowned.

Darnley, as usual, fell for what was said to him, and Mary thus encouraged him to accompany her eastwards. She had promised that she would resume a normal life with him, and it is possible she had resigned herself to doing so, at least for as long as it took for her ministers to find some legal, parliamentary means of ridding her of his presence. They set out at the end of January and took up residence in the house of Darnley's choice: the Old Provost's Lodging near the town wall, where he could recover his appearance (much of his hair had fallen out and his sores were still to heal) with the aid of baths.

The lodging was not a mean one. Mary, further, ordered furnishings from Holyroodhouse, and when Darnley complained that the bed was unfit for a king, she replaced it with one of her mother's – a prized possession. At this stage she must have felt very much in control of events. It was even possible for the married couple to resume a state of outwardly happy existence, cocooned in their relatively small home, fitted out as it had been like a little treasure chest. Mary kept a room beneath Darnley's, and he did all he could to conform to her wishes. Sensing that their sovereign had decided to reach an accord with her husband, Mary's ministers also bowed to the inevitable and paid homage to their king. Moray, however, was unable to stay in Edinburgh. On the 8th of February he received the distressing news that his countess, Agnes Keith, had miscarried. He set off immediately to condole with her.

On the evening of the 9th – scheduled to be Darnley's last night in the Old Provost's Lodging, his health having recovered – the king and queen entertained a number of guests at the house. Mary, though, was unable to spend the night, having promised two of her servants that she would attend the wedding masque she had organised for them at the palace. Her plan, of which she made no secret, was to stay at Holyroodhouse and ride for Seton in the morning. Darnley was disappointed but, after she had left, he ordered his own horses to be made ready so that he might rise early and join his wife on her trip. Once all the guests had departed, bells jangling and masque costumes sparkling, for Holyroodhouse, Darnley enjoyed a little music with his valet, William Taylor. He then retired for the night, knowing that he had an early rise. He would not see another dawn.

Murderer and Murderess?

It was difficult enough for the residents of Edinburgh to sleep during the Arctic blast of a Scottish winter. In the early hours of the 10th of February 1567, it became impossible. A massive crack erupted into the night sky, a brief flash flaring and making it as bright as day. The sound was followed by a more ominous rumbling: the clatter of heavy stonework crumbling downwards.

Mary Queen of Scots was woken by the noise, and she demanded knowledge of what was happening. Bothwell, coming from his own lodgings in the palace, told her that he would go and find out. It was not long before everyone in the town knew, and in only marginally less time the news had reached Moray. Darnley – or Henry King of Scots as he would have preferred – had been murdered. At first it looked like he had been killed in the explosion which had reduced the Old Provost's Lodging to rubble, but when his body could not be found in the wreckage, a further search revealed that he and his valet were lying some distance from the house, in the gardens. Both had, apparently, been smothered as they attempted to flee from a building they had realised was under threat. The question on everyone's lips was, and remained for centuries, 'whodunnit'.

The question had continued to animate scholars, historians, and amateur sleuths. Thanks to the magnificent detective work of Alison Weir, we can be as confident as the sources allow that the perpetrator of the murder itself was Archibald Douglas, a ruffian in the employ of the earl of Morton. Behind the ridiculous and unnecessary mining of the house was the earl of Bothwell, who employed a rag-tag string of men, amongst them Darnley's former friend and one of the most duplicitous men in Scottish history, Sir James Balfour. What motivated the two earls to deploy competing murder plots on the same night can only ever be conjectured upon. Mary, we can be fairly certain, was kept in ignorance. There is no reason to expect men like Bothwell and Morton, wedded to Knox's brand of Calvinism and its distrust of female involvement in politics, would consult her even if she were likely to approve.

Where Weir's conclusions become less convincing are when they implicate Moray, evidence for whose involvement being, she admits, is 'largely circumstantial'.[144] Although she gets the murderers right, her assertion that a conspiracy, involving Maitland and a number of others (such as Argyll and Huntly), later named in a scaffold confession, was designed from the start to implicate Bothwell with the goal of then blaming and being rid of him, are difficult to believe. Such a conspiracy would rely on predicting events to an almost demoniacal degree. The confessions later attained are all murky, and the provenance of the alleged Craigmillar Bond on which the conspiracy hinges has been disputed.[145] It was only after the murder that it was every man for himself in casting blame elsewhere, muddying the waters, and making what political capital out of it that he could. Thus, it is safest to assume that Bothwell and Morton, each directing underlings, were the architects and, although events would change things, the goal was simply to get rid of Darnley. As Maitland later met with the two at a crucial point in the affair, we can suppose he knew something and possibly approved the assassination. But Moray's and Mary's complicity ahead of the killing would return the Scottish verdict 'not proven' if tried today.

A number of reasons make Mary's involvement in the murder improbable. It stretches credulity beyond breaking point to believe that she was behind or even approved the plot which actually unfolded. It could only ever have brought scandal, infamy, and the unwanted attention of the world. Indeed, Mary's sanctioning of what happened to Darnley would be the equivalent of Richard III eliminating his young nephews by blowing up the Tower of London and displaying their corpses on Tower Green. A more contemporary comparison might also be made with the case of Robert Dudley and Amy Robsart: had Cumnor been blown up and Amy found smothered in the garden, it is doubtful that historians would find any likelihood of Dudley having planned a murderous escapade so obviously prejudicial to his hopes of marrying Queen Elizabeth. If it is true that Darnley frequented taverns, then it would have been far better for him to meet his end in a staged bar brawl. Failing that, a lethal dose of medicines might have been administered to him at the Old Provost's Lodging. Had either method been used to kill Darnley, we might more reasonably assume Mary's complicity; but to encourage or approve the mining of a house, she would have to have been insanely reckless. Nothing we have thus far seen in her behaviour suggests that she was a reckless woman, prone though she was to short bursts of manic depression and its concomitant symptom, excitable energy.

Similarly, Moray's sudden departure from Edinburgh has led many to assume that he had been briefed on the plot and decided to leave to avoid visible complicity. There is no evidence for this, and if we are to exculpate Mary on the basis of there being only controversial evidence (the infamous casket letters will later be discussed), we must treat her brother with the same benefit of the doubt. It was not in his nature any more than it was in his sister's to devise a murder: he was a cautious man not given to private vengeance by violent means, and he was opposed to anything that might draw negative attention to himself. Approving or organising the murder of a king, especially by explosion and suffocation, would do exactly that. It is possible, of course, that Moray had been tipped off by his friends Morton or Maitland, even if not about the specifics of the plan; but, again, there is no good evidence of this. Accepting Mary's ignorance of the murder is accepting her brother's. No matter their behaviour afterwards, nothing exists from before the fact to suggest guilt on either sibling's part.

Mary's immediate reaction to the death of Darnley was one of fear. She claimed to believe that the blast had been meant for her as well as Darnley, and she voiced her intention of discovering and punishing the killer. Opinions diverge as to whether this was an honest response or a staged one. However, those who believe she was feigning it face an obvious problem: if Mary had known what was coming and planned her reaction, which involved a determination to find the killer, then she would have perforce have had scapegoats lined up. She would have agreed, or been briefed, on how to handle the aftermath – primarily who was to be blamed. Only by having someone (or several people) to condemn could she herself avoid the entirely predictable accusations that she was part of the plot. Yet she named no one.

What the queen did do was attempt to discover the truth of what had happened, before belatedly ordering the court into mourning. A couple of local women came forward, and their depositions were taken the day after the blast. However, their claims of seeing men running and hearing Darnley cry out for mercy from a 'kinsman' were dismissed, their evidence suppressed. The problem, though Mary did not know it, was that her Privy Council were not interested in Morton and Bothwell being named as murderers-in-arms. They were very interested in hiding the fact. The queen went somewhat over her council's heads, publishing a proclamation inviting anyone with knowledge of the murder to come forward, with a reward of £2000 promised (an extraordinary sum, when one considers that the entire baptism had required only £1200 in taxation); and if anyone involved were to name the principals, a pardon was promised. Mary was genuinely interested in discovering the truth of the matter – and she must have suspected, at least, that the vengeful Morton, so recently returned from exile, had a hand in it.

The people of Edinburgh were not happy. This was the second hideous political murder that had occurred in the environs of the burgh in a year. The majority of the political community had hated Darnley, it is true, but the ordinary people with whom he is said to have mixed too freely were incensed. Their leaders were behaving with murderous abandon that shamed the nation in the eyes of Europe. Their handsome young king, useless and disease-ridden as he had become, had been done to death by one or more amongst the men who were meant to uphold the country's honour. Not only that, but the murder had taken place as an act of grotesque spectacle. Something had to be done to pacify them, and the assassins were quick to realise it. It was inevitable that, after the murder, Bothwell and Morton would each rush to pin the blame on the other as subtly as possible.

Bothwell's name was the first to gain currency in the heightened climate of suspicion and speculation. In the middle of the month men of the Lennox clan took it up, nailing placards openly accusing the earl and shouting in the streets that he had killed the king. This, to say nothing of the fact that Bothwell was as guilty as sin, could not but blacken Mary's name. He was and had been one of her most trusted councillors. It is likely that those on the council who wished to force the queen away from the earl had a hand in the poster campaign; much like modern-day newspapers, placards were as much designed to shape as to reflect the views of the populace. Public opinion not just in Scotland but across Europe rapidly became the familiar refrain: 'she must have known'. Monarchs across the continent began to send admonitory dispatches, and even Elizabeth was to forward her famous rebuke, which openly used words identical to those used by Maitland: 'I will not conceal from you that the people for the most part are saying that you will look through your fingers at this deed instead of avenging it, and that you do not care to take action against those who have done you this pleasure'.[146] Implicit in Elizabeth's note was a plea that Mary denounce Bothwell, and preferably send him to the block. To Mary, this can only have looked like another attempt to rid her of a key adviser. Killigrew, the ambassador who delivered the message, was to report that he could barely see the queen in her darkened mourning room – in fact, he could not even see her face. It is possible that Mary had veiled a substitute. She herself had already, or would soon, fall into the darkest depressive episode of her life.

As the dust from the rubble at Kirk o' Field settled, and rumour swirled about Mary and Bothwell, Moray did little. Probably he was as shocked by the madness of events as anyone. Happy as he might have been to see Darnley gone, he could not have welcomed the instability that the actual assassination, in all its vibrant horror, had brought. Yet near the end of February he did meet Morton and others at Dunkeld. Unfortunately, there is no record of what was said; it is tempting, however, to suppose that Morton, as he had done to Darnley, attempted to blame Bothwell entirely for the bloody deed that unfolded. After this meeting, Moray went to his sister. It appears he attempted to gauge her mood and find out what she knew or did not know, before he wrote to Cecil, assuring the English secretary that he had had no hand in the killing. This is interesting, as it is further evidence that he did indeed know nothing, and he never had. Had Morton disclosed the plot to him beforehand, Moray would doubtless have drawn a diagram and submitted it for Cecil's approval. It was also a necessary act, though, for Bothwell had been trying, as expected, to blame Moray and other well-known figures for the murder. At the end of his letter, Moray requested a passport to England. He had seen what way the wind was blowing and reckoned it prudent to be away again until matters settled.

As far as Mary was concerned, the wind was blowing in Bothwell's favour. Their relationship had taken a sinister turn. It is often stated that she fell into a kind of catatonic state after Darnley's murder. She did not. She fell into one of her fits of depression only after the accusations had been turned on her, and by people – including Elizabeth, on the 5th of March – she thought she had won over as allies. The trigger for her deep depression was the censure of her only peers: Europe's other monarchs. It is therefore not surprising that on Palm Sunday she had one of her collapses at a requiem mass for the late king, reported by her ladies as another bout of 'melancholy'. The sequence of high and low moods had returned with frightening severity. This made her easy pickings for Bothwell, who had all along hoped that he might make her his wife if he could eliminate Darnley. In the unlikely relationship – and unlikelier marriage which followed – Bothwell should be denounced for what he was: an abuser taking advantage of a woman in the nadir of a mental illness. She would grasp willingly at anyone who showed support and forcefulness, and he was determined that that would be him. About all that can be advanced in his defence is that the period had no real conception of mental illness, and so he might well have taken her bleak despondency for submissive affection. It was not. It was a growing dependence: the dependence of a deeply depressed person on one who has declared themselves their only protector and friend. If a monarch's health, physical or mental, broke down, it was perfectly usual for those around them to take advantage by seeker power for themselves, and it was under this nefarious principle that Bothwell began his own rough wooing.

Throughout March, the queen played second fiddle to the earl, who must have found it remarkably easy to dominate her. The earl of Mar was forced to resign Edinburgh Castle into the hands of one of his henchmen, and although at the end of March a trial was set for Bothwell (with his approval), it was made clear that it would be an ordinary civil suit with Lennox bringing the case against the man he alleged had killed his son. Such suits were settled in Scotland according to who could muster the larger display of men and arms, and from its announcement the trial was rigged so that this could only be Bothwell. When the rumours began that he was seeking a divorce from Jean Gordon, Moray decided that it was time to go.

Mary bid a tearful goodbye to her brother. He was the latest person to desert her, and in her low spirits it cannot have been surprising. Yet he did make a will shortly afterwards, which named her as executor. Clearly, he did not think that anything too dreadful or irrevocable would happen to her in his absence. It is very likely he thought that she would see sense quickly enough; she had always been, he knew, a shrewd operator. He did not understand the grip depression had on her any more than the earl of Bothwell, who was even then exploiting it. By the second week in April he was on English soil in Berwick. There he reported to the Spanish ambassador, da Silva, that rumours had been current at the time of his leaving Scotland that Bothwell sought the queen's hand, but that he himself doubted Mary would so debase herself. He certainly hoped that his sister would suitably recover her wits before allowing herself to be married off. A fortnight later he was bound for France, where he was to wait out the remarkable sequence of events unfolding in Scotland. There he befriended the Huguenot faction – chiefly Admiral Coligny and Louis, Prince of Condé, and resisted attempts by Catherine de Medici to win him over. The disgruntled queen mother shrugged that Mary Stewart's brother was England's man. In that assessment she was shrewd. Her attempts, though, indicate that he was considered a man worth courting, especially when his sister was proving to have fallen into disgrace.

It was in Moray's absence, on the 12th of April, that Lennox failed to bring his suit against Bothwell; the latter was prevented from bringing any more than six followers to Edinburgh, whereas the former had packed the town with several thousand men loyal to him. The earl of Argyll presided, alongside lords Lindsay, Henry Balnaves, Robert Pitcairn, and James McGill. The earl of Caithness led the jury as chancellor, and the jury itself comprised a cluster of notables: the earls of Cassillis and Rothes, a quiver of lords, and a number of the lairdry whose lands stretched from Banff to Berwickshire.[147] Ominously, one juror refused to appear: Bothwell's associate in the killing, Morton, who excused himself on the ironic basis that he would not take place in a rigged trial against the accused killer of his kinsman (not even the promise of the return of Tantallon sweetening him). In the absence of Lennox and his evidence, Bothwell was acquitted of any wrongdoing.

On the 16th of April the formal parliamentary procession – the 'riding of parliament' – took place, with Bothwell prominent. In an attempt to bolster the queen's flagging authority, Acts were passed forbidding the making and posting of placards and bills; amongst others, Moray's, Huntly's, and Morton's possession of their estates were ratified; and Acts concerning the law of oblivion (which abrogated the crimes of those previously accused) and religion were passed. Bothwell scored a victory with the latter, as it provided legal protection for Protestantism and its followers. He followed this up on the 19th with the curious episode of the Ainslie bond, which has recently been re-evaluated as a genuine attempt on the part of all signatories – including Bothwell – to reconcile the various factions and re-establish a kind of order on a political community in turmoil.[148] It was a blatant statement of intent, demanding that all signatories support Bothwell in what he was minded to do – which was marry the queen.

Mary did try and seek her own recovery, travelling to Stirling on the 21st to see her son. His new keeper at Stirling, the earl of Mar, recently relieved of the captaincy of Edinburgh Castle, allowed the queen access to play with Prince James, but utterly refused her requests to hand him over. After a stay at Linlithgow, she made to return to Holyroodhouse, and as she crossed the river Almond, Bothwell enacted his famous abduction, taking her and her retinue – including Maitland – to Dunbar. There, Mary alleged later, he ravished her. Others, both at the time and since, have suggested that she colluded in the whole thing, it being staged as a prelude to their marriage. The truth is likely somewhere in the middle. She went willingly. She had just been reminded of the gulf in Scottish politics that now divided her from her son. She had, in any case, already being going through the most dramatic attack of depression of her life. Bothwell had decided to imprint his authority on her sexually, and she was in no condition to say or do otherwise. If it is rape to take advantage of someone whose mental state has bred in them an inability or unwillingness to resist something they would normally oppose most strongly, then it is fair to say that Mary is correct in her assessment of his actions as ravishment. What did not occur was a moment of romantic climax. Mary was never a woman who displayed marked sexual desires. Her milieu was courtly love and practical politics, not devil-may-care passion.

At any rate, Bothwell made his proposal. To give it more weight, he showed her the bond listing the support for the match. At some point during her captivity in Dunbar, she accepted. Bothwell galloped off to secure his divorce from Jean Gordon, granted on the 7th of May by Archbishop Hamilton. His spirits must have indeed been high. He did not realise that already support for the marriage was melting away and an oppositional party gathering. As he did not know, Mary certainly did not.

Three days after the abduction, a group committed to freeing the queen and ending Bothwell's roughshod treatment of her met at Stirling, and at the start of May a new bond was produced, this one pledging all signatories to defend the little prince and the queen from the earl's emerging tyranny. This group crossed the religious divide: Morton, Mar, and Argyll were all Protestants, but Atholl was a Catholic. What brought them together was a shared dislike of Bothwell's political aspirations. For Morton, who had just helped rid the country of a powerless king who had crossed him, the raising up of a competent and violent one was to be avoided at all costs. What was more, Morton knew more than anyone of Bothwell's involvement in Darnley's murder; he therefore had the means to silence and ruin him.

It is probably fair to say that events moved so quickly that those who opposed the marriage had no real time to forcibly separate queen from councillor-turned-suitor. Mary was not totally inactive. She could not understand the sudden *volte-face* of men who had signed a bond entreating her to marry Bothwell, and her letters to Morton did not provide answers. Bothwell, for his part, was determined to keep her absolutely in thrall; then as now it was the goal of the abusive partner to prevent as much as possible their victim from communicating with the outside world and, if that proved impossible, to ensure that they distrust and fear everyone but their abuser.

On the 6th of May the couple entered Edinburgh in ceremonial procession, with Bothwell leading Mary's horse. A better visual metaphor for what their relationship had become could not have been devised. The crowds were sullen. The sight must have been odd to them; they could not understand their queen's behaviour, she having always been a model of decorum in her public appearances. More worrying for Bothwell was the resistance of the Kirk minister, John Craig, to announce the banns of marriage. It was only with the brutal caveat that he heartily opposed what he had been commanded to do that the brave minister finally published them. After that, Mary ennobled Bothwell as duke of Orkney, a dukedom elevating him sufficiently that he might become her husband. On the 15th of May the pair were married, by Protestant rites. Few courtiers attended, many of them flocking to Stirling where the opposition party was still figuring out a way forward. The only pair of any note to remain were Maitland and Huntly, who looked on in a kind of disgusted puzzlement. But the queen herself appeared in a splendid black gown. Evidently, as with the ennoblement ceremony, she had manically thrown herself into preparing the minutiae, whilst Rome was kindling around her.

Again, this was no love affair. Bothwell was said to behave so discourteously to the queen, and to have used such foul language, that Sir James Melville walked out. It seems that part of Bothwell's strategy in dominating his fragile bride had become abusive language. She did not even rise to argument. That came after the wedding, when the earl felt safe to abandon any pretence that he was her saviour and protector in a world that despised her. Still, though, Bothwell was determined that his wife should now be utterly captive, and reports arose that he 'would not allow her to look at or be looked on by anyone'.[149] Once again Mary's appearance was affected: the English observer William Drury echoed Randolph's assessment when Mary was at a low point before Moray deserted her: 'the queen is the most changed woman of face', he wrote, 'that in so little time without extremity of sickness'. Again, Mary was heard to have expressed a desire to commit suicide, calling sometimes for a knife and sometimes wishing she might drown. Again, a black depression seemed to have overwhelmed her.

Later, the queen of Scots would write to the bishop of Dunblane, 'this realm being divided in factions as it is, cannot be contained in order, unless our authority be assisted and forthset by the fortification of a man who must take upon his person in the execution of justice ... the travail therof we may no longer sustain in our own person, being already wearied, and almost broken with the frequent uproars and rebellions raised against us since we came in Scotland'.[150] This is probably how she justified her inexplicable behaviour to herself as well. It was behaviour which, when her mental health was stronger, she could never explain; in fact, later, she would studiously avoid discussion of Bothwell. At this time, though, the triggers for her depression are not hard to find. She had tried to retain power during her previous marriage and failed. Now the youth who was to have been her puppet had been killed under her nose, and she believed herself threatened. This would have taxed anyone. For a woman of long-standing mental instability, these cruelties led to a bout of illness that left her vulnerable to a man who promised to exert the control that her policy of autonomy had not allowed.

The lords gathered at Stirling had not been inactive. Rather, they had continued to gather support (Maitland would slip away to them on the 6th of June) and military personnel. Amongst their number were Morton, Argyll, Mar, Atholl, Glencairn, Ruthven (successor of the old man who had been at Riccio's murder), and Lindsay. Catholic support came in the form of Hume, Eglinton, and Montrose. Bothwell knew of this, and his response was to act try and win the Kirk to his side with anti-Catholic pledges, to try and win the people over by issuing fiscal decrees against counterfeit coinage, and to try and win England over by writing high-handed, kingly letters to Elizabeth as though he were already a fellow sovereign. It was a losing battle, though. Civil war was unavoidable, and after a series of skirmishes, escapes, and secret meetings, on the 15th of June it culminated in the battle of Carberry Hill, where the Marian army met the opposition in arms.

The day was blisteringly hot, and the soldiers on either side were reluctant to fight an actual battle. Instead they glared at one another, the queen's forces pitched on higher ground and her rebels opposite. The French ambassador, du Croc, attempted to mediate between sides, but he was unsuccessful. The anti-Bothwell lords were resolute that they intended and would accept nothing less than the queen abandoning Bothwell to his fate: as they had declared openly that he was Darnley's murderer, this would be a traitor's death. This she could not do. Not only did she suspect she might be pregnant, but she had married the man. As her forces melted away, their chosen spot unshaded and in the full glare of the June sun, it became obvious that the lords had the upper hand. Bothwell was allowed to escape, but Mary surrendered, in the belief that the opposition would, as its members promised, return to their former allegiance.

She was wrong in trusting them. When they led her back to Edinburgh it was as a captive, and along the route the soldiery began to heckle and verbally abuse her. This was to lead Kirkaldy of Grance, a veteran soldier and an honest man, to silence them: it was the first indication not only that Mary was to receive no honourable treatment, but that the lords who had opposed her and Bothwell were themselves already splitting in consideration of what was to be her fate. Mary herself showed some spirit, crying, 'how is this, my lord Morton? I am told that all this is done in order to get justice among the king's murderers. I am also told [by Bothwell?] that you are one of the chief of them'.[151] This was a witty utterance. It was a brave one. It was, however, an ill-considered if not foolish revealing of her hand. Henceforth Morton knew what he already probably suspected: Mary knew of his collusion with Bothwell in the murder of Darnley. She would have to go to. Luckily, she had provided her own replacement the previous year in the form of baby James.

In Edinburgh, too, enough Calvinist supporters had been found and were encouraged to hurl abuse at their queen. If Mary had been in the grip of manic depression over the preceding weeks, it was about to get much worse.

When news of Carberry Hill reached France, Catherine de Medici called Moray to her presence, and again made an effort to win him over. Moray, however, was deaf to her; he was far more concerned with the rapidity with which the affairs of Scotland had degenerated. It had been bad enough that Mary had married Bothwell, and that certainly had required to be dealt with. A rebellion, however, in which the queen was taken captive was a step too far. Even his own Chaseabout Raid had never been intended to depose or imprison the sovereign, despite her beliefs that it had. Most worrying of all, the captivity of his sister by his subjects would gall Elizabeth, who was ever sensitive to *lèse-majesté*. He dispatched a messenger, Elphinstone, to Scotland. He was charged with gaining access to Mary and assuring her of her brother's loyalty. Naturally he stopped in London first, to keep Elizabeth and Cecil up to date on Moray's position.

With a considerable brass neck, Moray then extricated himself from France by promising to restore his sister, and voicing hope that French help might aid him to do so if necessary, the two countries having been such reliable allies in the past. He was released from the French court with a passport, but forced to take as a companion an envoy, Philibert de Lignerolles, whose job was to ensure that he made good on his hollow rhetoric about a Franco-Scottish pact.

Moray reached London on the 25th of July. Waiting for him was knowledge of something that would change his relationship with his sister for the rest of their short time together. Morton had apparently been led by a frightened servant of Bothwell's to a house in Edinburgh on the 20ᵗʰ of June. There he had found a casket under a bed and broken it open the following day. Inside were allegedly a series of letters and love poems from Mary to Bothwell, eight documents in all, which proved beyond doubt that she had not only known of Darnley's murder, but that she and her third husband were the architects of it. It had been the convenient discovery of this casket and its contents that had brought about the decision to depose the queen and the excuse needed to do it. When it had first occurred to Morton – and he was the primary mover – that the queen could be got rid of entirely rather than just divided from Bothwell, we do not know, but it was likely at the time of Carberry Hill. As soon as she had been brought to Edinburgh after the battle, openly stating his guilt in Darnley's murder, the writing was on the wall as far as he was concerned. She had been forced to endure a night in a cell, during which she reached her lowest ebb, shrieking and crying at the window. Thereafter she had been manhandled to Holyroodhouse before being taken, on the 17ᵗʰ of June, to Lochleven, the seat of Moray's mother and half-brother.

Yet Moray found that not everyone had fallen in behind Morton. The lords who had met at Stirling had split since the queen had been removed from Bothwell's side (Bothwell himself having flown north). A faction calling themselves the confederate lords had splintered off. They were enemies not only of Bothwell, but of Mary herself. This group comprised Morton, Mar, Glencairn, Ruthven, Lennox (still bent on revenge), Lindsay, Maitland, and the Catholic Atholl (who was a Stewart but a Lennox ally).[152] Remaining loyal to the queen were, surprisingly, Moray's old friend Argyll, the entire Hamilton clan (led by Archbishop John in the absence of Châtelherault), and a smattering of friends and allies of Bothwell. So it was that the coronation of the queen's son as King James VI was rushed, taking place on the 29ᵗʰ of

July. It was a poorly attended and rather seedy affair, presided over by the amoral Bishop of Orkney who had wed Mary to Bothwell. Elizabeth, like Mary and her adherents, was disgusted. Moray, still in England when the news arrived, probably shared their feeling.

Into this fevered atmosphere the English queen had sent Sir Nicholas Throckmorton at the end of June, his mission being to quell the unrest and assure Mary of her English cousin's support. He was to become embroiled in the claims and counter claims that made this month in Scottish politics such a mire; even, he wrote to England, the confederate lords were divided amongst themselves, with Maitland favouring a limited restoration of the queen, Atholl banishment, and others imprisonment. Throckmorton was not, however, allowed to see the queen in person; this allowed the confederate lords to try and control the narrative they were spinning around her. None of this went down well with Elizabeth, who saw only varying shades of unacceptable treason. This was bad news for Morton and his faction. Elizabeth's condemnation of them for imprisoning their lawful sovereign was no mean thing. Their plans – to depose the queen and install a regent to govern in place of baby James – must have seemed dangerously ambitious. Their trump card was the mysterious casket.

Much as been written about the casket letters. The originals, however, disappeared in 1584; consequently, for centuries scholars have been trying to prove or disprove the validity of the content of French copies, and English and Scots translations. This is far from ideal. Yet it has not deterred historians. Some avow that the long-vanished originals were what they were claimed: proof that Mary was a murderous adulteress. Others favour the argument that they were a series of interpolations and ambiguous forgeries.[153] Probably the latter school of thought is correct. Their composer remains subject to debate. The semi-literate Morton is an unlikely candidate. Some favour Maitland, a skilled man of letters, and it is tempting to imagine that the sheer ambiguity and oddness of the documents stemmed from some Machiavellian policy on his part to produce material which looked damning but could, if sides needed changing, be rejected as false. There is, however, as much firm evidence that his hand was put to the sexing up of real documents as there is that it was done by another suspect, Mary Beaton: none.[154] At any rate, it does not matter: they are gone, and thus ruminations on their validity and source can only ever be speculative.

However, when Moray learnt of their existence whilst in England, he professed himself convinced. The reasons behind his conviction are not difficult to find. Although he did not want his sister deposed, he himself could not otherwise account for her marriage to Bothwell than their having been secret lovers. Many modern scholars have, after all, been unable to see anything other than a guilty woman consumed by lust, and it is understandable that a sixteenth-century Calvinist would do likewise. This was, after all, a world in which some still believed that a woman's uterus travelled freely around her torso, giving rise to hysterical behaviour.[155] His belief in the letters being genuine does not make them so.

As he had after helping arrange Darnley's murder, Morton moved quickly. The supposed author of the casket letters, Mary, remained at Lochleven; between the 20th and 23rd of July she miscarried twins. Immediately after, as she lay in bed in pain and despondency, Lindsay of the confederates burst in. Using threats of violence, he forced her to sign three documents: one was a declaration of abdication in favour of her infant son; the next was an acceptance of her brother as regent (he being the nominated choice as the quondam leader of the old Congregation, uncle of the prince, and a legitimated Stewart); the third accepted Morton and the other confederate lords as Scotland's governors until Moray (who was just a day off reaching England at the time) returned. Mary signed, believing, as Throckmorton's smuggled missives had told her, that anything signed under duress could later be rescinded. Following this brutal visit, Moray's wife Agnes visited.[156] It is to be hoped that her role was that of a friend, but more likely that she hoped to sound out Mary's mind ahead of her husband's return.

From the point at which Mary's pen touched the paper, her relationship with her brother was to become that of rivals for power: of enemies. He had been part of a 'coup pushed through by a narrow clique' and she was its victim.[157] The following year they were to each face choices that would determine not only the future course of their lives, but whether they would see one another again.

One Up, The Other Down

Mary sat in the chamber that had become hers, in a tower room in Lochleven Castle. She had visited before, in happier times. Now she was a captive. It was mid-August. She had faced the worst that anyone could in the past few months: her husband had been killed, she had been accused, the man whom she had come to rely on had taken advantage of her in every way possible before fleeing, she had lost two babies, and been forced to sign away her own throne. If she looked back on her own behaviour throughout much of what had happened, it must have been with a kind of shameful wonder. The door opened and in strode the brother she had not seen since the beginning of April, when she had been in the grip of depression. His fellow travellers, Morton and Atholl, remained outside.

Moray remained silent. He had accepted the regency of Scotland, which Morton and his allies had secured for him, but it was a hollow victory. The only time he had desired the full powers of a regency had been back in 1560, when the reformation had just been born. Then he had sought it with the queen's approval. It was a quite different thing to receive it by deposition. It was an unpopular, contentious thing. It was an anti-English thing. Moreover, he had learnt a valuable lesson from Mary's struggles. Whilst a counsellor, it was always possible to escape from difficult circumstances – to achieve an alibi and avoid being mired. To be in sole charge, whether as regent or monarch, was to be where the buck stops. It was to be in a highly visible and therefore vulnerable position.

He listened as Mary recited a litany of complaints. She had had no one with whom to speak beyond her ladies and her brother's family, who were her gaolers. Then she wept, reproving him for the treatment she had endured. According to Moray's account, filtered through Throckmorton to the English government, he 'used covert speech, and such as he judged she would not discover neither the good nor the ill he had conceived of her, nor meant unto her'.[158] This was, on his part, a fact-finding mission. He wanted her side of the story. She poured it out for two hours, until the announcement of her supper brought it to an end.

Mary was not finished. She summoned her brother to her again after supper, and they spoke until 1 o'clock in the morning. Moray, so he claims, took the opportunity this time to air his opinions on her 'misgovernment, and laid before her all such disorders as either might touch her conscience, her honour, or surety'.[159] In Throckmorton's poetic estimation, Moray behaved 'more like a ghostly father ... than like a councillor'. It is said he left her hoping for 'nothing but God's mercy'. This might seem cruel, but from Moray's perspective, it was a necessary antidote to his sister's outpouring of recrimination. As far as he was concerned, she was an adulteress and a murderess who had invited all that had happened. Many historians who are critical of the queen of Scots would no doubt have said much the same to her were they ever given the opportunity. However, his harshness is indicative of something more interesting. Either Moray showed a callous disregard for his sister's rape, or he did not believe it had happened at all. Rape in the period is often mistakenly considered to have been viewed as the woman's fault, but a wealth of literary sources indicate that it was considered a brutal and sinful act carried out by men who could not contain their own passions. It is therefore reasonable to conclude that Moray did not think his sister had been ravished by Bothwell and not

226

care; he truly believed she had been art and part (as the Scottish term goes) of a deception born of a secret love affair.

The next morning, he met with her again. This time, the meeting – it could not be described as an audience, given that she had abdicated – was more amicable. The air had been cleared the previous night; the bitterness on both sides had been released. Moray spoke 'words of consolation' and assured her that her life was not in any danger as long as it was in his power to protect her. Her liberty, though, was not his to offer – and, in fact, he suggested that she would probably be safer in captivity at Lochleven, under his protection, than if she were amongst those who were less inclined to see her live.

It is here that Moray's account of events becomes difficult to believe. According to him, Mary fell into a bout of grateful weeping, throwing her arms around his neck and kissing him. She entreated him not to deny the regency, insisting that only by his acceptance of it might Scotland be well governed. Naturally, he listed the reasons why he should not take it. Again, Mary supposedly pooh-pooed them, demanding that he put her wishes in the matter before his own. She even asked him to take everything of value which was hers, only for him to 'show himself very unwilling to have the custody of her jewels'.[160] It is the prolonged mention of the jewels in Moray's account that betrays him veering off into fantasy territory. It reads much more as a justification than an honest account: a blatant attempt to convince Elizabeth and the English government that he was a reluctant and humble man, on whom greatness was thrust. Probably he did not want the regency; however, if there were no alternatives, he would much rather accept it than otherwise. The accompanying material possessions he wanted with all the fervour of a seasoned Scrooge. It was not pure fantasy, though. Mary did surrender some of her jewels to him. Some of them he eventually gave to Agnes and others he sold; governing Scotland was proving to be a pricey business.[161]

It is also possible that Mary did make some assurances that she would accept her brother's elevation to the regency. She had to. At this stage, there was little point in resisting. She had vented her anger the previous night, and now turned to craft. From this point onwards, her depression lifted, and she became the more familiar Mary: the political animal who would and could master her emotions and dissemble in order to escape difficulties or work out her future course. If Moray spun his account of the meeting into an almost heroic tale of his own humble rise, Mary helped him by giving him the bare bones. She played the penitent subordinate, whilst her mind was secretly turning to escape.

A week after this series of meetings between Moray and Mary, the former was formally proclaimed Scotland's regent in Edinburgh. Again, he made a conventionally humble statement about his unwillingness to take up the office and serve the crown (which had fallen to the baby James) and his faith. This is often taken as his apogee: the crowning moment of all he had wished for. It was not. Throughout his career, Moray had been risk-averse. He did not like driving state events and had learnt the value of being a weathervane rather than the wind which blew it. By that strategy he could reap the rewards of politics without attracting the catastrophes. Driving events meant exposure. His revolt in 1565 was thus his political anomaly as his sister's Catholic interlude had been hers. In his speech he insisted too that he would attempt nothing that would alter Mary's status as a former queen of Scots without the approval of the Privy Council. This was undoubtedly a point desired by his colleagues, but it represented again his desire not to make decisions for himself, and to share collective responsibility. All must have seemed orderly. However, he had inherited control of a deeply divided country.

Two main orders of business were to consume the nascent regency government. Firstly, it had to establish international recognition. Secondly, it would have to do something about those members of the political community – lords, gentry, and clergy – who remained absolutely opposed to Mary's deposition. They had formed themselves into a 'queen's party', which now became the opposition to Moray's 'king's party'.

Naturally, Moray's primary concern was getting English approval of his new office. Throckmorton, however, was implacable; Elizabeth, he knew, wanted the anointed queen restored to her throne. Moray and Maitland attempted to sway him, justifying all that had occurred in Scotland, but it was to no avail. Nevertheless, the pair stressed that they meant goodwill towards England. By this means they hoped that Elizabeth could be won round. It was far better, they hoped she would realise, to have a compliant, friendly, Protestant cousin as a neighbour than a disgraced Catholic queen. Yet neither Throckmorton or Elizabeth would recognise 'King' James or the men who ruled under that title: to them, the anointed sovereign was Queen Mary. Thankfully for Moray practicalities intervened, and by November affrays in the Borders – along with Cecil's wheedling – forced her to let her wardens work with Moray's.

The Marian party were a clearer and present danger. Mary had won many to her side during the programme of courting she had enacted since returning to Scotland in 1561. Some had, of course, deserted her over the course of the previous summer, whether for religious reasons, out of disappointment at her marriage to Bothwell, or simply because they preferred the rising sun of Prince James to the early setting of Queen Mary. Moray mustered forced against the Marians in Glasgow, where they were scheduled to meet. By showing force of arms, he brought Huntly and Herries to the negotiating table, and elicited submission from Argyll, Kilwinning, and Boyd. Next came his taking of Dunbar Castle, a Marian stronghold. That left only Dumbarton Castle, which was relatively marooned in the middle of Lennox country in the west. By October, he wrote to Cecil that the Scottish political scene was quiet. Even Bothwell had turned up in Norway, only to be imprisoned despite his pathetic entreaties that he was the consort of the queen of Scots. Domestic peace allowed Moray to turn his attention southwards, to the perennial problem of the Borders, where he showed himself an able and brutal enforcer of justice.

Scotland's political community could never quite stand stability. With Mary still in the deck, albeit not in play, its members continued to disagree over what was to be done with her. Despite the regent's apparent successes, men would not stop changing sides, and his initial gains against the queen's party only served to give the cause lustre. Catholic lords who had supported Morton in separating Bothwell from the queen now came out for her. To counter this, Moray tried to keep outrage over Darnley's murder fresh in everyone's mind, hunting down and prosecuting men associated with Bothwell. In October he visited his sister at Lochleven, ostensibly to see how she was faring, but in reality to try and gauge whether her spirits indicated burgeoning or falling support. As he was now in power, so was she out of it. Any pretence at amity between them was a charade.

At a parliament called for December, the Kirk, too bore the fruit of Moray's regency, the Acts of the 1560 parliament again ratified and the mass declared – again – illegal. By these means Moray was assuring support from the Kirk as a powerful lobby; predictably, however, it meant that Catholics would rally ever more to the captive queen's cause. Hence, he had to buy support from waverers and adherents alike, rapidly depleting the treasury simply to keep his government afloat and united against the opposition party. To further besmirch the queen and her supporters, Moray had the casket letters exhibited in the parliament, hoping to advertise what he truly believed was evidence that his sister's deposition had been an acceptable act. Parliament, in turn, backed the action.

Moray's regency at this time is probably best described as insecure. He was managing capably, but management was not the same thing as overall control. Still Mary was a thorn in the government's side. Still there were men in the king's party whose loyalty could not be trusted. Still Elizabeth was pushing for her restoration – even to the extent of sending money to the captive queen's Hamilton supporters. Although she began writing to him cordially in January 1568, the English queen continued to refuse to recognise Moray as anything more than a rebel leader, and James as nothing more than the puppet king he was. But the insecurity of the new regime was to get its biggest shock at the beginning of May 1568. It was on the 3rd of the month that a messenger from Lochleven rode to the regent, who was then in Glasgow, with the news that his sister had slipped her bonds and escaped.

Mary had never been a contented captive. It was not in her nature, as demonstrated by the frequent politically-motivated progresses she enjoyed. During the course of her captivity, she had carefully devised a means of escape. This involved employing her legendary charm on the household. It was no mean feat, given that Lochleven was governed by the regent's brother-in-law, William Douglas of Lochleven. Luckily, one of the laird's younger brothers, George, was utterly captivated by the tall, tragic heroine with whom he lived. Warnings of a looming escape supposedly reached the regent in late March or early April, which resulted in a visit to the castle to investigate. The story runs that Mary had openly asked for the young man's hand, alerting Moray to possible danger, and he had banished George from the household.

At the end of March, Mary had tried to escape disguised as a laundress, but the attempt had been discovered by the boatman who conveyed the servants back and forth across the loch. He had not, however, told the laird of her behaviour. Her successful attempt came later. It involved young Willie Douglas, an illegitimate son of the laird, working with the banished George, who waited at Kinross on the mainland. On the 2nd of May, during the May Day revels, Willie drilled holes in all the boats but one. Then, at supper, he swiped the laird's keys from under his nose and signalled to Mary in the tower. The queen dressed in her gentlewoman Mary Seton's clothes and walked boldly out of the main gate. Willie locked it and threw away the key, before the pair rowed their way across the loch to George, who had retrieved horses from the laird's mainland stables. Off the queen went towards Hamilton, the cry going out to her supporters that their mistress was free at last, and ready to take down the pretended regent. Within days she had gathered thousands of supporters to her side. At Hamilton on the 8th of May her men signed a bond pledging themselves to her: nine earls, nine bishops, twelve abbots, eighteen lairds, and over ninety others were the official signatories: each brought with him personal followings. Mary, however, was not intent on a bloody civil war. Still less did she want another Carberry Hill. She made requests instead that the regent give up his power peacefully and accept her restoration.

Moray now faced a tough choice. It was submitting to his sister, making an apology, and accepting her restoration, or continuing to oppose England's queen and maintain his regency. Ultimately, the question came down to what he wanted. As we have seen, that was power. However, it is not good enough to simply say he wished to be the power behind a throne: that notion needs to be unpacked. What he wanted was power without the burden of chief responsibility. He wanted to wield it whilst someone else provided the public face and thus attracted public censure. It would be a lot more difficult to share blame with, and cast it on, a baby than it would a grown woman. But then there were financial considerations, to which he was ever sensitive. Already he had discovered how expensive it was to govern Scotland without the aid of Mary's French dower revenue. Yet too much troubled water had passed under the bridge for him to trust that the queen's restoration could do him any good. The army behind her would not accept her returning to power on a wave of good faith. On balance, it was better to retain the poisoned chalice of the regency, as troublesome as governing Scotland would be without his sister to share in the slings and arrows, than give it up. Therefore, he could and would not accede to his sister's demands. Similarly, he had no reason to believe that in the event of his submission she would be any kinder to him than he had been to her. In fact, he might expect the block at worst, and long-term imprisonment at best. It would be far better and safer, in the end, to enrich himself and mould his young nephew than receive back a dangerous sister. His refusal to come to terms favourable to Mary made battle inevitable.

Dumbarton Castle had been in Marian hands throughout the queen's captivity, and it was to this mighty fortress that the queen's party decided to go. To get there, though, they had to march past Glasgow, where Moray had remained on hearing the news of his sister's escape. He had not been idle, either, but gathered his own men and their followings. He was also a veteran general, having taken part in military adventures since his fights against English troops during the Rough Wooing. He led his men towards Mary's, and they met at the village of Langside, south of Glasgow, on the 13th of May. His friend Kirkaldy of Grange, an excellent soldier himself, led Moray's troops. They were smaller than the queen's, but far more experienced and better organised. Most importantly, they knew how to make effective use of terrain.

Mary's forces marched along the south bank of the river Clyde. Leading them was Châtelherault's second son, Lord Claude Hamilton. Present too were the earls of Argyll, Cassillis, Rothes, and Eglinton, and the lords Sommerville, Yester, Livingston, Herries, Fleming, and Ross. They were all being watched by Kirkaldy, who then hid his forces in the gardens and cottages of the village itself. When the Marian army arrived at Clincart Hill (present day Mount Florida) they arrayed themselves for battle. Artillery fire was exchanged but was on neither side conclusive. Argyll and Hamilton then forced a front assault along what is now Battlefield Road, hoping to break the regent's ranks and march through. They were, however, mown down by the hagbutters hidden in the foliage and housing on either side of the road.

Hamilton, in charge of Mary's cavalry, fell back before attempting another attack, whilst Herries appeared to be making headway in causing confusing amongst the regent's forces. However, Kirkaldy then sent forward his infantry to launch another assault on the queen's men. This proved decisive. The brutal hand-to-hand combat gradually forced the Marians back along the road, the blood of three-hundred men dripping from hedgerows and sinking into the mud. Mary watched the retreat of her army from a nearby hill, as they fled from the regent's men who had ordered them to be taken prisoner rather than slain. Moray later rewarded the bakers of Glasgow with a new wheat mill, in recognition of their having supplied his men with bread prior to the clash – ever the magnanimous victor. He had won. Mary had lost.

What her brother did not know was what she would do next. In the immediate aftermath of the battle, it is likely that she did not know. With lords Herries, Livingston and Fleming at her side, she left the environs of the battlefield. She rode south.

A number of options remained open to her. She could stay in Scotland, regrouping her fighting men and taking on her brother at a more auspicious time and place. This was probably the wisest choice. Her party was strong, and she had only just displayed that, if she were present to give it heart, its men would take up arms. She might, though, go to France and beg for continental aid. This would be a mistake. Aside from the fact that it would be a humiliating act to return to the country of which she had once been queen having lost the crown of Scotland, there was no evidence that France, with its own problems, would spend anything on a country which had broken the auld alliance. If she were to go to France, then, it would be to retirement as a dowager queen. She was not ready to retire.

The third option was to seek aid in England. Elizabeth had protested vocally – and financially – about the injustice of Mary's deposition. The Scottish queen must have confidently decided that a brief meeting between the pair would be enough to muster a loan of money, men and arms. After all, Elizabeth had been willing to give just that to the Congregation in 1559-60. The world would look askance at her refusing to do the same for her cousin.

England was the option on which Mary settled, and she wrote a letter at Dundrennan Abbey to Elizabeth before crossing the Solway Firth on a fishing boat without waiting for a reply. With her were sixteen attendants, and a sense of apprehension as to what kind of reception Lowther, the deputy governor of Carlisle Castle, would give her. What could never have crossed anyone's mind is that she would never return. Nor would she see her brother again. Their paths would now only cross by means of legal proceedings and nugatory letters. To the bafflement of Europe, Elizabeth and Cecil would set up a rigged inquiry into the behaviour of both siblings that would settle their fates in Scotland and England.

Siblings on Trial

In October 1568, England – and the world – bore witness to one of the strangest events known to European history. Two siblings, one a queen and the other her bastard brother, then regent of her country, were put on trial by their cousin, queen of a foreign country. The affair rested on whether the sister had murdered her husband, and consequently whether the brother was right to depose her. It was beyond the imaginations of the period's greatest writers of romance, tragedy, or comedy. What on earth had led to this?

In the wake of Mary's flight into England, her brother had taken his army of roughly seven-thousand on a campaign of destruction across Clydesdale, Galloway, Nithsdale, Annandale, and Tweeddale.[162] His lenience in sparing the survivors of Langside had given way to rage. After all he had conceded to the Marians in trying to build up the king's party, they had rewarded him with insurrection in the name of his sister. It was not to be borne. He executed no one – he was not a bloodthirsty man – but castles were burned, and his enemies turned out of their homes. Even Dumbarton was sieged, albeit it to no avail. The whole thing was rather pyrrhic: Huntly remained in the field against him in Fife, Argyll and the returned Fleming menaced Glasgow, Claude Hamilton recovered Hamilton Castle from the pro-regency Sempill, and Hepburns were garrisoning East Lothian.[163] Moray had no choice but to fight hard. This policy bought him no new friends. Indeed, it brought out his enemies. At the start of August, the Lyon Herald fled into Dumbarton Castle, accused of 'conspiracy against the life of the regent': a conspiracy which was rumoured to involve Moray's intimates. The bruit [rumour] of the regent's murder had, according the herald, who denied being part of the plot, been 'tossed up and down at Edinburgh'.[164] He was burnt on the 15th, the means by which he was extracted from Dumbarton unrecorded.

But winning friends was never the aim of Moray's policy following his sister's flight to England. It was enacted to cow him enemies. He felt emboldened, further, by the tentative support of Elizabeth and Cecil, who now recognised his government, at least quietly. Both were utterly bamboozled by the sudden appearance of Mary – they had no more idea of what to do with her than had Moray earlier in the year. What was clear was that they did not want her, and if they had to have her, it would be on sufferance. Moray wanted nothing to do with her either.

Whilst her brother launched his campaign of repression against the queen's party north of the border, Mary had made a good impression south of it. Likely she thought she might draw breath in England, enjoying an unofficial royal visit, before having to get back into the thick of things in Scotland again. With Elizabeth's backing, she would even give a fillip to her party at home. After an overnight stay at Workington Hall, the queen arrived at Carlisle Castle on the 18th of May. Custody of her was wrangled over by Lowther and the earl of Northumberland: an ominous hint of what was to be her future. More ominous still were rumours that she met with the duke of Norfolk, who supposedly hastened to make the acquaintance of the glamourous Scottish arrival. Whether the meeting took place or not, stories of it circulated, and were to do nothing to warm Elizabeth to her cousin's cause.

Elizabeth was in quandary. She had not asked for this – in fact, throughout her life, she had not asked for any of the problems associated with Mary Stewart. As always, her primary concern was keeping her own house in order, and it no doubt irked her that her cousins could not do the same. Nevertheless, she sent north a package of mean clothes, in a move that many have probably correctly considered a catty snub. Letters flew between the queens, with Mary entreating her cousin not to trust her brother of his party. 'They deceive you', she wrote, 'in the hope of proving their false slanders to you … your ministers too … are writing and counselling them to pay no heed to your persuasions'.[165] In this Mary was quite right. Cecil was the driving force behind English support of Moray's regency. Elizabeth wrote on the 8th of June that she would do all in her power to protect Mary and work towards her restoration, but only if the charges that she had conspired to kill Darnley were proven false. This was a stalling tactic. Elizabeth needed time to work out what on earth was the safest course of action for England's future, whilst balancing the need to be seen to support an anointed monarch against subjects whom she alleged had seized her son and forced her abdication. In the meantime, the Scottish queen had to be removed from Carlisle, where escape back over the border might be too easily accomplished. Accordingly, and despite Mary's protestations in letter and in person to the men who had become captors rather than hosts, she was moved in the middle of July to the more isolated Bolton Castle.

What Elizabeth's claim of requiring proof of Mary's innocence amounted to was a trial, although she and her government were studiously careful to avoid calling it that. It was to be a commission, designed, supposedly, to benevolently help settle the affairs of her sister monarch. No one was fooled. To sweeten what looked like unjust treatment of a monarch by a peer who had no jurisdiction over her or her country, Elizabeth assured Mary that she would help restore her regardless of what evidence Moray might bring to bear – although if it were convincing, there would be conditions to the restoration. It is doubtful if Elizabeth ever intended this – but perhaps she believed it at the time. Moray could not but realise this was a possibility. On the 11th of June Lennox, who had decamped to England himself, wrote to him 'advising that they arm themselves with arguments against the kyngis mother and suche as are comin with her into this realme'.[166]

The English government had not only been dealing with Mary, however. In the middle of June Elizabeth had been publicly rebuking Moray, telling him to cease attacking the queen's party and prepare to face charges of rebellion. The effect of this was undermined by earlier, more private messages from Cecil to continue doing what he was doing. The great problem for England was this: its queen and chief secretary were broadly happy with Moray's governance and his strategy of pressing for Scottish friendship with England. They were happy with his religious goals, and they were very happy with his willingness to kowtow to them. The English queen, however, was absolutely opposed to the means by which his government had been installed, and must, moreover, consider the opinions of her fellow monarchs, who would balk at seeing one queen support the deposition of another. The solution, again, was the commission. It was to be a stage upon which some form of impartial, friendly justice could be seen to be offered by Elizabeth to help reconcile the difficulties faced by her neighbours. And so Moray was invited to send commissioners of his own southwards, ready to justify their deposition.

Although a friend to England, Moray was not prepared to cease harrying the queen's party. He was marginally happier to participate in Elizabeth's legal charade (the Tudors had always been great lovers of the machinery of law as a solution to thorny problems, and Moray was willing to play along) as long as he and his government would not be unfairly treated. He had dispatched his secretary, John Wood, to

England to treat with the English queen, and a flurry of unequivocal doublespeak passed back and forth between the two governments. Hedging his bets, he also sent to Mary coffers of clothing she had left in his mother's house at Lochleven. It was an insurance policy. Even now, he might be required to accept back a chastened and pliant Mary, a broken Mary under strict conditions from Elizabeth, to front and fund the monarchy whilst he managed affairs quietly. It was far from ideal – it was horrifically dangerous, as long as his sister could raise men-in-arms – but it might well be what the English queen thrust upon him, and he had to consider how he might make the best of it. Keeping his options open, he submitted formally on the 13th of July to Elizabeth's request for an inquiry, whilst arranging for a parliament (against her wishes) to legally forfeit the queen's supporters, who were themselves massing in the west and seeking help from Spain.

Moray's agreement to an inquiry was followed by Mary's, which came on the 28th of July. It coincided with her request to her party to lay down their arms if Moray would do likewise. Both had, after all, agreed to an arbitration, and so a ceasefire made sense. This prompted her brother to write to her, feigning warmth. His sister did not reciprocate. Neither did her followers do as she bade: Argyll and Huntly continued to make trouble across Scotland. However, they were cut off from any external help. Spain provided nothing to aid Mary's cause, and despite Châtelherault, who was still in exile, pleading for aid from the French government, that too was a dead letter. Moray's August parliament, which he had hoped would give legal weight to his government, proved equally ineffectual. The Hamiltons, Fleming, and John Leslie, bishop of Ross, were forfeited, but his desire for a complete rout of his opponents was vitiated by moderates in his government.

In September, Mary was confidently looking towards the inquiry as the prelude to her restoration. Moray was worrying about it for the same reason. He sought assurance by requesting a passport through England prior to taking part (which would grant him, in modern parlance, diplomatic immunity from arrest) and a private conference with Cecil. The last is particularly noteworthy. What Moray wanted was for he and Cecil to sew up the result ahead of the inquiry itself, the pair of them ensuring that the outcome would not in any way harm his government. Elizabeth wrote to him on the 20th of September assuring him that if Mary were found guilty she would not be restored. This revealed her earlier promises to Mary to have been lies, but her strategy is more devious. Quite simply, she never intended the inquiry to return a verdict on Mary's guilt either way. The whole thing was to be a sham from its announcement. Elizabeth, as her motto, 'semper eadem' attests, wanted nothing to change. She had inherited a situation not of her own making – Mary's lodging in her country – and, though she had not wanted it, she had no intention of changing it now.

Moray gathered his commissioners – a difficult task, given many still believed Mary might return at any point full of hatred of those who had proceeded against her – and set off for England at the end of September. Amongst his party were Morton, Lindsay, the bishop of Orkney, and the commendator-prior of Dunfermline. Mary's tutor-turned-enemy George Buchanan accompanied these commissioners, as did Maitland, who was edging ever further away from his old friend the regent and towards the captive queen. A key player in the farce which followed, Maitland almost certainly knew all about the plot to murder Darnley in advance of it, and thus he had a vested interest in burying the matter. Further, since he had always been a stalwart support of the Stewart succession, he wanted nothing which would give the xenophobic English parliament cause to decry the Scottish dynasty as untrustworthy. In the luggage train of the regency delegation were some jewels Moray hoped to hawk (he would be unsuccessful, giving them to Agnes afterwards). Present also was the notorious casket.

The location Elizabeth had chosen for the inquiry was York – the same place that had been mooted in 1562 as a meeting place for the two queens. Elizabeth sent as her delegation the duke of Norfolk, England's premier peer, that old hand in Scottish affairs, Sir Ralph Sadler, and the earl of Sussex. Mary, who was denied the right to attend in person (and did not at this stage want to), sent the recently-forfeited bishop of Ross and her friend Lord Herries, neither of whom were entirely sure of her innocence at the time, having not seen the casket letters.[167] From her perspective, the meeting was to be no more than a conference; as anointed queen of Scots, she absolutely refused to recognise the English justice system as having any right to try her.

In the course of the York conference, which had its first session on the 7th of October, Moray and his faction were charged with treasonous rebellion against their sovereign. Nervously, the regent asked Norfolk to reiterate Elizabeth's promises that if Mary were found guilty, she would be not be aided by English attempts at restoration. The duke complied. Moray then revealed his knowledge that the English queen had made a contradictory promise to Mary. This threw Norfolk, and Moray pressed the advantage. Did the inquiry have the legal power to find Mary guilty of Darnley's death? If they had that power, would they use it? If they did, would they hand the Scottish queen back, and recognise the sovereignty of King James VI? Norfolk had no idea how he was supposed to answer these questions, and Moray refused to condemn his sister without guarantees. It was a stalemate.

Thereafter followed double-dealing of the worst kind. Maitland began courting Herries – not necessarily in Moray's favour. Moray, equally shadily, privately showed the casket letters to the English commissioners, who professed themselves shocked at this proof of

242

Mary's guilt. Maitland let Mary's commissioners know of this skulduggery – and the queen was understandably disgusted. She had always maintained that her handwriting was generic enough so as to be easily copied, and the flurry of letters and poems (if the copies extant are accurate) were occasionally damning, occasionally confusing, and internally inconsistent. The secretary then proceeded to work on Norfolk, who for his own reasons resiled from his disgust and began again to become a secret Marian. The duke was to become, if he had not already begun to consider himself, a potential suitor to the queen of Scots. Moray was not closed to the idea; in fact, as long as Mary was kept in England, unable to punish him for his profiting from her forced abdication, he even expressed himself willing to accept the ideas Norfolk proposed.

In a further undermining of the veneer of legality that cloaked the York inquiry, Moray then send an envoy, Robert Melville, directly to his sister. He was to deliver the following message: the regent will use the casket letters against you unless you agree to remain in England, form an accord with Norfolk, and accept a Scottish pension. Mary agreed, not because she feared the casket letters being treated as accurate (she was confident they could not be) but to buy time. When Melville then went south to present Elizabeth with this compromise, he was to find that Mary, through Herries, had outflanked him. She wanted nothing to do with the sordid compromise scheme. Norfolk, too, had played Moray false; he had no designs upon an alliance, marital or otherwise, with a powerless exile. If he was to consider Mary at all, she must be a queen regnant. Moray had been led by the nose into believing that his sister would ever ratify her abdication in exchange for a potential marriage with a duke and a paltry Scottish pension. Henceforth, however, the duke and the queen were to be locked in a dangerous game.

Elizabeth was understandably confused and irate by all the dodgy dealings taking place so far from her own sphere of influence and power, and the rumours blowing southwards about secret meetings and broken compromises induced her to declare that the proceedings at York should be moved to Westminster. On the 3rd of November, this is exactly what happened. The leg of the conference that was to take place in the south would, however, have a different complexion. Irritated by his sister's trick, Moray was now more willing to hold up the casket letters to public scrutiny. The English government, too, was prepared to provide answers to his questions about Mary's fate and recognition of King James VI. The Scottish queen would, Elizabeth and Cecil agreed, be kept in England, and Moray would be allowed to resume his regency unhindered. As this had already been decided upon, it rendered the actual conference a show trial. Further illustrating the kangaroo nature of the court, Mary's pleas to attend in person and see the evidence against her for herself were refused. Tacitly, a grubby deal had been brokered between the queen's brother and cousin: Mary Queen of Scots must be utterly disgraced so that Moray and Elizabeth's predetermined future actions (rule in Scotland and imprisonment of Mary) would be accepted by the world.

The English delegation during the Westminster proceedings, which opened on the 25th of November, had swollen. Much to Moray's delight, Cecil himself was now a participant. The questions Norfolk had been unable to answer were now answered exactly to satisfaction, and this emboldened him to formally accuse his sister of murder. A story recounted by Herries holds that he instituted an insurance policy even then: allegedly his formal written accusation had to be wrested from the hand of his secretary, Wood, by his co-commissioner, the bishop of Orkney.[168] Whatever the truth, this represented the end of Moray's close association with Maitland. Even amidst the regency delegation, there were splits as to whether or not Mary's name should be dragged through the mud in an English courtroom, and Moray's old friend was implacably opposed. Union and amity with England were what Maitland had always wanted, but not at the cost of Scotland's honour and independence. In throwing his sister to the wolves, Moray appeared to be inviting the loss of both. The fact that the secretary's own foreknowledge of Darnley's murder meant he knew Mary was innocent probably did not factor in to his growing support for her. He reasoned, simply, that if the Scottish queen were held in England on the basis of the flimsy letters, Elizabeth would always hold the whip hand. Her policy would be, 'do as I say, or I will send her home'.

Insurance was not the only reason behind Moray's hesitance to accuse his sister and hand over the casket letters. Since 1542, his life and Mary's had been intertwined. Accusing her in a public forum of murder – a crime, it must be remembered, that her marriage to Bothwell made him believe she had committed – meant a severing of the knot. There could be no going back. It was a firm and irreversible decision on an international stage: precisely the type he detested having to make.

The accusation made, the inquiry descended into a circus of Mary-bashing. Mary's commissioners were rightly incensed, and howled in protest that the dealings were unjust, and that their mistress ought to be allowed to appear in her own defence. No one listened. This followed the bishop of Ross's equally ineffectual, but legally nice, claims that the whole inquiry ought to have been dissolved at the time of the accusation, given that Elizabeth had promised that nothing prejudicial to the Scottish queen should be publicly exhibited. Again, his and his fellows' huffy declarations of dissolvement were ignored. Instead, Lennox was invited to claim the queen had killed his son, and on the 6th of December Moray handed over his *Book of Articles*: a narrative of Mary's supposed crimes. Even Cecil found the tissue of lies and hyperbolic accusations too ridiculous to attach weight to, however, and on the 7th the casket letters themselves were handed over. Moray did this only reluctantly. This had led many to believe that he knew of their falsity and feared it being uncovered. Sexed up they were, but whether Moray knew for certain is unclear (though we know he was not reluctant to hand over the blatantly false *Book of Articles*). Neither Morton or Maitland had any reason to confess to him the massaging of them that they had undertaken when he was still planning his return from France; however, he must have had his suspicions that they would collapse under the scrutiny of England's legal minds. It did not matter. The English had made it clear that the only way he could secure Mary's imprisonment was by giving them to the commissioners. They were taken to Hampton Court where, in the middle of the month, they were laid out on a desk for the perusal of the inflated English delegation. Professing themselves convinced, the commissioners declared that the material proved that it was not commensurate with Elizabeth's honour to receive the Scottish queen.

The implication was that, in English eyes at least, Mary was a murderess. But it was only an implication. It could be denied. This, at least, was what Elizabeth hoped. As Maitland had astutely pointed out at York, it was the English queen's desire that 'all things be held in suspense' and no more. She would deliver no final judgement, and she said as much to Herries and Ross on the 16th of November, when she called them to her presence and feigned disappointment at Moray's revelations. As she often did, she attempted to divest responsibility for the matter onto others, requesting that their mistress answer her brother's charges by messenger – something she knew Mary would not do, acknowledging as it would Elizabeth's jurisdiction over her person. Her compromise solution was that Mary should formally ratify her abdication and Moray's regency, with the only reward for doing so being that the inquiry would be dissolved, and no pronouncement made against her.

The festive period interrupted proceedings. It did not, though, provide an escape for any of the participants. Elizabeth, in particular, could not avoid making some declaration. When she did, on the 10th of January, it was equivocal. Nothing, she said, had been proven either way against either Moray or Mary. The latter was to remain in ward; the former was free to resume the reins of Scottish government. Few have assessed the result as well as Lady Antonia Fraser: 'thus ended what was surely one of the strangest judicial proceedings in the history of the British isles, with a verdict of not proven given to both parties, yet one plaintiff allowed to return freely to rule in the place of the other plaintiff, who in the meantime continued to be held a prisoner'.[169] But even this is not quite fair. The flagrantly cruel and unjust outcome did fewer favours for Moray than it might have appeared. He was able to return to Scotland and authority, but with the knowledge that his sister was disgraced rather than having been proven guilty of anything. She might at any point be restored by Elizabeth – exactly as Maitland had suspected. In fact, the English queen would begin proceedings to do just that within a year.

The farcical trial, or inquiry, or commission, was over. Elizabeth emerged unscathed, her options open. Given she had not asked for any of the troubles her warring cousins had thrust upon her, one is tempted to say, 'good for her'. However, the injustice and partiality of the whole affair cries against this. At any rate, the relationship between brother and sister was now over. Henceforth, they would be locked in a deadly battle, each seeking the destruction of the other entirely. By accusing her of a crime she did not commit, but which he believed she did, Moray had become Mary's bitterest enemy. She had become the most likely means of his ruination. Their contact now was to be only through proxy-sniping, insincere correspondence, and armed conflict between the supporters of each. Even that would not last long. In a year's time, one of them would be dead.

The Good Regent and the Captive Queen

As preparations were put underway to move Mary to her most hated prison, Tutbury, her brother was finally able to leave England behind. Throughout the prolonged proceedings he had indicated his desire to return, worried as he was about the state of affairs in his civil-war-torn country. Luckily, his generals had kept a steady hand on the tiller in his absence until December, when the accusation he had feared to make against Mary released the barely-bridled hostility of the queen's party. In direct response to Moray's accusation, the queen of Scots had sent word to her supporters at home to beware of Moray, whom she claimed planned to usurp the crown. Here she was adroitly playing on her brother's reputation – which Cecil himself had incorrectly believed in – for wanting to sit on the throne of Scotland. By the end of the month the Hamiltons (who were more threatened by the subversion of the crown than their peers) had joined Argyll and Huntly in renewed hostility to government forces. In January the *Protestation of Huntly and Argyll* appeared, likely transmitted by Mary, which recounted the meeting at Craigmillar in late 1566 and added, 'we judge in our consciences and hold for certain and truth that the earl of Moray and Secretary Lethington [Maitland] were authors, inventors, counsellors, and causes of [Darnley's] murder, in what manner or by whatsoever persons the same was executed'.[170] Beneath was an implicit threat about the prospect of Spanish and French aid. This was pure spite on Mary's part: an attempt to do to her brother what he had done to her.

Still in England, Moray's response was to request that Elizabeth publicly proclaim his innocence, which she did towards the end of January. Before leaving, he bluntly asked Herries and Ross if their mistress wished to formally accuse him of colluding in Darnley's murder, and the browbeaten pair had to admit that they did not. He therefore set out for home, his pocket heavier by virtue of a loan of £5000 from the English queen.

As Mary was being moved deeper into Yorkshire, Moray was himself dreading a trip through the infamous Catholic north of England. Travelling through her sister's new home-region, he gave voice to his apprehension, stating that, 'I might, peradventure, find such trouble on my way that my throat might be cut before I came to Berwick'.[171] Mary might well have hoped so. He met with the duke of Norfolk at Hampton court, informing him that he had accused his sister only out of necessity, and that he bore her affection. The first was definitely true, and the second might have retained some vestiges of truth. More dangerously, he let the duke know that he would not be averse to his marrying Mary – a scheme which was to simmer in Norfolk's head for year and ultimately lead him to the block. Moray's purpose, however, was simply to ensure that the men of the north under the duke's command did not harass him as he made his trip back to Scotland. When she got wind of Moray's overtures to Norfolk, Mary, likewise, advised her supporters at home to settle down and wait on events.

At end of January, Moray was on his way north with an English escort and promises from Elizabeth that her march wardens would only allow the passage of Scots who carried safe conducts issued by his government. With him went a letter from Elizabeth to the earl and countess of Mar, 'denying that she made a covenant with the earl of Moray, who is said to aspire to the throne of Scotland, and asking them to care for the prince, her godson'.[172] Clearly both Moray and Elizabeth knew that there was distrust even on the part of the former's friends about his intentions and hers. At the same time, Mary was on her way south, accompanied by six of her ladies and sixteen borrowed horses. Her road took her to Ripon, Wetherby, Pontefract, Chesterfield, and finally Tutbury.

When he arrived home, Moray's first action was entirely predictable. He summoned the Privy Council to approve all that he had done. As usual, he was intent on sharing responsibility for anything that might happen in the future. By the middle of February, whilst his sister was complaining at length about the spartan conditions of her new home, he was back in the Borders raiding Jedburgh, where sixty Marians were taken. His goal now was not to crush his opponents, but to convince them that they had backed a lame duck and thereby bring them round to accepting his regency. Not only were his raids less destructive, but he used his sponsorship of the Norfolk marriage as a means of convincing the queen's party that he shared a project with them.

One of Moray's main targets in this charm offensive was Châtelherault, who returned to Scotland in February (his exile having come to an end with the deposition of the queen to whom he had voluntarily tendered it). The old duke was largely a spent force and had been for years. Nevertheless, he seems to have benefitted from that political phenomenon common even today: the acquisition of a veneer of statesmanship due to advanced age rather than any marked history of talent or ability. He came to the table willingly in March, and as the highest-ranking Marian he agreed to take part in a meeting between the government and its opponents, scheduled for April. It was hinted strongly by the regent that it would be in the best interests of the Marians to accept his rule and the coronation of King James VI – by so doing, they might expect their forfeitures to be rescinded and they might even hope to be preferred to government posts. At the end of March arrived troops sent from Berwick on Elizabeth's command. With these – and outright lies about the English queen having declared Mary guilty – Moray hoped to smash the belief still held by some in the queen's party that Mary's flight to England meant her cousin would send men to force her restoration.

When the April meeting arrived, Châtelherault proved uncooperative because, he claimed, Mary had written to him privately, playing on his loyalty. Given he had never displayed much loyalty in the past, this is hard to believe. Probably he was holding out for greater concessions. Moray was not inclined to grant them. Instead he arrested the duke along with Herries, who also refused to sign the documents he proffered, which pledged loyalty to the regency government and James VI. Good news did arrive in the form of the safe delivery of another child, Margaret, to Agnes in April, but domestic cheer was likely cold comfort in light of the parlous political situation. The next month he brought down Huntly and Argyll by sheer force, the power of the former broken by humiliating financial exactions. In June, Moray went on a progress of his own, mirroring that he and Mary had taken in 1562. His aim was the pacification of Huntly's stomping grounds, and the north more generally. This took him much of the summer.

Mary's summer involved progresses of her own, although she was in charge of neither the destinations nor the dates of travel. She was, however, introduced to two new homes which were become extremely familiar during her captivity: Wingfield Manor and Chatsworth. Her hosts had become the genial earl of Shrewsbury and his countess, Bess. In their company her status felt less like that of a prisoner and more like that of a respected houseguest: she was even permitted to keep her own little court, and her leisure activities included embroidering, riding and hawking (under guard), gossiping, and writing impassioned letters of protest to Elizabeth. The latter she had not stopped since the end of the inquiry, and it appeared that the first shoots of its success were sprouting in early May. Cecil drew up three potential means to the problem of the Scottish queen: her acceptance of her abdication and retirement in England; joint rule between her and her son (in other words, James VI's coronation was not to be erased, but Mary was to become an anointed regent); or restoration under the condition that she embrace Protestantism and attempt nothing against her brother and his allies.

When Moray received these alternatives, he was incensed – particularly as Mary's commissioner, Ross, made it clear that she would only countenance restoration. What motivated Elizabeth is questionable, but it seems that the pendulum of her mind had again swung in favour of monarchical authority and the rights of princes. Marian restoration was a serious consideration. It would rid her of her guest; it would look good to her fellow sovereigns on the international stage; and, if Protestantism could be safeguarded, it would ensure a grateful, beholden monarch north of the border. It was, however, a major decision that could not be reversed. Like her cousin Moray, Elizabeth, as we know, disliked making any such decisions.

In addition to the vexing note from Cecil came a note from Mary by means of Lord Boyd: he was charged with proposing to 'James, earl of Moray' (rather than the regent) 'the conditions … for means of reconciliation betwixt the queen and himself'.[173] In it she offered promises that, if she were restored under the third option, she would abide by its conditions; she wanted also a divorce from Bothwell so that she might be free to marry again. Her role was now that occupied by her brother the previous year, when he had sent her a message at Bolton telling her he meant her no ill will. It was now his turn to give her the cold shoulder. He wanted no part of quixotic schemes to restore a pliant Mary and marry her off to Norfolk. It was a fool's dream that, if it ever reached Elizabeth's ears, it would destroy the Stewart claim to the English throne that it was ostensibly to aid.

In June, Moray took up his pen and expressed his surprise directly to Elizabeth. He requested time to sound out his government and people as to the project of a Marian restoration. Really, he wanted to make sure it would not happen. This involved feigning support of Norfolk in the hope that the imprudent duke would advance his plans and thereby bring down the censure of Elizabeth on Mary, sinking any idea of restoration. In July he wrote to Norfolk in terms of friendship, in the same month calling for a convention of the Scottish estates (a shadow parliament). This, he hoped, would allow him to reject Elizabeth's pro-Marian proposal without taking sole responsibility: the rejection would be a collective decision rather than his own. He somewhat gave the game away by removing Ross's bishopric, however. Elizabeth had forbidden him from doing so, but the thought of collecting revenues for the treasury was too great an incentive.

At the end of July, whilst Mary was still feigning raptures of love in order to make a match with Norfolk, the convention met at Perth. Present were Moray, Morton, the weakened Huntly, Atholl, Mar, Cassillis, Crawford, Glencairn, and Buchan; also there were a number of lords, four bishops, seven abbots and commendators, and commissioners from the burghs. Discussion resulted in an outright refusal of anything other than Mary's recognition of her infant son's sovereignty. Moray held his peace when, on the 30th, talk turned to Mary's divorce. Instead, he watched Maitland and the clerk register, McGill, laird of Nether Rankeilour, make the case for accepting the deposed queen's entreaties that she might be divorced and seek remarriage. Ultimately, they were voted down. What must have been extremely clear to Moray, however, was Maitland's absolute commitment to the Marian cause – a commitment which he had suspected for some time, having sent his secretary, Wood, to spy on him earlier in the year.

Nevertheless, Moray had his victory. He could refuse any requests made by Elizabeth regarding the peaceful restoration of Mary by pointing out that the Scottish political community, and not he, were unwilling to accept her return. The duke of Norfolk, too, would be disappointed; for all Moray's fair words and fair friendship, neither he nor his government would help bring his marriage to Mary to fruition. Elizabeth was furious and wrote to tell him so. In this matter, however, he was immovable. His determination was to settle affairs in Scotland rather than allow them to be stirred up. Accordingly, he ordered another seige of Dumbarton Castle, still in Marian hands, and at the end of August he drew up plans to pacify the Borders as he had done the Highlands in summer. As he was arranging this trip, he summoned Maitland to him at Stirling.

The secretary, as we know from his presence at Whittinghame with Bothwell and Morton prior to Darnley's murder, undoubtedly knew all about it. Whatever had driven him into Mary's arms since the queen's flight into England, he was now to face Moray's wrath. It came in the form of a trap. After Maitland arrived at the Stirling council chamber, an unfamiliar man was admitted. His name was Thomas Crawford, and he was a Lennox follower. On his master's behalf, he accused the secretary of having played a role in the murder of Darnley, and the entire council voted in favour of his arrest. He was immediately put in ward and taken to Edinburgh. In a two-pronged move, Moray had also sent men to arrest the lawyer, Sir James Balfour, who was also accused of involvement. So began the mopping up of the smaller fish in the plot; Morton was left untouched. In fact, opinion held that it was Morton who had been behind the arrest of Maitland, as he had been behind the accusations of Bothwell and Mary. Very probably he did have a hand. Moray did not like working alone in any great matter.

News of Maitland's fall from grace was dispatched southwards, but it was overwhelmed by events in London. Elizabeth had finally discovered the secret marriage negotiations taking place between Mary and Norfolk, as Moray had hoped she would. Also as he had hoped, all prospect of Elizabeth helping Mary to recover her throne were lost in the fire and smoke of her rage. Moray was now potentially Elizabeth's best friend, and Mary an untrustworthy viper. All he had to do was reveal what he had known about the Norfolk match, and he was quite willing to spill all to Lord Hunsdon, whom he met at Coldstream in September. He followed this up with letters of explanation, in which he confided that he had known of the plans but had assented to nothing that did not have Elizabeth's approval. Only to Cecil would he secretly admit that he had given the duke tacit encouragement at the end of January. All of this, however, was secondary to Moray's reasons for being at Coldstream. His goal was to bring the troublesome Borders to heel, which he did with ruthless efficiency and almost unseemly haste. He returned to Edinburgh at the start of November, there to wait on Maitland's trial date, which was set for the 22nd. But Maitland had got the message out to his friends and adherents (he was, after all, a laird himself) and they flooded the town. As ever, a show of force was the Scottish plaintiff's guarantee of escaping justice. In response Moray postponed the trial, making an honest speech about the dishonesty with which his country's justice system had too long been riddled.

Elizabeth's anger over Norfolk and Moray's irritation over Maitland were themselves overtaken by events. In September, Mary had been returned to Tutbury. Two of the greatest leading Catholic magnates in Northern England, the earls of Northumberland and Westmorland, spurred on by their wives, Anne Percy and Jane Neville, raised and united armies in favouring of freeing Mary from captivity and restoring Norfolk, who had gone into hiding when Elizabeth learnt of his marital plans, to their respective places. The rebellion was religious in complexion. Lady Westmorland, who was Norfolk's sister, made this clear: 'we and our country,' she said, 'were shamed forever, that now in the end we should seek holes to creep into'. This was a deliberate jab at the English government which had made the practice of Catholicism a secret vice. The Rising of the North, as the revolt came to be known, began in earnest in the mid afternoon of the 14th of November.

Whilst the rising was in progress, Moray issued proclamations against Scottish aid being given to the rebels. Then he began to muster his own forces – which remained strong – for dispatch south against the Catholic insurgents. Though he must have feared it might happen, none of Mary's supporters at home rose up to join the English rebels. Even as the regent's army was assembling at the border on the 20th of December, news arrived that the rebellion had been defeated. Mary herself had been literally sent to Coventry under armed guard, and the rebels had wasted time taking towns and saying masses; their hesitation had allowed Elizabeth to raise a royalist army, and in fear of it, the northern forces disbanded on the 24th. The leaders had themselves just crossed the border into Scotland. Moray eagerly hunted them down, locating Northumberland on the 24th (thanks to the perfidy of a Borders chief, who had given him shelter). This raised outrage amongst those on the border, with whom it was tradition that political enemies might seek shelter and be protected; it was something which Moray had availed himself of after the Chaseabout Raid. After trying to send Northumberland south, the cry went out from the Scottish people 'of all sorts, both men and women' that the regent had sold 'the liberty of their country'.[174] One wonders at their taking so long to realise. Catherine de Medici had had the measure of his foreign policy after only a brief spell in his company. The unfortunate earl was instead sent to Lochleven and lodged in Queen Mary's old tower. Moray was forced by the violence of the reaction against his subservient behaviour towards Elizabeth to state publicly that he did not intend to send Northumberland south.

In modern terms, Moray's behaviour in the wake of England's Rising of the North was a PR disaster. He tried to get out of it by casting the blame for the rebellion itself on his wayward sister, and even flirted with the idea of exchanging the captured earl for the captive queen. The fact that he would even countenance allowing Mary's return to Scotland illustrates with some gravity the depth of his blunder. Worse still was that the fire it put into the bellies of Scotland's Marians, who relished the opportunity to bash the regent. He wrote a demanding letter to Elizabeth, who cared nothing at all for his domestic problems and wanted only the swift return of her rebel. In it, he laid out the difficulties he faced, lamented the state of his finances as a result of being constantly in arms, and requested a lump sum, an annual pension, and formal recognition of James VI as king of Scots. His desperate appeal is interesting not for its litany of woes, but for its similarity to the appeals made by the last Scottish regent, Mary of Guise, to the French monarchy. Mary of Guise had faced religious and xenophobic insurgents; Moray was facing largely political ones. Elizabeth wrote back, offering to discuss his demands, but he would never read the letter. His past deeds were about to redound on him.

After inspecting progress – which was non-existent – at the siege of Dumbarton, Moray visited Stirling. As always, he put off business, in this case the calls of English ambassadors to send Northumberland south, by insisting that he could only make a conciliar decision. This was, as we have seen, his style. Sir James Melville would later say of Moray that 'he was like an unskilful player in a game of catch-poll, running after every ball' and too reliant on familiars.[175] Meant as a criticism, it reveals the success of the impression the regent sought to create. It also, though, showed an understanding of Scottish governance, which was predicated upon conciliar rather than autocratic action. Moray's error was in taking it too far.

On his way to Edinburgh, he stopped off at the traditional resting point of Linlithgow, where he stayed the night. The English ambassadors would later state that he had been warned that danger lurked in the town, and that even the precise house from which it would spring was pointed out. Agnes, his wife, who was then pregnant (she would give birth to their third daughter after her husband's death) heard the rumours. She begged his secretary to ensure his safety. In response, Moray altered the route of his procession. However, so many people pressed on the regent's train that in the end he had to take the main road.

What he did not know was that one of the Hamilton clan, James Hamilton of Bothwellhaugh, a pardoned Langside prisoner, had covered the upper floor of a house overlooking the street with a mattress. There he lurked in shadow, his footsteps muffled, and trained a gun out of the window. When the regent hove into view he fired, immediately dropping the gun, flying downstairs and outside to his waiting horse, and riding off. His mission had been set by the duke of Châtelherault's brother, John Hamilton, the archbishop of St Andrews who had officiated at Prince James' baptism. The archbishop would later be hanged by Morton, who got the regency after Lennox and Mar had each tried it and died themselves. But personal reasons gave heart to the murder; after Langside, Bothwellhaugh's estate had been declared forfeit, and his wife had been one of those thrown out of her home, Rutherglen Castle. He had long sought an opportunity for revenge, and its success was to be rewarded with a pension from Mary.

Moray did not succumb to his wound immediately. He stepped down from his horse without assistance and made his way into his lodgings. There, according to Buchanan (whose goal was to portray Moray as a martyr), his friends pressed on him, saying that his own good nature and leniency to criminals had brought about his end. Moray, supposedly, declared that nothing would make him repent of lenity. Words and life finally fled him shortly before midnight. Agnes went on to give birth to his last child, the short-lived Annabel; she remarried in 1572, choosing as a husband Colin Campbell, 6th earl of Argyll. Moray's eldest daughter, Elizabeth, married another James Stewart. He inherited the earldom and went on to become hero of the ballad 'The Bonny Earl o' Moray'. Margaret Stewart, his second daughter, married the 9th earl of Errol.

Mary, as we know, reacted with muted delight to the death of a man who had once been her most trusted counsellor, but who had become her main accuser. Elizabeth, according to the French ambassador, was deeply upset at the loss of her cousin. When, on Valentine's day 1570, Moray was laid to rest in St Giles Church (where Agnes commissioned a monument, sadly now destroyed, with only the plaque remaining), Mary was in Tutbury.[176] The death of her brother brought little more than hope that she might finally be freed from captivity, but it was not to be. Her communication with Norfolk continued until the foolish earl finally tested Elizabeth's patience too far. He was to be another man who sought to use the Scottish queen for his own gain, and he too met his end because of it, in 1572. In Scotland, the queen's party continued to exist, but without her presence or any real hope of her return, it was a losing battle. In June 1573, the last holdout, which had become Edinburgh castle, secured by Maitland and her other former enemy, Kircaldy of Grange, was stormed by the then regent, Morton, with the aid of English forces. By this time the Marians were a diminished opposition voice; their cause was nominal and their members in perpetual flux due to shifting personal, religious, familial, and political affiliations. The honourable soldier Kirkaldy was hanged, and Maitland died, possibly by his own hand, before he met the same fate. Morton, who showed a remarkable competency as regent, was finally brought down by the king in whose name he wielded power, and whose father he had killed. He lost his head in 1581, accused, finally, of murdering Darnley.

The rest of Mary's story is well known. She remained in thrall for the rest of her life, occasionally dabbling in plots which other people spun around her, more often than not a pawn in the power games of others. Her health, both physical and mental, continued to fluctuate. She would, probably, have been far happier accepting the life of an apolitical country gentlewoman – the kind of bourgeois woman she had once delighted in pretending to be – rather than dabbling in political affairs, from which she was in any case increasingly isolated. But her sense of entitlement as an anointed queen would never have allowed that. In 1586, she was entrapped by her most devious enemies, Cecil and Elizabeth's spymaster, Sir Francis Walsingham. Despite a spirited defence, she went to her death playing to the gallery as a Catholic martyr. It was in captivity that policy fell away – to an extent – and the queen underwent her true spiritual awakening, far beyond anything instilled in her by her uncle Charles. By this time, her famous beauty had dimmed, not due to a bout of manic depression, but to years of inactivity and ever-closer imprisonment. She went to the block in February 1587, a woman committed to nineteen years of imprisonment for a crime she did not commit, accused by a brother she had once showered with favour.

Epilogue

History is riddled with irony. James and Mary Stewart forged a relationship based on their shared desire to see the Stewart dynasty's right to succeed to the English throne. For both of them it became an all-consuming obsession, and disagreement over the means by which they might achieve it ultimately tore them apart. What is ironic is that what they both sought with such blinkered intensity – Queen Elizabeth's recognition of what they both viewed as an inalienable hereditary right – in the end did not matter one jot. Elizabeth never gave any formal recognition of any of her successors. When the English queen died in March 1603, her councillors were none the wiser as to what she really wanted to happen after her death. In the absence of a will, or even a spoken indication, they had been for years courting James VI of Scotland. James had never questioned his right to succeed; it was his entitlement, as it had been his mother's. He did little to help Mary during her captivity: a king from the cradle, he felt just as entitled to govern Scotland as his mother did. There could be no relationship there.

In studying the relationship between the queen of Scots and her bastard brother, the idea of entitlement recurs with astonishing frequency. Understanding it is understanding the period and all its political players. Mary's most eloquent modern critic, the late Jenny Wormald, advanced the idea that the queen of Scots was so fixated on England that she neglected Scotland, to the extent of having an utter disinterest in the realm. This is unfair. As we have seen, Mary managed

Scotland well, showing an interest in courting its political community even whilst still in mourning for his first husband. Further, she felt entitled to rule the country as an autonomous sovereign even after taking another husband, who was naturally confused and angry at her unwillingness to share – or hand over – control of the realm. Her obsession with the English throne, though, was indeed the foundation of her foreign policy throughout her personal reign. This was not unusual. Early modern monarchs shared obsessions with what they believed to be the inalienable entitlement of their dynasties. Henry VIII, for example, sought continually to be recognised as France's king, as well as nurturing a profound belief in his entitlement to rule Scotland. Henry II of France and the Guises – and briefly Mary herself – had styled the queen of Scots as the queen of England too. Elizabeth was determined to subdue her 'rebels' in Ireland, and never ceased believing that that country was hers and its people her lawful subjects. From the time James VI was old enough to understand the world around him, he believed himself entitled to rule Scotland and, in time, England. Indeed, Mary's son was to develop the belief into a carefully-developed theory of kingship, the divine right of kings, explicated in his 1599 treatise, *Basilikon Doron*.

If monarchs had a sense of entitlement writ large, so too did their subjects. James Stewart, earl of Moray, felt entitled both spiritually and politically to have his sister's ear, and thereby to govern Scotland via conciliar involvement. When he rebelled, it was because this was threatened. Darnley felt entitled to have his position legally recognised, and to subordinate his wife as a king was expected to do. The duke of Châtelherault felt entitled to have his position in the Scottish succession respected no matter how often he changed sides.

The charge of ambition is often levelled at both Mary Queen of Scots and her brother. This too is unfair. Ambition in the period was well understood to be a vice, quite distinct from pursuing one's rights and privileges. It is unlikely that either brother or sister (or anyone else involved in their story) felt themselves to be personally ambitious. Their goals were only ever to exercise power and privileges which they felt were theirs by right, tradition, convention, and custom. Mary's reign was brief and her end unfortunate, but so too was her brother's regency. Moray, ironically, understood the importance of conciliar governance, albeit he preferred it only as a means of escaping responsibility. He was never interested in his sister's crown; in fact, he showed absolutely no interest in any of the pursuits of a renaissance prince. The idea that he sought to be king, or even that he would have made a good sovereign, is therefore an odd one. He conformed to none of the requirements of Scottish monarchy in the period. He was a recognised bastard, legitimated only in order to be able to acquire property. He showed no great liking for or inclination to patronise the arts. He embarked on no great cultural pursuits. He built little or nothing. He wrote no verses. He was a good administrator and canny diplomat, and this is the role he wanted and fulfilled: a high-ranking politician motivated by a spiritually-guided entitlement to safeguard and manage domestic affairs. As a de facto ruler he managed to pacify the Highlands as well as might be expected, but his position was that of a chief manager, not a monarch of the standards expected by early modern Scotland. He neither stamped out the Marians – indeed, it was under his governorship that Maitland became one – and, as some have accused Mary of political ineptitude for being unaware of dangerous plots developing around her, we cannot ignore that, despite warnings, he walked directly into the path of an assassin's bullet.

Mary, by contrast, was skilled in the arts of renaissance queenship: she embroidered, wrote verses, and displayed restrained majesty and an innate understanding of personal splendour and display. She, however, tried to resist Scottish conciliar tradition, attempting to raise up men like Riccio in order to have assuredly loyal counsel. Her downfall was her marriage to Bothwell, and this was the result of his taking advantage of one of her periods of the inherited deep depression that had hastened her own father's death. There is little doubt that the queen suffered some kind of mental illness – quite likely a form of bipolar disorder – but the system of hereditary monarchy, especially in the early modern period, cared nothing for the condition of the incumbent. Responsibility was hers whether her health was good or bad, this being a flaw of the system, not the woman. As a person, she is deserving of sympathy. The person cannot, however, be separated from the office in what was an age of inherently personal politics. Her struggles therefore highlight the cruelty and cut-throat nature of the monarchical system of which she was part. At the first sign of failing health, physical or mental, the jostling for power began, the person of the sovereign in no way hedged by divinity. During the peak years of her personal reign, she made a far better monarch than ever her brother could have; but those years would have been far less of a success without his (admittedly frequently self-serving) guidance in domestic matters.

At the height of their relationship, Mary Queen of Scots and James Stewart presented a strong and united front. Together they represented the best of the Stewart dynasty. They were, unfortunately, to be divided by religion, by suspicion, by politics, and by competing senses of entitlement. The famous tragedy of Queen Mary is not one of grand passion and star-crossed love, and nor is it one of sexual misconduct, murder, and Machiavellian scheming. It is the tragedy of a brother and sister torn apart.

Notes

Full details are given for the first citation of a book or article. Thereafter, short references are used.

---

[1] Strickland, A., Strickland, E. 1858 [2010]. *Lives of the Queens of Scotland and English Princesses, VII* (Cambridge: CUP), p. 62.

[2] Massie, A. 2010. *The Royal Stuarts* (New York: Thomas Dunne Books), p. 114.

[3] Stedall, R. 2012. *The Challenge to the Crown, I* (London: The Book Guild), p. 435.

[4] Guy, J. 2004. *My Heart is My Own* (London: Harper Perennial), p.10.

[5] Strickland, *Lives*, p. 509.

[6] Bowen, M. 1934 [1971]. *Mary Queen of Scots* (Aylesbury: Sphere), p. 190.

[7] Lang, A. 1901. *The Mystery of Mary Stuart* (London: Longmans, Green & Co.), p. 9.

[8] Herries, J. M. 1836. *Historical Memoirs of the Reign of Mary Queen of Scots and a portion of the Reign of King James the Sixth* (Edinburgh: Edinburgh Printing Company), p. 54.

[9] Bain, J. 1898. *Calendar of the State Papers Relating to Scotland and Mary, Queen of Scots, 1547-1603, I* (Edinburgh: H. M. General Custom House), p. 821.

[10] Leslie, J. 1596 [1888-95]. 'The Nynt Buik' in E. G. Cody (ed.) *The Historie of Scotland Wrytten First in Latin by the Most Reverend and Worthy Jhone Leslie Bishop of Rosse* (Edinburgh: William Blackwood and Sons), p. 261.

[11] Buchanan, G. 1582 [1733]. *History of Scotland, II* (London: H. Parker), p. 162.

[12] Lyndsay, D. 1536 [1871]. *The Poetical Works of Sir David Lyndsay of the Mount, Lion King at Arms* (Edinburgh: W. Patterson), p. 109.

[13] In fairness, rumours circulated after the deaths of Mary and James' sons that he had taken up with other women. However, these putative lovers remain nameless, and Mary's biographer, Rosalind Marshall,

makes the case that they were designed to sow discord between the royal couple. Another rumours, reported by English spies, appeared shortly before the king's death. After the defeat at Solway Moss, he was said to have visited Tantallon Castle, 'where he has a mistress ... and sets not much store by the queen'. The problem here are two-fold: the king was at this time in a deep state of depression, which makes his cavorting with a secret lover unlikely, and afterwards he passed through Edinburgh to visit his wife (which he would hardly do if the reports were true that he had lost all interest in her). At any rate, if he did return to his womanising ways, it was towards the end of his life and marriage. See Marshall, R. 1977. Mary of Guise (London: Collins), p .99.

[14] The date of James' birth cannot be known with absolute accuracy. See Weir, A. 2011. *Britain's Royal Families: The Complete Genealogy* (London: Pimlico), p. 244.

[15] Mahon, R. H. 1924 [2011]. *Mary Queen of Scots* (Cambridge: Cambridge University Press), p. 30.

[16] Hay, Denys (ed.). 1954. *The Letters of James V: Collected and Calendared by R. K. Hannay* (Edinburgh: HMSO), pp. 320, 324.

[17] Bingham, C. *James V, King of Scots* (London: Collins), pp. 98-9.

[18] An excellent account of James V's strategy of aggrandisement can be found in: Thomas, A. 2005. *The Princelie Majestie: The Court of James V of Scotland 1528-1542* (Edinburgh: John Donald).

[19] Lee, M. 1953. *James Stewart: A Political Study of the Reformation in Scotland* (New York: Columbia University Press), p. 17.

[20] The claim that James was the eldest is common. For example, it is made by Dunn, J. 2003. Elizabeth and Mary (London: Harper Perennial), p. 98. Cameron provides evidence, however, that another James Stewart, that James V begat with Elizabeth Schaw, was the eldest. See Cameron, J. 1998. *James V: The Personal Rule, 1528-42* (East Linton: Tuckwell Press), p. 205.

[21] Le Roy Ladurie, E. 1997. *Saint-Simon and the Court of Louis XIV* (Chicago: University of Chicago Press), p. 106.

[22] Brown, M., Stevenson, K. 2017. *Medieval St Andrews: Church, Cult, City* (Woodbridge: The Boydell Press), p.173.

[23] For full discussion of this, see Merriman, M. 2004. *The Rough Wooings* (East Linton: Tuckwell Press), esp. pp. 39-57; Goodwin, G. 2013. *Fatal Rivalry* (London: Weidenfeld and Nicolson), pp. 89-105.

[24] Merriman, Rough Wooings, p. 44.

[25] Sadler, R. 'Embassy to Scotland in 1543' in A. Clifford (ed.) *The State Papers and Letters of Sir Ralph Sadler, Knight-Banneret* (Edinburgh: Archibald Constable), p. 105.

[26] Holinshed, R. 1577 [1803]. *Chronicles of England, Scotland, and Ireland in Six Volumes* (London: J. Johnson), p. 582.

[27] Froude, J. A. 1862. *History of England from the Fall of Wolsey to the Death of Elizabeth, I* (London: Parker, son and Bourne), p. 394.

[28] Sadler, *Letters*, p. 88.

[29] Sadler, R. A. 1543 [1877]. *A Memoir of the Life and Times of the Right Honourable Sir Ralph Sadleir Compiled by his Descendent Major F. Sadleir Stoney* (London: Longmans, Green & Co.), p. 156.

[30] For a history of the name of the conflict and the conflict itself, see Merriman, *The Rough Wooings*.

[31] As Lee notes, the records at St Andrews indicate that James matriculated in 1545; however, he astutely points out the haphazard nature of the enrolment records, noting that it might be that he was nearer the end of his studies than the beginning at this time. See Lee, James Stewart, p. 18.

[32] Graham, R. 2001. *John Knox: Democrat* (London: Robert Hale), p. 29.

[33] Taylor, J., Lindsay, W., Eadie, J., Anderson, J., and Macdonald, G. 1868. *The Pictorial History of Scotland: from the Roman Invasion to the Close of the Jacobite Rebellion, I* (London: James S. Virtue), p. 469.

[34] Dunlop, A. I. (ed.). 1964. *Acta Facultatis Artium Universitatis Sanctiandree, 1413-1588, I* (Edinburgh: T. and A. Constable), pp. lxi-i.

[35] Brown, K. M. 2013. *Noble Power in Scotland from the Reformation to the Revolution* (Edinburgh: Edinburgh University Press), p. 242.

[36] Porter, L. 2013. *Crown of Thistles* (London: Pan Books), p. 307.

[37] Patten, W. 1547 [1798]. 'The Expedicion into Scotlande', in J. G. Dalyell (ed.) *Fragments of Scottish History* (Edinburgh: Archibald Constable), p. 67-8.

[38] Macdonald, A. R., Harris, B. 2006. *Scotland: The Making and Unmaking of the Nation, c.1100-1707* (Edinburgh, EUP), p. 196.

[39] Russell, E. 1912. *Maitland of Lethington* (London: James Nisbet & Co.), p. 102.

[40] The 'bad beer' is attested by none other than John Mair. See Graham, *John Knox*, p. 27.

[41] Gerber, M. 2012. *Bastards: Politics, Family, and Law in Early Modern France* (Oxford: Oxford University Press), p. 68.

[42] Robertson, J. (ed.). 1863. *Inventaires de la Royne Descosse Douairiere de France* (Edinburgh: The Bannatyne Club), p. xxxix.

[43] *CSP, Scotland, I*, p. 144.

[44] Knox, J. 'Letter to the Faithful in England' in *Select Practical Writings of John Knox* (Glasgow: William Collins & Co.), p. 85.

[45] Presumably an early adherent of the maxim 'God loves a trier', Knox wrote to Mary of Guise requesting that she convert. She showed the letter to archbishop of Glasgow with the quip, 'care you to read a

pasquil?' This is recounted in Kyle, R. G. 2014. *God's Watchman: John Knox's Faith and Vocation* (Eugene: Pickwick Publications), p. 226.

[46] Staines, J. D. 2009. *The Tragic Histories of Mary Queen of Scots, 1560-1690: Rhetoric, Passions, and Political Literature* (Farnham: Ashgate), p. 80.

[47] McIlvenna, U. 2016. *Scandal and Reputation at the Court of Catherine de Medici* (London: Routledge), p. 162.

[48] Staines, *Tragic Histories*, p. 81. Staines proposes Geneva as the place of publication.

[49] Frasier, *Mary Queen of Scots*, p. 88.

[50] The Scottish political community had various methods of acting collectively: parliament was supreme, whereas conventions of the three estates were parliaments in all but name but lacked permanent legislative competency. In addition were the general assembly, conventions of the royal burghs, and the privy council. See Goodare, J. 2004. 'The Scottish Parliament and its Early Modern "Rivals"', *Parliament, Estates & Representation, 24, 1*, pp. 147-172.

[51] Marshall, *Mary of Guise*, p.212.

[52] There is some confusion over the number of commissioners sent. Antonia Fraser and John Guy (amongst others) cite nine. Chroniclers Knox and Pitscottie claim eight: two bishops and six lords. The Acts of Parliament (*APS, II*, 504-5) suggest the following: James Stewart, Cassilis, Rothes, Seton, Fleming, Erskine of Dun, the archbishop of Glasgow, and the bishop of Orkney. Erskine of Dun, however, was not a lord. The laird of Easter Wemyss, whom Pitscottie claims died as a result of poisoning, might be the mysterious ninth commissioner – however, as the poisoning story is highly suspect and those who categorically did die did not do so until the end of the year, a certain mystery remains as to where the figure of nine comes from.

[53] Skelton, J. 1893. *Mary Stuart* (London: Boussod, Valadon & Company), p. 22.

[54] Warnicke, R. M. 2006. *Mary Queen of Scots* (London: Routledge), p. 52.

[55] Roberston, W. 1760. *The History of Scotland, during the reigns of Queen Mary and King James VI, I* (London: T. Cadell), p.69.

[56] Guy, *My Heart is My Own*, p. 87.

[57] Guy, *My Heart is My Own*, p. 93.

[58] Pitscottie, R. L. 1728 [1899-1911]. *The historie and cronicles of Scotland, from the slauchter of King James the First to the ane thousande Fyve hundreith thrie scoir fyftein zeir* (Edinburgh: W. Blackwood), p.124.

[59] Pistcottie, *Historie*, p. 125.

[60] Pitscottie, Historie, p. 127.

[61] *Dictionary of National Biography*. 1885. (Oxford: Smith, Elder, & Co.), p. 419.

[62] Mason, R. 2005. 'Renaissance and Reformation' in J. Wormald (ed.) *Scotland: A History* (Oxford: Oxford University Press), p. 110.

[63] Loades, D. M. 2006. *Mary Tudor: the Tragical History of the First Queen of England* (London: National Archives), p. 196.

[64] This claim is made by, amongst many, Lee, *James Stewart*, p. 5; Ross, S. 1993. *The Stewart Dynasty* (Michigan: Thomas and Lochar), p. 215; Hartley, C. 2003. *A Historical Dictionary of British Women* (London: Europa), p. 153.

[65] Cecil, W. 1558. 'A memorial of certain points meet for the restoring the realm of Scotland to the ancient weale' in W. Robertson, *History of Scotland*, p. 350.

[66] Fraser, A. 1969. *Mary Queen of Scots* (Manchester: Philips Park Press), p. 114.

[67] Frasier, *Mary Queen of Scots*, p. 115.

[68] Fraser, *Mary Queen of Scots*, p. 122.

[69] Fraser, *Mary Queen of Scots*, p. 123.

[70] Stevenson, J. (ed.). 1863. *Calendar of State Papers, Foreign Series, of the Reign of Elizabeth, 1558-9* (London: Public Record Office), p.358.

[71] Lee, James Stewart, p. 47.

[72] *CSP, Foreign, Elizabeth*, p. 144.

[73] McSherry, J. A. 1985. 'Was Mary Queen of Scots Anorexic?', *Scott Medical Journal, Oct*, 30 (4): pp. 243-5; Guy, *My Heart is My Own*, p. 66.

[74] Hume, M. A. S. 1896. *Calendar of State Papers, Spain (Simancas), III, 1580-6* (London: H. M. Stationery Office), p. 100-01.

[75] This was Cecil's second trip to Scotland. He had accompanied his then master, Somerset, during the invasion of 1548, albeit as a non-combatant.

[76] Kellar, C. 2003. *Scotland, England, and the Reformation, 1534-61* (Oxford: Clarendon Press), p. 220.

[77] For discussion of the relationship between lairds and parliament, see Goodare, J. 2001. 'The Admission of Lairds to the Scottish Parliament', *The English Historical Review, 116, 469*, pp. 1103–1133.

[78] This section might have been toned down or deleted entirely in the end. See Lee, *James Stewart*, p.64-5.

[79] Lee, *James Stewart*, p.67

[80] BL, Egerton MS 1818, fo. 21, to Dudley, 25th May 1562. Quoted in Adams, S. 'The Release of Lord Darnley' in M. Lynch (Ed.) *Mary Stewart: Queen in Three Kingdoms*, p. 134.

[81] Loughlin, M. 1991. *The Career of Maitland of Lethington, c.1526-73* (Edinburgh: PhD Thesis), p. 128.

[82] For discussion of Cecil's approach to unionism, see Dawson, J. 1989. 'William Cecil and the British Dimension of Early Elizabethan Foreign Policy', *The Journal of the Historical Association, 74, 241*, pp. 196-216.

[83] *CSP, Foreign, Elizabeth*, p.468.

[84] *CSP, Foreign, Elizabeth*, p. 472.

[85] Lee, *James Stewart*, p. p. 73.

[86] Lee, *James Stewart*, p. 74

[87] Lee, *James Stewart*, p.77.

[88] *CSP, Foreign, Elizabeth*, p.77.

[89] Lee, *James Stewart*, p.85-6.

[90] Froude, *History of England*, p.353-4.

[91] 'It was shown to her in France that Scotland was but a barbarous country, but now she confesses she saw the contrary, for she saw never so many fair personages of men and women and also young babes and children as she saw that day in these bounds where she had been.' Quoted in Marshall, *Mary of Guise*, p.61.

[92] Innes, J. T. 2018. John Knox (London: Oliphant Anderson), p.90.

[93] Pollnitz, A. 2015. *Princely Education in Early Modern Britain* (Cambridge: Cambridge University Press), p.215.

[94] Strickland, *Lives*, p.261-2.

[95] Lee, *James Stewart*, p.93

[96] Mary I. 1562 [1904]. 'A letter from Mary Queen of Scots to the duke of Guise' in J. H. Pollen, S. J. (ed.) *Publications of the Scottish History Society, XLIII, Queen Mary's Letters to Guise, 1562* (Edinburgh: T. and A. Constable), p. xiv.

[97] *CSP, Scot, I*, pp. 561-4.

[98] Buchanan, G. 1856 [1582]. *The History of Scotland, II* (Glasgow: Blackie and Son), p.518.

[99] Lang, *The Mystery of Mary Stuart*, p. 20.

[100] Knox, J. [1905]. *The History of the Reformation in Scotland, II* (London: Adam and Charles Black), pp. 313-5.

[101] This took place in September 1561 and was designed to foster understanding between Huguenots and Catholics. James got his copy of the pamphlet from Randolph. See Lee, *James Stewart*, p.96.

[102] Callahan, J. M. 1912 [1978]. *Genealogical and Personal History of the Upper Monongahela Valley, West Virginia* (New York: Lewis Historical Publishing Company), p.408

[103] Pitscottie, *Chronicles*, p.176.

[104] Lee, *James Stewart*, p. 101.

[105] An account of Sir John's activities can be found in Warnicke, *Mary Queen of Scots*, pp. 82-4.

[106] There is uncertainty as to the exact date in September on which James was publicly given the earldom of Mar. Lee and Warnicke favour

the 10th, but others believe it to have been after the fracas at Inverness (which began on the 11th).

[107] Strickland, *Letters, II*, pp. 354-5.

[108] Knox, *History, II*, p.360.

[109] This is offered by Lee, *James Stewart*, p. 114 as a possibility. It seems the likeliest in terms of squaring what we might expect from James' attitude versus what it appears to have actually been.

[110] See Weir, A. 2003. *Mary Queen of Scots and the Murder of Lord Darnley* (London: Jonathan Cape), p.45-6. Maitland appears to have been behind the story that Chastelard confessed before his execution that he had been a Huguenot troublemaker. The secretary was, though, busy trying to protect Mary's reputation by squelching rumours that she had led the poet to believe himself her lover.

[111] Goodare, J. 2005. 'The First Parliament of Mary Queen of Scots', *The Sixteenth Century Journal, 36, 1*, pp. 55-75.

[112] Knox, *History, IV*, pp. 77-8.

[113] The Duke of Hamilton provides an amusing table listing the defects of Mary's suitors: see Hamilton, A. D.-H. 1991. *Maria R: The Crucial Years* (Edinburgh: Mainstream Publishing Company), p. 34.

[114] *CSP, Foreign, Elizabeth*, p.291.

[115] Darnley's birth is generally accepted as having been in 1545. Alison Weir makes a compelling case for dating it to 1546. See Weir, *The Murder of Lord Darnley*, p. 55.

[116] Cowan, I. B. 1971. *The Enigma of Mary Stuart* (London: Gollancz), p.66.

[117] Chalmers, G. 1818. *The Life of Mary, Queen of Scots: Drawn from the State Papers, I* (London: John Murray), p. 123.

[118] *CSP, Scot*, p. 129-34.

[119] Lang, A. 1907. 'New Light on Mary Queen of Scots', *Blackwood's Magazine, 182*, p.21.

[120] Skelton, J. 1894. *Maitland of Lethington and the Scotland of Mary Stuart: A History* (London: W. Blackwood), p. 214.

[121] Cowan, *Enigma*, p. 87.

[122] Lee, *James Stewart*, p. 141.

[123] Carroll, S. 2011. *Martyrs and Murderers: The Guise Family and the Making of Europe* (Oxford: Oxford University Press), p. 5.

[124] Lee, *James Stewart*, p. 143.

[125] Calderwood, D. 1843. *The History of the Kirk of Scotland, II* (Edinburgh: Wodrow Society), p. 572-3.

[126] Guy, *My Heart is My Own*, p. 234-6.

[127] Lee, *James Stewart*, p. 156-7.

[128] Goodare, J. 'Queen Mary's Catholic Interlude' in M. Lynch (ed.) *Mary Stewart: Queen in Three Kingdoms* (Oxford: Basil Blackwell), pp. 154-70.

[129] Bingham, C. 1995. *Darnley* (London: Phoenix), p. 121.

[130] Herries, *Memoirs*, pp. 73-4.

[131] Melvile, J. 1683 [1922]. *Memoirs of His Own Life* (London: Chapman and Dodd), p.146-7.

[132] In his defence, one might argue that Moray's eagerness to have Morton as a friend and ally, and Morton's own ability to attain the regency in later life, suggests that he must have had enough charm about him to win support. He was said also to take good care of his daughters, and he had a keen interest in gardening; there was a human side to the ruthless politico.

[133] The preceding sequence of events is drawn from Bingham, *Darnley*, pp. 140-2. John Guy reorders them, although the tenor of what occurred is similar. The difficulty of being sure of the order in which meetings took place is due to the multiplicity of accounts, chief amongst them Morton's, Ruthven's, and Mary's. All came with agendas, the former pair eager to exculpate themselves by pinning the blame for the whole affair on Darnley.

[134] Loughlin, 'Maitland of Lethington', p. 224.

[135] Flood, V. 2016. *Prophecy, Politics and Place in Medieval England: From Geoffrey of Monmouth to Thomas of Erceldoune* (Cambridge: D. S. Brewer), p. 120.

[136] Lee, *James Stewart*, p.179.

[137] Lee, *James Stewart*, p.181.

[138] *National Records of Scotland*, SP13/94, 13 Aug 1566.

[139] Weir, *The Murder of Lord Darnley*, p.148-9.

[140] *APS, II*, 545, c.1.

[141] Chalmers, *The Life of Mary Queen of Scots, II*, p. 170.

[142] Keith, *History, I*, p.xcvi-xcviii.

[143] It is often stated that Darnley suffered syphilis, which he likely contracted on one of his visits to France. This is based on examination conducted in the late 1920s of a skull said to be his. The pitting on the skull, according to Karl Pearson, was conducive to an advanced stage of syphilis. However, it is telling that his physicians at the time did not record syphilis as the cause of his disease, and commentators, typically, ascribed it to poison. If Mary and her physicians had any inkling that her husband suffered a familiar, communicable disease, it would have given her sufficient reason to have him immured for good, or at least to break with him.

[144] Weir, *The Murder of Lord Darnley*, p. 279.

[145] Guy, *My Heart is My Own*, p.289.

[146] Guy, *My Heart is My Own*, p. 312.

[147] MacRobert, A. E. 2002. *Mary Queen of Scots and the Casket Letters* (London: Tauris), pp. 53-4.

[148] Goodare, J. 2014. 'The Ainslie Bond' in S. Boardman and J. Goodare (eds.) *Kings, Lords and Men in Scotland and Britain, 1300–1625: Essays in Honour of Jenny Wormald* (Edinburgh: Edinburgh University Press), pp. 301-319.

[149] Guy, *My Heart is My Own*, p. 336.

[150] Stanhope, J., Buckingham, F. 1844. *Memoirs of Mary Stuart, II* (London: Richard Bentley), p. 187.

[151] Fraser, *Mary Queen of Scots*, p. 397.

[152] Lee, *James Stewart*, p.199.

[153] Weir, *The Murder of Lord Darnley*, p. 107; Guy, *My Heart is My Own*, pp. 396-436.

[154] Fraser, *Mary Queen of Scots*, pp. 481-3.

[155] Peterson, K. L. 2016. *Popular Medicine, Hysterical Disease, and Social Controversy in Shakespeare's England* (London: Routledge), pp. 110-12; Dixon, L. S. 1995. *Perilous Chastity: Women and Illness in Pre-Enlightenment Art and Medicine* (Ithaca: Cornell University Press), p.22.

[156] Porter, *Crown of Thistles*, p. 458.

[157] Goodare, 'Admission of Lairds', p. 1104.

[158] Keith, R. 1844-50. *History of the Affairs of Church and State in Scotland, II* (Edinburgh: Spottiswoode), p.736.

[159] Keith, *History, II*, p.737.

[160] Keith, *History, II*, p.738.

[161] I am grateful to Michael Pearce for sharing with me an advance copy of his forthcoming article, 'Jewels in and out of Edinburgh Castle 1567-1573'.

[162] Donaldson, G. 1983. *All the Queen's Men: Power and Politics in Mary Stewart's Scotland* (London: Batsford Academic and Educational), p. 88.

[163] Donaldson, *All the Queen's Men*, p. 88.

[164] Lang, *The Mystery of Mary Stuart*, pp. 374-9.

[165] Quoted in Templeman, D. 2018. *Mary Queen of Scots: The Captive Queen in England, 1568-87* (Exeter: Short Run Press), p.10.

[166] *National Records of Scotland*, GD406/1/27, 11-12 Jun 1568.

[167] Lee, *James Stewart*, p.236.

[168] Melville, *Memoirs*, p.210-11.

[169] Fraser, *Mary Queen of Scots*, p.463.

[170] Robertson, *History of Scotland*, p. 326.

[171] Robertson, *History of Scotland*, p. 403.

[172] *National Records of Scotland*, GD124/10/26, 22 Jan 1568/1569.

[173] *National Register of Scotland*, GD8/201, 1569.

[174] *CSP, Foreign, Eliz, IX*, pp. 157-8.

[175] Melville, *Memoirs*, p. 222.

[176] When the vault was opened up in 1850, Moray's body was not found. Likely it was moved to the churchyard during restoration of the cathedral earlier in the Victorian period. See Marshall, R. K. 2006. *Queen Mary's Women* (Edinburgh: Birlinn), p. 103.

Printed in Great Britain
by Amazon